T0388686

Innovation, Technology, and Knowledge Management

Series Editor

Elias G. Carayannis, George Washington University, Washington, DC, USA

More information about this series at http://www.springer.com/series/8124

Chun LIAO (廖春)

The Governance Structures of Chinese Firms

China's Innovation System and Chinese Model

Second Edition

 Springer

Chun LIAO (廖春)
Shanghai Lixin University of Accounting and Finance
Shanghai, China

ISSN 2197-5698   ISSN 2197-5701   (electronic)
Innovation, Technology, and Knowledge Management
ISBN 978-3-030-52217-9   ISBN 978-3-030-52218-6   (eBook)
https://doi.org/10.1007/978-3-030-52218-6

This Springer imprint is published by the registered company Springer Nature Switzerland AG
The registered company address is: Gewerbestrasse 11, 6330 Cham, Switzerland

This book is dedicated to LIU Xinyu (刘新玉),
LIAO Guangfu (廖光甫), YANG Laike (杨来科),
LIAO Lei (廖雷), ZHU Ziye (朱子叶)
– LIAO Chun (廖春)

Series Preface

The Springer book series *Innovation, Technology, and Knowledge Management* was launched in March 2008 as a forum and intellectual, scholarly "podium" for global/local, transdisciplinary, transsectoral, public–private, and leading/"bleeding"-edge ideas, theories, and perspectives on these topics.

The book series is accompanied by the Springer *Journal of the Knowledge Economy,* which was launched in 2009 with the same editorial leadership.

The series showcases provocative views that diverge from the current "conventional wisdom," that are properly grounded in theory and practice, and that consider the concepts of *robust competitiveness,*[1] *sustainable entrepreneurship,*[2] and *democratic capitalism,*[3] central to its philosophy and objectives. More specifically, the aim of this series is to highlight emerging research and practice at the dynamic intersection of these fields, where individuals, organizations, industries, regions, and nations are harnessing creativity and invention to achieve and sustain growth.

---

[1]We define *sustainable entrepreneurship* as the creation of viable, profitable, and scalable firms. Such firms engender the formation of self-replicating and mutually enhancing innovation networks and knowledge clusters (innovation ecosystems), leading toward robust competitiveness (E.G. Carayannis, *International Journal of Innovation and Regional Development* 1(3). 235–254, 2009).

[2]We understand *robust competitiveness* to be a state of economic being and becoming that avails systematic and defensible "unfair advantages" to the entities that are part of the economy. Such competitiveness is built on mutually complementary and reinforcing low-, medium- and high-technology and public and private sector entities (government agencies, private firms, universities, and nongovernmental organizations) (E.G. Carayannis, *International Journal of Innovation and Regional Development* 1(3). 235–254. 2009).

[3]The concepts of *robust competitiveness* and *sustainable entrepreneurship* are pillars of a regime that we call *"democratic capitalism"* (as opposed to "popular or casino capitalism"), in which real opportunities for education and economic prosperity are available to all. especially—but not only—younger people. These are the direct derivative of a collection of top-down policies as well as bottom-up initiatives (including strong research and development policies and funding, but going beyond these to include the development of innovation networks and knowledge clusters across regions and sectors) (E.G. Carayannis and A. Kaloudis. *Japan Economic Currents,* p. 6–10 January 2009).

Books that are part of the series explore the impact of innovation at the "macro" (economies, markets), "meso" (industries, firms), and "micro" levels (teams, individuals), drawing from such related disciplines as finance, organizational psychology, research and development, science policy, information systems, and strategy, with the underlying theme that for innovation to be useful it must involve the sharing and application of knowledge.

Some of the key anchoring concepts of the series are outlined in the figure below and the definitions that follow (all definitions are from E.G. Carayannis and D.F.J. Campbell, *International Journal of Technology Management*, 46, 3–4, 2009).

Conceptual profile of the series Innovation, Technology, and Knowledge Management

- The "Mode 3" Systems Approach for Knowledge Creation, Diffusion, and Use: "Mode 3" is a multilateral, multinodal, multimodal, and multilevel systems approach to the conceptualization, design, and management of real and virtual, "knowledge-stock" and "knowledge-flow," modalities that catalyze, accelerate, and support the creation, diffusion, sharing, absorption, and use of cospecialized knowledge assets. "Mode 3" is based on a system-theoretic perspective of socioeconomic, political, technological, and cultural trends and conditions that shape the coevolution of knowledge with the "knowledge-based and knowledge-driven, global/local economy and society."
- Quadruple Helix: Quadruple helix, in this context, means to add to the triple helix of government, university, and industry a "fourth helix" that we identify as the "media-based and culture-based public." This fourth helix associates with "media," "creative industries," "culture," "values," "lifestyles," "art," and perhaps also the notion of the "creative class."
- Innovation Networks: Innovation networks are real and virtual infrastructures and infratechnologies that serve to nurture creativity, trigger invention, and catalyze innovation in a public and/or private domain context (for instance, government–university–industry public–private research and technology development coopetitive partnerships).
- Knowledge Clusters: Knowledge clusters are agglomerations of cospecialized, mutually complementary, and reinforcing knowledge assets in the form of "knowledge stocks" and "knowledge flows" that exhibit self-organizing, learning-driven, dynamically adaptive competences and trends in the context of an open systems perspective.
- Twenty-First Century Innovation Ecosystem: A twenty-first century innovation ecosystem is a multilevel, multimodal, multinodal, and multiagent system of systems. The constituent systems consist of innovation metanetworks (networks of innovation networks and knowledge clusters) and knowledge metaclusters (clusters of innovation networks and knowledge clusters) as building blocks and organized in a self-referential or chaotic fractal knowledge and innovation architecture (Carayannis 2001), which in turn constitute agglomerations of human, social, intellectual, and financial capital stocks and flows as well as cultural and technological artifacts and modalities, continually coevolving,

cospecializing, and cooperating. These innovation networks and knowledge clusters also form, reform, and dissolve within diverse institutional, political, technological, and socioeconomic domains, including government, university, industry, and nongovernmental organizations and involving information and communication technologies, biotechnologies, advanced materials, nanotechnologies, and next-generation energy technologies.

Who is this book series published for? The book series addresses a diversity of audiences in different settings:

1. *Academic Communities:* Academic communities worldwide represent a core group of readers. This follows from the theoretical/conceptual interest of the book series to influence academic discourses in the fields of knowledge, also carried by the claim of a certain saturation of academia with the current concepts and the postulate of a window of opportunity for new or at least additional concepts. Thus, it represents a key challenge for the series to exercise a certain impact on discourses in academia. In principle, all academic communities that are interested in knowledge (knowledge and innovation) could be tackled by the book series. The interdisciplinary (transdisciplinary) nature of the book series underscores that the scope of the book series is not limited a priori to a specific basket of disciplines. From a radical viewpoint, one could create the hypothesis that there is no discipline where knowledge is of no importance.

2. *Decision Makers—Private/Academic Entrepreneurs and Public (Governmental, Subgovernmental) Actors:* Two different groups of decision makers are being addressed simultaneously: (1) private entrepreneurs (firms, commercial firms, academic firms) and academic entrepreneurs (universities), interested in optimizing knowledge management and in developing heterogeneously composed knowledge-based research networks and (2) public (governmental, subgovernmental) actors that are interested in optimizing and further developing their policies and policy strategies that target knowledge and innovation. One purpose of public *knowledge and innovation policy* is to enhance the performance and competitiveness of advanced economies.

3. *Decision Makers in General:* Decision-makers are systematically being supplied with crucial information, for how to optimize knowledge-referring and knowledge-enhancing decision-making. The nature of this "crucial information" is conceptual as well as empirical (case-study-based). Empirical information highlights practical examples and points toward practical solutions (perhaps remedies), conceptual information offers the advantage of further-driving and further-carrying tools of understanding. Different groups of addressed decision-makers could be decision-makers in private firms and multinational corporations, responsible for the knowledge portfolio of companies; knowledge and knowledge management consultants; globalization experts, focusing on the internationalization of research and development, science and technology, and innovation; experts in university/business research networks; and political scientists, economists, and business professionals.

4. *Interested Global Readership:* Finally, the Springer book series addresses a whole global readership, composed of members who are generally interested in knowledge and innovation. The global readership could partially coincide with the communities as described above ("academic communities," "decision-makers"), but could also refer to other constituencies and groups.

Elias G. Carayannis

Preface

This is a new preface written for the 10th anniversary of the first edition of my book and also for this second edition. Coincidentally, the first edition was completed during the 2008 global financial crisis, and now the second edition is complete in the midst of the 2020 coronavirus pandemic. However, the very quickly developing reality time and again proves the topic of this book. This book will never be out of date.

This book, which was originally published in 2009 by Springer, analyzes China's super innovation system and the Chinese model. Marketing the idea of this book can witness several ups and downs. In the year 2004, when I first noticed and spoke about how powerful Chinese-specific innovation system is, no one else really believed. During the 2008 global financial crisis, many foreign scholars took interest in this topic. Post recovery, such opinion was left alone. With the development of artificial intelligence (AI), the development of high-technology-involved infrastructure, and now China as one of the leading powers in high-technology development globally, many scholars realize China's great innovative capacity, which had earlier been ignored and even denied. For example, Kai-Fu Lee published a book in 2018 entitled *AI Superpower: China, Silicon Valley, and the New World Order*. Put into this background, the price of my book, which was published much earlier, springs to a new high level. The marketing of this book mirrors how the world sees China.

The original framework of the book was the thesis for my second master's degree in International Economics during my stay in Germany. I began writing toward the end of 2004 and completed in spring 2005. I planned to write this book to study the topic in greater depth. At that time, I was also pursuing my Ph.D. in Economics, following my doctoral supervisor and economist Hu Peizhao at Xiamen University, and therefore had the opportunity to collect comprehensive data about China that could support my argument. In October 2005, I started my another Ph.D study at the Free University of Berlin in Germany, following my doctoral supervisor and economic sociologist Heiner Ganßmann, hoping to study German innovation system typified for the European model (say, coordinated market economies, including advanced European countries and Japan) and the American innovation system that is topical for liberal market economies (including advanced English-speaking countries). After completing my Ph.D. study in Germany in July 2008, I started working hard to finalize the book. I sent my book proposal to four world-renowned publishers: Springer, Cambridge University Press, Macmillan, and Routledge. Then, I got four positive answers, though Springer came first.

The "Chinese model" and "China's innovation system" are the two core concepts discussed in this book. "Chinese model" does not mean government-led economy. The private sector and state sector must coexist, each exemplifying their respective innovation mechanism and comparative advantage. In the state sector, there is state coordination based on state controlling shareholding, not based on government behavior. In the private sector, coordination is based on the free market mechanism. Both private and state sectors are framed by the concept of market economy. Thereby, the coexistence of both sectors builds up such a super innovation system: In the state sector, there is state strategic innovation system that is similar to but also superior to the Germany leading European innovation system. In the private sector, the high-technology innovation system operates similar to the American model. Therefore, China has two types of innovation systems, while there is only one in other countries. Dual innovation system creates two types of core competitiveness. This dual strength builds up the superpower.

Coexistence of the two sectors without friction in between relies on "coordination boundary" between the coordination mechanisms of the two sectors. State coordination based on its controlling shareholding has long replaced the previous government-led framework. It is this creative institutional arrangement that contributes fully to the clear coordination boundary between the two sectors. This sounds nothing special, but actually it is a determined point. If there is no clear coordination boundary, then both coordination mechanisms in the two sectors will perform inefficiently. Only if there is a clear coordination boundary, the Chinese dual innovation system could be superior to other economies with only one type of innovation system. China's super innovation system just means its dual innovation system, which is actually a creative and powerful institutional arrangement.

Some scholars understand the "Chinese model" as "aggression of the state sector and recession of the private sector." That is not my version of the "Chinese model." Without the private sector, there would be no such high-technology innovation system typified in this sector. If China would have only one type of innovation system, it would lose its specific powerful dual innovation system and hence its comparative advantage in innovation.

The book is authorized to have been translated, updated, and published in Chinese in 2013 by Shanghai People's Publishing House (上海人民出版社) together with Truth & Wisdom Press (格致出版社). The title of the Chinese version is modified to *The Governance Structures and Innovation Systems of Chinese Firms: The Comparison with American–British Model and German–Japanese Model* (中国企业的治理与创新模式:与"美英模式"和"德日模式"的比较).

China's super innovation system and the Chinese model were built up roughly in the period from the mid-1990s to the middle of the first decade of the 21st century. The book focuses on how such an innovation system had been built in those years. It is because of that build up that China has now become one of the leading powers in the field of AI and high-technology development. In the meantime, China has the strong capability to control crises (e.g., Coronavirus crisis) and also the strong stability to avoid global economic crises (e.g., the 2008 global financial crisis), compared to the USA, the European countries, and others.

Last but not least, my cordial thanks to Nicholas Philipson, Editorial Director of Business/Economics & Statistics, Springer New York, USA, and Innovation Series Editor Prof. Elias G. Carayannis at the George Washington University, Washington D.C., USA, for recognizing the book and taking the decision to publish it. This proves that the decision was a right one.

Munich, Germany   Chun LIAO (廖春)
March 2020

Acknowledgments

First, cordial thanks are due to my whole family. With their love and support, I could overcome all difficulties and finally achieve this goal in my life. My father passed away when my younger sister and I were still kids. Our mother raised us alone, and she has naturally implanted her love and optimistic attitude deeply in our minds.

Second, cordial thanks to the Ludwig Maximilian University (Munich, Germany) and to Prof. Dr. Thorstan Sellhorn and Vice President Prof. Dr. Hans van Ess for the efforts in inviting me to stay in such a prestigious university, so that I could concentrate on writing this new edition.

Zweitens, meinenherzlichen Dank zu Prof. Dr. Thorsten Sellhorn und Vice President Prof. Dr. Hans van Ess in Ludwig Maximillian Universität in München Deutschland, für die Einladung, damit ich in Ludwig Maximilian Universitätbleibenund ichmichdaraufkonzentierenkann, die neue Edition dieses Bucheszuschreiben.

Third, thanks for the great support from my university, especially the encouragement from President Zhao Rongshan, and my colleagues Cheng Zhenqiang and Chen Shuanghua, which helped me focus on writing the book.

Fourth, thanks to former President Tang Haiyan and Vice President Xu Mei of my university; thanks to my former teachers Hu Peizhao, Heiner Ganßmann, Jan Priewe, Song Wenzhou, HouZheng, XuJingde, Chen Xiaokun, Li Yaxin, He Chunlian, Jiang Chuangdao, GuoShudu, GaoJianqiang, and others; thanks to all my classmates from the Shuguang Talent Project 2009 in Shanghai, that is, Zou Jun, Yang tao, ZhongChunlong, Wu Xiaohui, Jiang Chuanhai, Yang hua, XieShaorong, Zhang Qinghua, Zhao qian, Dai Congrong, and others; thanks to my former students Zhou Jingwen, Li Yanlin, Li Wenhua, BaoHanguang, and others and also to my former classmates Wu Zongwen, Chen Yingyao, Song Chongbi, Yan Xiaojun, Li Yang, Yang Xiaoping, and others; thanks to Lu Hong at Reiji Hospital in Shanghai and thanks to all my teachers, classmates, and students for their support and positive energy.

Fifth, thanks to Prof. Dr. Wilhelm Stolz and his team, that is, D. Beer, Dr. med. Martin Kuehn, Dr. med. Christian Hacker, Dr. med. Julia Ernst, and Dr. Markus J. Pfeiffer, for giving me a positive experience and making me understand how Germany can be successful in the incremental innovation system in the medical field.

Sixth, thanks to Daniel Brandenburger, Anton Eltekov, GeroldStreif, Age Mariussen, Lv Xuemei and Li Jingsheng, LubaTrauner, Iris Bauer and Jens Bauer, Maria Tauber Wiese, Claudia Danner and Thomas Danner, Martina Suter, Celine Garbutt, Egor Fast and Dado and Giovanna Diso, Kai Kunicki and Thomas Pertassek, and also Bernhand Kurzer, Blair Gaulton, Michael Pauschand, and Karen Oxford in my circle of friends for their help and great friendship during my time in Germany.

Seventh, thanks to the China National Research Fund of Social Science (key project 16AGJ002) for supporting this book.

Last but not least, many thanks to Nitza Jones-Sepulveda, Nicholas Philipson, Faith Su, Shobha Karuppiah, and Springer for deciding to publish this third edition and offering a king production schedule. Thanks to Parick Chen, Ma Junsheng, and Wang Meng for their work to have had the original edition published in Chinese.

March 25, 2020

Munich, Germany   Chun LIAO (廖春)

Introduction

Part I

China's development and achievement in artificial intelligence (AI) and other high-technology innovations have attracted the whole world's attention. The following questions would quickly pop up in people's mind: Why has China become one of the leading powers in high-technology innovation? Is the Chinese innovation system unique and more powerful compared to other countries? How to compare China's innovation system with American innovation system and Germany leading European innovation system? How can China catch up so quickly? What are the advantages of the Chinese model? Is the Chinese model unique or can it be replicated in other countries? Why does the Chinese model have the strong stability to avoid the economic crises and the strong capability to control crises? Is the Chinese model sustainable? What is the future of the Chinese economy?

This book, which systematically defines and analyzes China's innovation system and the Chinese model, answers those questions. China's innovation system and the Chinese model were built up roughly in the period from the mid-1990s to the middle of the first decade of 21st century. The goal of this book is to shed light on how they were built in those years. It is because of that build up that China has now become one of the leading powers in innovation. In the meantime, China has the strong capability to control crises (e.g., Coronavirus crisis) and also the strong stability to avoid global economic crises (e.g., the 2008 global financial crisis), compared to the USA, Europe, and others. Therefore, the topic of this book will never be outdated.

For the 10th anniversary of the first edition of my book, it would be meaningful to publish its second edition, letting more people understand what drives China's innovation and what the Chinese model really means. In addition, it lets people connect the second edition with the first one and realize that it is this very early book, perhaps the first one, that recognized and identified China's super innovation system and the Chinese model.

The "Chinese model" and "China's innovation system" are the two core concepts discussed in this book. The "Chinese model" does not mean government-led economy. Private and state sectors must coexist, each exemplifying their respective innovation mechanism and comparative advantage. In the state sector, there is state coordination based on its controlling shareholding and not on government behavior. In the private sector, the coordination is based on the free market mechanism. Both private and state sectors are framed by the concept of market economy. Thereby, the coexistence of both sectors builds up such a super dual innovation system: In the state sector, there is state strategic innovation system, which is similar yet superior to the Germany leading European innovation system. In the private sector, the high-technology innovation system operates similar to the American model. Therefore, China has two types of innovation systems, while there is only one in other countries. Dual innovation system creates two types of core competitiveness. This dual strength builds up the super innovation power.

Coexistence of the two sectors without friction in between relies on "coordination boundary" between the coordination mechanisms of the two sectors. State coordination based on its controlling shareholding has long replaced the previous government-led framework. It is this creative institutional arrangement that contributes fully to the clear coordination boundary between the two sectors. This sounds nothing special, but it is a determined point. If there is no clear coordination boundary, then both coordination mechanisms in the two sectors will operate inefficiently. Only if there is a clear coordination boundary, the Chinese dual innovation system could be superior to other economies with only one type of innovation system.

Based on the basic concept and dimensions, this book can define the Chinese model and innovation system and can compare that with the US leading liberal market economies and Germany leading European coordinated market economies. The basic concept is a firm's governance structure. It includes five dimensions: ownership and shareholding structure, interrelation between employer and employee, interrelation between firms, firms' financing pattern and performance criteria, and innovation system and core competitiveness. Based on the first four dimensions, Innovation systems and core competitiveness of different countries can be compared. Upon these five dimensions, business models of different countries can be defined and compared. We can then find out that the Chinese state sector operates in a logic similar to Germany leading European model, which is basically a coordination-based business model, and leads to a coordination-based incremental innovation system and quality competitiveness. While the Chinese private sector operates in a logic similar to the American model, which is basically free market-based business model, it leads to a market-oriented radical innovation system and price competitiveness. We can see that while in other countries there is one business system, one type of innovation system, and one type of core competitiveness, China has a dual system with double strength.

Does the USA have the potential to build up a similar dual innovation system that China has? Why does Chinese state strategic innovation in the state sector appear superior to the Germany leading European innovation system? During the 2008 financial crisis, the US government injected stocks into the economy, which helped the economy recover. Effort in this direction could build up a dual system. Even though the state-coordinated Chinese state strategic innovation system in the state sector works quite similarly to the coordination-based European model, the coordination type in the Chinese state sector is different from the European model. In the Chinese state sector, state coordination is based on its controlling shareholding, whereas in Germany and many other European countries, it is institutional coordination. The state-coordinated Chinese state strategic innovation appears more powerful than institutional coordination–based European innovation.

The state coordination is based on its controlling shareholding, this creative institutional arrangement creates a clear "Coordination Boundary" between the state sector and the private sector in China. It is this insight that makes this book break through the standard approach / view (ie. each country has only one type of business system & innovation system), and makes it from originally impossible to become now possible to define Chinese dual business system / innovation system. The creative logic flows into the heart of the unique Chinese model.

Compared to the first edition, the second edition highlights the core concepts of China's super innovation system and Chinese model. Because of the many jargons that appear in the title, introduction, and conclusion of the first edition, nonscholarly readers might find it difficult to go through, leaving the core concepts behind the hard texts. The second edition makes the book easy to read and popular.

Recently, several articles came out talking about China's innovation and the Chinese model. This book can be distinguished from those. First, most of the other articles understand the "Chinese model" as "aggression of the state sector and recession of the private sector." But, this description is different from the "Chinese model" briefed in this book, which emphasizes the coexistence of the two sectors. Without a private sector, there would be no such high-technology innovation system typified in the Chinese private sector and, as a consequence, China would lose its specific dual innovation system and its comparative advantage in innovation.

Second, other articles are mostly descriptions and introductions of innovation achievement in China, while this book deeply finds out the institutional arrangement that supports and drives the innovation development in China. Because the other articles lack a suitable approach that can be used to analyze China's phenomenon, they cannot see through and gain insight. This book finds a typical approach, breaks through it, and helps to find out the secrecy about what makes Chinese innovation unique and powerful.

Third, many other articles emphasize the state's role, ignoring the boundary between the two sectors. This book highlights the restriction to the state role and emphasizes the state coordination boundary. The state's role in this book refers only to a shareholder function, which is based on its controlling shareholding and not on government behavior. This kind of creative design draws a clear boundary between the two sectors: If there is state controlling shareholding, it belongs to the state sector, otherwise it belongs to the private sector.

Fourth, other articles separately talk about China's innovation. This book compares China's innovation system with the American model and Germany leading European model. While other countries have only one innovation system, either radical innovation system such as the American model or incremental innovation system such as the European model, China has both: radical innovation in the private sector and state strategic innovation in the state sector, which is similar yet superior to the incremental innovation. The American radical innovation system can generate price competitiveness and the European incremental innovation system can generate quality competitiveness, whereas China has both price competitiveness and quality competitiveness. Therefore, China is able to compete broadly and successfully in the global market.

Part II

This book compares firms' governance structures in China with those in US leading liberal market economies (including the advanced English-speaking countries) and those in Germany leading coordinated market economies (including the advanced European countries, but also Japan) to define the innovation system and core competitiveness of the Chinese model evolving from its specific business systems.

The core of a business system/market economy is a firm's governance structure. There are two basic types of market economies: the US leading liberal market economies and Germany leading coordinated market economies. Accordingly, there are two basic types of governance structure for firms: the market-based governance structure and the coordinated governance structure.

The comparison of different firms' governance structures in distinct business systems is mainly based on five dimensions: ownership and control, interfirm coordination, employer–employee relation, firm's financing pattern and performance criteria, and firm's innovation system and core competitiveness. Considering variations in the types of owner control, the first dimension is particularly important. It has quite a strong implication for the other dimensions.

The market-based firm's governance structure emphasizes the exclusivity of ownership boundaries and limits interfirm cooperation and employer–employee interdependence. The firm's financing mainly relies on the capital market–based financing pattern or the self-financing pattern (for small owner-managed firms). Maximization of the short-term profitability is the main performance criterion. Firms tend to develop a market-oriented radical innovation system and market-oriented core competitiveness. The coordinating mechanism of this model is based on a market mechanism.

The coordinated firm's governance structure encourages the overlap of ownership boundaries and mutual cross-shareholding as well as interfirm collaboration and employer–employee interdependence. The firm's financing mainly relies on the credit-based financing pattern, in which banks play a control-oriented role in corporate governance. Long-term growth and long-term technological improvements are the main performance criteria. Firms tend to develop a coordination-based incremental innovation system and organizational competitiveness. The coordinating mechanism of this model relies on nonmarket-mode coordination.

The market-based firm's governance structure is prevalent in a business system that is dominated by arm's length market–controlled firms (the US case) and by firms that are under the owner's direct control (the British cases). The market-based firm's governance structure is the general model of the firm's governance structure in liberal market economies.

The coordinated firm's governance structure is prevalent in the business system that is dominated by alliance-controlled firms (German and Japanese cases). The coordinated firm's governance structure is the general model of the firm's governance structure in coordinated market economies.

In the Chinese state sector, a firm's governance structure is similar to the coordinated firm's governance structure model in coordinated market economies. The only difference is the type of coordination. In a firm's governance structure in the Chinese state sector, the primary coordination is "the state coordination through its controlling shareholding," while in coordinated market economies, a firm's governance relies on the institutionalized coordination. The institutional environment in China is impoverished with the institutional coordination arrangements that are pervasive in coordinated market economies, hence it cannot support the type of institutional coordination like in coordinated market economies. But the coordination role in a firm's governance structure in the Chinese state sector can be organized and played by the state on the basis of its controlling shareholding. This results in differing coordination mechanisms between the state-controlled shareholding-coordinated firm's governance structure in the Chinese state sector and the coordinated firm's governance structure in coordinated market economies.

The Chinese private sector is dominated by direct owner-controlled firms, and such firm's governance structure is market-based governance as in liberal market economies.

This dual Chinese model was built through reforms since the mid-1990s until the middle of the first decade of 21st century. It generates a dual innovation system and dual core competitiveness, which cannot easily be found in other countries. The state-controlled shareholding-coordinated firm's governance structure plays an important role in pursuing the state strategic goal of technological modernization and also generates a coordination-based innovation system and organizational core competitiveness like that in coordinated market economies. The market-based firm's governance structure in the private sector generates a market-oriented innovation system and market-oriented core competitiveness similar to liberal market economies. Such a dual innovation system and dual core competitiveness have enabled the Chinese economy to compete more successfully than US leading liberal market economies and Germany leading coordinated market economies, which have only one type of innovation system and core competitiveness, respectively. With such an overall innovation system and competitiveness, the Chinese economy can develop successfully in much broader industrial sectors, technological sectors, and scientific research fields than other liberal market economies and coordinated market economies.

On the basis of the concept of institutional complementarities, the author will explain why in coordinated market economies and liberal market economies only one model of a firm's governance structure/one type of innovation system exists, and why China can have both kinds of governance structure model and innovation system. The concept of institutional complementarities implies that, in general, each economy has one specific model of governance structure and accordingly one type of innovation system. This is because the coordinating mechanism in the model of a firm's governance structure applies and covers the whole economy, which does not have clear coordinating boundary and cannot be split and constrained within a certain part of the economy. Thus, in liberal market economies, such as the USA and the UK, and in coordinated market economies, such as Germany and Japan, only one model of governance structure and its related one type of innovation system exist for firms.

But if it is possible to find a business system with such a specific coordination mechanism, which has clear coordination boundary and only covers a certain part of the economy, then it is also possible for the other part of the economy to develop a different type of coordinating mechanism; therefore, two models of firm's governance structure can coexist in the economy. China provides the typical case here. Because the state is a controlling shareholder, the state plays the coordination role through its controlling shareholding in the governance structure of corporatized state-controlled enterprises. Because such a specific coordination mechanism is based on the state-controlling shareholding, it has a clear coordination boundary. It can be constrained within the state sector, while outside the state sector private enterprises develop and rely on a different type of coordinating mechanism that is built upon a market-based governance structure/radical innovation system. Because of the clear coordination boundary between the two sectors, the institutional complementarities in each sector are intact, and this prevents the interaction-driven convergence between the two sectors. Thus, the case of China does not actually contradict the concept of institutional complementarities. As a specific case, it supports and supplements the concept.

On the basis of another concept of institutional continuity and divergence, it will be analyzed how the dual-structured Chinese model can support the economic convergence of the Chinese economy toward both advanced liberal market economies and coordinated market economies, and how foreign direct investment and technology transfer can realize such a dual convergence.

The concept of institutional continuity and divergence means a path dependency in running a certain type of business model. It does not support economic convergence between economies with different business models/innovation systems, but it supports the conditional convergence between economies with similar business models. Therefore, it also supports the dual convergence of the Chinese economy toward both advanced liberal market economies and coordinated market economies. The Chinese business system has a dual structure, which makes it compatible with both advanced liberal market economies and coordinated market economies. This is the ground on which the Chinese dual economic convergence toward these two evolves. Foreign direct investment and technology transfer drive the dual convergence.

The joint strength of the dual innovation system, the dual core competitiveness, and the dual convergence, which develops from the dual-structured Chinese model, contributes to China's remarkable economic growth and super innovation achievement.

Author's Notes: Contribution to the Comparative Studies Approach

The author focuses on the firm's governance structure dimension (Whitley 1999, pp. 65–77) as a distinguishable criterion to differentiate between the business systems in the liberal market economies and those in the coordinated market economies and to compare the Chinese model and innovation system with that in liberal market economies and in coordinated market economies (Hall and Soskice 2001). In this book, the concept of a firm's governance structure combines the five principal spheres in Hall and Soskice's approach with Whitley's concept of the firms' governance system. It also entails the important sphere "ownership and control," which is emphasized in Whitley's approach. On the basis of the approaches from Hall and Soskice and Whitley, the author adds the dimension of a firm's innovation system and core competitiveness to its governance structure, which are used as an important dimension for the comparison of the varieties of market economy or business system in both Hall and Soskice's and Whitley's approaches. The firm's governance structure dimension therefore becomes an inclusive and generalized approach in the comparative analysis of business systems.

The author uses this comparative approach to analyze the Chinese model/innovation system on the basis of comparison of the Chinese model with the models of the US leading liberal market economies and Germany leading coordinated market economies. The author finds out that in the Chinese state sector, the firm's governance structure is a state-controlled shareholding-coordinated firm's governance structure, which is similar to the coordinated firm's governance structure in coordinated market economies, while in the Chinese private sector, the firm's governance structure is market-based, which is similar to the market-based firm's governance structure in liberal market economies.

Different economic models have different kinds of innovation systems and core competitiveness. Therefore, a particular economic model not only enhances its competitiveness in certain industrial sectors but also limits its capacity to compete in others (Hall and Soskice 2001). The US leading liberal market economies have a market-oriented radical innovation system and market competitiveness, but they are constrained to develop a coordination-based incremental innovation system and organizational competitiveness like that in Germany leading coordinated market economies. The Germany leading coordinated market economies have a coordination-based incremental innovation system and organizational competitiveness, but they are constrained to develop a market-oriented radical innovation system and market competitiveness like that in liberal market economies.

Thus, the dual structure of the Chinese model has an important implication. It generates a dual institutional comparative advantage, a dual innovation system, and dual core competitiveness. They have enabled the Chinese economy to compete more successfully than liberal market economies and coordinated market economies, which have only one type of innovation system and core competitiveness, respectively. With such an overall innovation system and competitiveness, the Chinese economy can develop successfully in much broader industrial sectors, high-technology sectors, and scientific research fields than other liberal market economies and coordinated market economies.

The author contributes to the concept of institutional complementarities in the comparative analysis in analyzing the dual structure of the Chinese model. The concept of institutional complementarities implies that, in general, each economy develops only one specific type of model based on its specific firm's governance structure. The coordinating mechanism in the firm's governance structure applies and covers the whole economy, which cannot be split and constrained within a certain part of the economy. Thus, in coordinated market economies such as Germany and Japan and in liberal market economies such as the USA and UK, only one kind of firm's governance structure model exists. In this book, the author finds that if it is possible to find a business system with such a specific coordinating mechanism that only covers a certain part of the economy, then it is also possible for the other part of economy to develop a different type of coordinating mechanism; therefore, there can be two different models of a firm's governance structure coexisting in the economy. This is the case for the Chinese economy. With a controlling shareholding, the state plays a coordination role in the governance structure of corporatized state-controlled enterprises. Such a specific coordination mechanism has a clear coordination boundary, and it can be constrained within the state sector, while outside the state sector private enterprises develop and rely on a different type of coordinating mechanism built upon the market-based governance structure. Thus, the case of China does not actually contradict the concept of institutional complementarities. As a specific case, it supports and supplements the concept.

In this book, the author analyzes the conditional convergence across economies. The concept of institutional continuity and divergence in the comparative analysis does not support economic convergence between economies with different models. On the basis of this concept, the author analyzes the conditional institutional convergence across economies with similar models. The author further analyzes how the dual structure of the Chinese economy supports its dual convergence toward both advanced liberal market economies and coordinated market economies, and how the dual convergence had been driven by foreign direct investment and technology transfer from those economies to China.

This book also addresses the important implications on several other key issues, such as: Why has China become now one of the leading powers in artificial intelligence (AI) and high-technology innovation? Is the Chinese innovation system unique and more powerful compared to other countries? How did China catch up so quickly? What are the advantages of the Chinese model? Is the Chinese model unique or can it be replicated in other countries? Is the Chinese model sustainable? Why does the Chinese model have the stability to avoid an economic crisis, the capacity to control the crisis, and the potential to keep the economy growing strongly for decades while many other countries don't? What is the future of the Chinese economy? How to compare China's innovation system with the American and European innovation systems (exemplified by German innovation)? Does the USA have the potential to build up a similar dual innovation system such as China? Why does the Chinese state strategic innovation in the state sector appear superior to the European innovation system?

This is the first time that the comparative approach has been used to analyze the innovation system and core competitiveness of the Chinese model, to analyze the dual structure–supported dual convergence of the Chinese economy toward advanced liberal market economies and coordinated market economies, and to analyze the remarkable long-term Chinese economic growth and China's super innovation. The author finds that it is such a dual innovation system, dual core competitiveness, and dual economic convergence that drive the remarkable Chinese economic growth and contribute to China's super innovation. On the one hand, it is a creative perspective of the analysis of the Chinese phenomenon, and on the other hand, the dual structure analysis of the Chinese case is a breakthrough of the standard approach in the comparative economies/business systems.

Contents

About the Author

Chun LIAO (廖春) was born on 4 February 1969 in the People's Republic of China. She is now a Professor of Economics at Shanghai Lixin University of Accounting and Finance. She is a Shuguang Scholar (曙光学者) in Shanghai. She holds a Ph.D. from the Free University of Berlin in Germany, and her research field is international business with a focus on comparative innovation systems, comparative firms' governance structures, and comparative business systems. Prof. Liao also passed the entrance examination for and was admitted to studying for Ph.D in Economics at Xiamen University in China. She has published more than 40 papers and books on Chinese business and economics. From each of her research work, there is a creative clue leading the whole topic. Since she started teaching, almost in every academic year she has got the best teaching rating from her students. This book is the second edition of the original book *The Governance Structures of Chinese Firms – Innovation, Competitiveness, and Growth in a Dual Economy*, which was published in 2009. This book may be the earliest one that systematically talks about China's super innovation system and the Chinese model. She has translated the first edition of the book into Chinese, which was authorized by Springer to be published by Shanghai people's publishing house (上海人民出版社) together with Truth & Wisdom Press (格致出版社) in 2013. The title of the Chinese edition was revised to *The Governance Structures and Innovation Systems of Chinese Firms: The Comparison with American–British Model and German–Japanese Model*, the Chinese translation of which is "中国企业的治理与创新模式:与'美英模式'和'德日模式'的比较."

Chapter 1
Different Economic Models and Their Corresponding Innovation Systems: To Build the Way to Find China

Abstract How many types of economic models and innovation systems exist and what are they? What is China's basic position? An economic model or a business system is basically built upon a certain type of firm's governance structure. There-fore, a certain type of firm's governance structure corresponds to a certain type of business system or economic model. Every firm's governance structure has a corresponding innovation pattern. Therefore firm's governance structure is a basic concept that is used to define and to distinguish a certain type of economic model and its related innovation system. There are two basic types of economic models (the US leading liberal market economies and Germany leading coordinated market econo-mies). Accordingly, there are two basic types of firm's governance structure (market-based firm's governance structure and coordinated firm's governance structure). Market-based firm's governance structure emphasizes the exclusivity of ownership boundaries, limits interfirm cooperation and employer–employee interdependence, shows free market mechanism determination. It leads to a market-oriented innova-tion system with price competitiveness. Coordinated firm's governance structure encourages an overlap of ownership boundaries to share risks and to improve flexibility. It also encourages interfirm collaboration and employer–employee interdependence. These characteristics show nonmarket institutional coordination. It leads to a coordination-based innovation system with quality competitiveness. China provides an exceptional case for a dual-structured model and innovation system because it creates a clear "coordination boundary" between the two parts of the economy. The state sector is based on a coordinated firm's governance structure, with a state strategic innovation system that is a coordination-based similar to but superior to the Germany leading European innovation system, while the private sector is built upon a market-based firm's governance structure, with a market-oriented innovation system that is similar to the US innovation system. The dual-structured Chinese economy supports its dual convergence toward both types of advanced economy that contributes to its remarkable catching up. It also sparks its own engine for further innovation development. While the other econo-mies are with only one type of innovation system and core competitiveness, China has two. The dual strength builds up the innovation powerhouse.

Keywords Innovation · Chinese innovation · Economic model · Business system · Chinese model · Corporate governance · Competitiveness · Chinese catching-up · Ownership · Interfirm relation · Employer–employee relation

How many types of economic models and innovation systems exist and what are they? What is China's basic position? Because a certain type of economic model or business system is basically built upon a certain type of firm's governance structure, different firm's governance structures mean different business systems or economic models. Every firm's governance structure has a corresponding innovation pattern. Therefore firm's governance structure is a basic concept that is used to define and to distinguish a certain type of economic model and its related innovation system. Here we go to find the basic position of China.

1.1 The Business Model and Innovation System of Market-Based Firm's Governance Structure and Coordinated Firm's Governance Structure: To Build the Way to Find Where China Is

1.1.1 Liberal Market Economies and Coordinated Market Economies

The concept of the comparative market economies (Hall and Soskice 2001) draws a core distinction between two basic types of market economies, the US leading liberal market economies and Germany leading coordinated market economies, which constitute ideal types at the poles of a spectrum along which many national economies can be arrayed. In liberal market economies, like those of the USA and other advanced English speaking countries, firms coordinate their activities primarily via hierarchies and a competitive market mechanism that are well described by classic literature (Williamson 1985). The market mechanism in a context of competition provides a highly effective means for coordinating firms' endeavors in liberal market economies. In coordinated market economies, like those of Germany and many advanced European countries, also including Japan, firms depend more heavily on nonmarket institutional coordination to coordinate their endeavors with other economic actors to construct their core competencies. Firms make extensive use of nonmarket modes of coordination, including network coordinating and monitoring, reliance on collaborative as opposed to competitive relationships, and relational or incomplete contracting (Hall and Soskice 2001, p. 8).

1.1.2   Firm's Governance Structure Defined by Five Dimensions

The comparative analysis of the varieties of market economies involves the identification of the characteristics of their different patterns of economic coordination and control, summarized as business system, of which the firm's governance structure is the key variable and can be constructed so that variations in the nature and behavior of firms can be described and explained (Whitley 1999, p. 31).

Owners, managers, and employees are organized differently based on different firm's governance structure across varieties of market economies. For example, ownership can be exercised directly over economic activities as in the owner-managed firm or may be delegated to managers with varying degrees of interdependence and commitment. Employer–employee relations can vary between the sort of adversarial zero-sum conflicts and the more institutionalized forms of cooperation represented in Germany's Codetermination Acts and firm–employee interdependences in postwar Japan (Whitley 1999, p. 32–3). Interfirm relations can be dominated by one-off and adversarial bargains as in pure market contracting or by repeated and cooperative connections as in obligational contracting (Dore 1986; Sako 1992). Competitor relations may also be adversarial and zero-sum or may encompass collaboration (Whitley 1999, p. 33).

There are five main dimensions for defining and comparing firms' governance structures in different business systems. The first one is ownership coordination, including primary means of owner control: direct control, alliance control, or market contracting control (Whitley 1999, p. 34). The second dimension is employment relations and work management, such as employer–employee interdependence, delegation to and trust of employees, distributional structure, strength of trade unions and labor organizations, and vocational training in firms (Whitley 1999, p. 34, 48; Hall and Soskice 2001, p. 7). The third one is interfirm coordination, including the extent of alliance coordination between firms and between competitors (Whitley 1999, p. 34; Hall and Soskice 2001, p. 7). The fourth dimension is the financing pattern and performance criteria. The financing pattern shows the patterns of how firms obtain access to finance and how investors seek assurance for returns on their investments. Financing patterns vary between capital-market-based financing and credit-based financing (Whitley 1999, p. 49; Hall and Soskice 2001, p. 7). Because the self-financing pattern also mobilizes capital directly according to changing market signals and trade capital through liquid markets (Whitley 1999, p. 49), it can also be included in the category of the capital-market-based financing pattern. Performance criteria vary between short-term profit maximization and long-term growth (Whitley 1999, p. 67, 71; Hall and Soskice 2001). The fifth dimension is innovation system and competitive capacity. Innovation system varies between the incremental innovation mode and the radical innovation mode. The competitive capacity of firms is also related to price competitiveness (which is pure market competitiveness) or quality competitiveness (which involves organizational competitiveness) (Hall and Soskice 2001, p. 38–44; Whitley 1999, p. 67). Among these five dimensions, particularly important is the dimension concerning the way in which property rights confer authority over the acquisition, use, and disposal of resources and activities, including labor power (Whitley 1999, p. 34). Thus, the first dimension, which considers variations in types of owner control and organization of property rights, has quite strong implications for a number of other firm's governance structure or business system characteristics (Whitley 1999, p. 39). On the basis of the five-dimension comparison, we can analyze if the firm's governance structure in a business system is mainly based on market mechanisms or makes more extensive use of nonmarket coordinating mechanisms. Accordingly, we can get two basic types of firm's governance structure: "market-based governance structure" and "coordinated governance structure."

The market-based governance structure is the general model of the firm's governance structure in the US leading liberal market economies. The market-based governance structure exists in firms with market arm's length portfolio control or direct owner control in the *fragmented business system* (Whitley 1999, p. 43). The Anglo-Saxon pattern of arm's length portfolio investment demonstrates the market type of owner control, while owner-managers of family businesses in the UK typify direct owner control (Chandler 1990; Whitley 1999, p. 35).

The coordinated governance structure is the general model of the firm's governance structure in Germany leading to coordinated market economies. The coordinated governance structure exits in alliance-controlled firms. The ownership of some shares by bank and allied companies in Germany and Japan exemplifies alliance control (Whitley 1999, p. 35). This governance structure also exists in artisanal firms in the European regional *coordinated industrial district business system*, in which even though ownership units remain owner-controlled, collaboration and coordination are still the main characteristics of the firm's governance structure because of their specific coordinated institutional environment and arrangements (Whitley 1999, p. 43, 84–5). In Chap. 3, I will analyze the reason for the differences in the firms' governance structures between the artisanal firms in the coordinated industrial district business system and the owner-controlled firms in the fragmented business system.

1.1.3 The Business Model and Innovation System of Market-Based Firm's Governance Structure Versus that of Coordinated Firm's Governance Structure

Both direct control of firms by owners in the fragmented business system and market arm's length control emphasize the exclusivity of ownership boundaries, limit interfirm cooperation and employer–employee interdependence, and show market mechanism determination; thus, both belong to liberal market economies. For example, the firm governance model in the USA is a market form of owner control with managerial management for large corporations. The firm governance model in the UK is a direct form of owner control with personal management for smaller family firms. Both the USA and the UK belong to liberal market economies. Moreover, both of them are different from the alliance control model in coordinated market economies, which encourages permeability and an overlap of ownership boundaries to share risks and to improve flexibility. It also encourages interfirm collaboration and employer–employee interdependence. These characteristics show nonmarket institutional coordination (Whitley 1999, p. 36–40). The discussion on this point is along the five main dimensions: the ownership coordination dimension, the nonownership coordination dimension, the employer–employee relation and work management dimension, the financing pattern and performance criteria dimension, and the innovation system and the competitive capacity dimension.

1.1.3.1 Ownership Coordination

Direct control of firms by their owners is typified by owner-managed firms, in which the owner involvement in management and the concentration of control over assets are high. Owner-managers usually maintain firm control over organizational boundaries. Control as well as shareholding is not often shared with others, except with family members or with those with whom family-like relationships have been established over a long time. Similarly, the market arm's length control type of ownership encourages strong ownership boundaries because capital holders focus on returns from separate and exclusive ownership in making investment decisions. Therefore, regarding the exclusivity and rigidity of ownership boundaries, the direct control model and the market arm's length control model are similar. Given the predominantly adversarial and exclusive ownership relations between the economic actors, long-term corporation and sharing of resources as well as activities and ownership between firms are difficult to develop and reproduce in economies that are dominated by the market control form and the direct control form of ownership.

In contrast, the alliance control form of ownership, as prevalent in postwar Japan and Germany, encourages permeability and overlaps of ownership boundaries to share risks, to improve flexibility, and to coordinate innovations (Whitley 1999, p. 34–6).

1.1.3.2 Interfirm Coordination

Interfirm coordination applies to interfirm relationships between members of a production chain or between competitors. The variations in nonownership forms of coordination are normally linked to differences in ownership relations. Direct owner control of managerial decisions often limits the interfirm relationships because of the strong sense of exclusivity of ownership boundaries, reluctance to share control, and low trust in formal institutions. Similarly, market forms of owner control are unlikely to encourage interfirm alliances. Because of the strong exclusivity of ownership boundaries and strong corporate control in markets, it is difficult to establish long-term and wide-ranging interfirm alliances and cooperation. Thus, the interfirm relations between firms with direct owner control or market forms of control are likely to be zero-sum, adversarial contracting, and competition. In contrast, alliance forms of owner control are likely to encourage more cooperative, long-term, and mutually committed relationships between partners and competitors.

Personal networks in market economies where owner-managed firms dominate, like in China, are different from institutional-coordination-based interfirm networks in market economies where alliance-controlled firms dominate, like in Japan and Germany. In comparing these two types of interfirm relation, the crucial issue is the extent to which economic activities are consciously and repeatedly coordinated, based on long-term organizational commitments. The personal networks in business systems that are dominated by owner-managed firms (like in China) do not imply such a high level of coordination because they tend to be based on personal rather than long-term organizational commitments. They also do not dominate the economy as their Japanese counterparts do. Their authoritative integration of activities and resources is therefore much less than that of interfirm networks in Japan and Germany (Whitley 1999, p. 37–8).

1.1.3.3   Employer–Employee Relations and Patterns of Work Organization and Control

Employer–employee relations and work systems vary with different business systems. Alliance-controlled firms, like firms in Japan, encourage mutual dependence between employers and employees and encourage mutual commitment in organizational capabilities. "Responsible-autonomy" strategies implemented in the working system trust employees to carry out tasks with more discretion and independence from managers. The long-term mutual interdependence of employers and employees means that employees constitute key assets and that firms' performance standards depend on employee skills and commitments. Thus, employee interests are significant influences on the firms' strategies (Whitley 1999, p. 69). In contrast, market-controlled firms encourage reliance on external labor markets in managing the bulk of the labor force. The Anglo-Saxon pattern represents flexible external labor markets and high rates of turnover of personnel. "Scientific management" strategies in the USA that are implemented in the working system remove all discretion from employees and fragment tasks to simplify them for unskilled and easily replaceable employees (Whitley 1999, p. 38–9). Firms treat employees' skills as short-term resources, to be acquired or removed in flexible external labor markets as business cycles change, and it is unlikely that they pay much heed to employee interests in deciding priorities (Whitley 1999, p. 69). In companies in the USA, firms treat white-collar employees and manual workers differently; as a result, managerial integration is greater than organizational integration (Lazonick 1991; Lazonick and West 1998). Similarly, owner-managed firms also rely on external labor markets in managing their labor force and discourage delegation of task performance to employees because employees are viewed as needing instruction and being unreliable in following organizational interests (Whitley 1999, p. 59).

These three dimensions are the basic characteristics of a firm's governance structure and exhibit particular interdependences with each other to form quite distinct ways of organizing business systems in market economies. In the fragmented business system, the dominating owner-controlled firms engage in adversarial competition with each other and short-term market contracting with suppliers and customers. Employment relations are short-term and dominated by external markets. Thus, organizational integration of economic activities is low in employer–employee relations and in interfirm relations. That sharing of risk with business partners and with employees is low and is also associated with short-term commitments to particular technologies, skills, or markets. The case of China Hong Kong represents such a low-commitment economy. Firms in Hong Kong moved quickly from making plastic flowers to wigs, toy manufacturing, and property development and financial services as the market was changing. Similarly, in the business system that is dominated by market forms of ownership, firms exhibit little commitment or collaboration between each other or between employers and employees, such as in the Anglo-Saxon economy.

In contrast, the business system that is dominated by alliance forms of ownership manifests more collective organization and cooperation in employer–employee and interfirm relations. Owner control of these firms is exercised through alliances, organizational coordination of economic activities is achieved through the economy, and employer–employee interdependence is high, as in continental European economies and postwar Japan's "alliance capitalism."

Both direct and market forms of owner control rely mainly on markets to coordinate firms' endeavors; they therefore tend to limit interfirm cooperation and employer–employee interdependence. Because control over economic activities is difficult to share between ownership units on a stable and long-term basis, collaboration between business partners is restricted, and commitment between employer and employee is limited, which manifests itself as flexible labor strategies and a "hire-and-fire" culture. In contrast, alliance forms of ownership make more extensive use of nonmarket modes of coordination to organize firms' endeavors, and thus they presume risk-sharing and mutual dependence between owners of enterprises, which implies an institutional framework for coordinating interfirm relations in a non-zero-sum mode. Interfirm collaboration can lead to greater employer–employee interdependence as employers and employees become locked into particular sectors or enterprises. Employer dependence on particular sectors encouraged the reliance on skilled worker's commitment to product improvements in those industries, which is difficult to elicit if employers do not retain employees over business cycles. High levels of employer–employee interdependence are associated with considerable worker discretion over task performance. Employers encourage the flexibility of employees to manage market and technology changes (Whitley 1999, p. 39–44).

1.1.3.4   The Financing Patterns and Performance Criteria of Firms

The financing patterns of firms vary with the different business systems. Capital can be allocated through the market and competition, or firms can be financed in the more institutional coordinated way. The capital-market-based financing pattern mobilizes and distributes capital directly through liquid markets, ownership rights are easily traded, and owners have little incentive to retain shares when they are offered higher-priced premiums by acquisitive predators. So investors are only weakly committed to the growth of any single firm in which they own shares and only have a short-term and narrow interest in their investments. This encourages a strong market for corporate control. Market arm's length controlled firms and some large owner-controlled firms depend on this financing pattern.

Small owner-controlled firms mainly rely on the self-financing pattern, which is also largely based on the market and competition. Owners of small owner-controlled firms change their investment directions rapidly as market conditions alter, which represents a low-commitment business system.

Alliance-controlled firms depend on the credit-based financing pattern. In contrast to the other financing patterns, the credit-based one coincides with weak and illiquid capital markets that only play a minor role in mobilizing and pricing investment capital. The dominant institutions here are banks. Because shares are not easily traded, owners and banks become locked into the fates of particular firms and have to be involved in the decision-making of the firms. Financial intermediaries become more committed to particular firms (Whitley 1999, p. 49–50).

The three basic characteristics of firms' governance structures and financing patterns affect the sorts of dominant goals and performance criteria of firms in different business systems. In arm's length controlled firms, the dominant goal and performance criteria are seen in profit maximization. Growth in share prices and dividend payouts are significant measures of corporate performance. Effectiveness is a matter of achieving financial objectives rather than market-share objectives. Large size without sufficient rates of return on capital is unlikely to appeal to shareholders. Investors in these firms have a very narrow interest in their shares and they easily trade shares for a higher price premium (Whitley 1999, p. 70–1). Similarly, the pursuit of short-term profits, high personal incomes, and personal wealth accumulation are the main objectives and performance criteria of owner-controlled firms (Whitley 1999, p. 69, 72).

Alliance-controlled firms pursue growth as their dominant objective and performance criterion. In Japan, firms long pursued market-share goals and sought to grow in size; in Germany and other economies where firms are closely tied to large banks, growth goals are also likely to be dominant (Zysman 1983).

Firms' governance structures and firms' prime performance criteria are interconnected. Both considerable employer–employee interdependence and authority sharing with business partners encourage growth goals. The mutual dependence between firms, suppliers, customers, banks, employees, and institutional organizations leads to strong collective interests in expansion (Abegglen and Stalk 1985;

Fruin 1992; Gerlach 1992) because employees and business partners gain more from expansion than from increased profits. Direct owner control is unlikely to be associated with authority sharing, either between firms or with employees. The arm's length type of owner control is not likely to encourage employer–employee relations or interfirm collaboration. In these two business systems, where firms are much more isolated, the pursuit of growth goals is limited by the market constraints and the need to meet the expectations of capital owners. The growth of these firms is subject to a profit constraint (Whitley 1999, p. 71–2).

1.1.3.5 Innovation System and Competitive Capacity

Firms vary in kinds of innovation system and competitive capacity across business systems because different firms' governance structures condition different comparative advantages in particular products, innovation, and core competitiveness. The coordinated governance structure should be better at supporting incremental innovation, that is, continuous small-scale improvements to existing product lines. The coordinated governance structure provides high levels of support for relational requirements that are needed to foster incremental innovation. Employee involvement in the firms' governance, employee autonomy from close monitoring, and the development of employer–employee relations elicit their cooperation and contribution to the firms' incremental innovation. Systems of corporate governance that insulate firms against hostile takeovers and reduce their sensitivity to current profits, as well as build up a close interfirm collaboration foster incremental innovation.

The market-based governance structure is highly supportive of radical innovation, which entails substantial shifts in product lines or major changes to the production process. Labor markets with a few restrictions on layoffs and high rates of labor mobility help companies in easily hiring personnel with the requisite expertise and in releasing them if the project proves to be unprofitable. Interfirm relations based mainly on markets help firms to buy other companies and to poach their personnel. Liquid capital markets with a few restrictions on mergers and acquisitions help firms in seeking new technologies by acquiring other firms. The presence of venture capital helps individuals to invest in new technology.

Different firms' governance structures in different business systems condition different competitive capacities and also give rise to the specialization of production across the business systems. Incremental innovation tends to be more important in the production of capital goods, such as machine tools and factory equipment, consumer durables, engines, and transport equipment. Incremental innovation also helps to generate continuous and incremental improvements in an established product line to maintain high quality. Radical innovation tends to be more important in fast-moving technology, as in software, biotechnology, semiconductors, telecommunications, and defense systems, and service sectors, as in airlines, advertising, corporate finance, and entertainment.

The other type of firms' competitive capacity is related to price competitiveness or quality competitiveness. Firms with a coordinated governance structure can secure high levels of quality control because of their close relationships with employees and collaboration with other firms. The quality competitiveness may offer them advantages in cases of products for which demand depends more heavily on quality than on price. Firms with a market-based governance structure achieve price competitiveness because they can cut costs by releasing workers, given fluid labor markets. Price competitiveness may offer them advantages in cases of products for which demand is price-sensitive (Hall and Soskice 2001, p. 38–44).

Firms with a coordinated governance structure pursue long-term growth and high quality as their dominant goals and performance criteria at the expense of short-term profitability. They therefore rely heavily on the commitment of employees and collaboration of other firms. In contrast, firms with a market-based governance structure are subject to strong profit constraint and have price competitiveness. They therefore pursue efficiency and low price as their dominant goals. They will not develop strong interdependencies with their employees and business partners. Since low price is the dominant goal for these firms, this encourages adversarial, cost-based relationships and limited cooperation with other firms (Whitley 1999, p. 74–5).

On the basis of the analysis of the five dimensions above, we can summarize the main characteristics of the two basic types of firm's governance structure: market-based firm's governance structure and coordinated firm's governance structure. The market-based firm's governance structure is prevalent in both owner-controlled firms in the fragmented business system, which are exemplified by Chinese family businesses (Whitley 1999, p. 75), and arm's length controlled firms, which develop in Anglo-Saxon economies because both of them rely mainly on markets to coordinate firms' endeavors. Owner-controlled firms in the fragmented business system are atomistic firms that are highly dependent on the market and that minimize commitments to employees and business partners. They are controlled by the owners, who compete by being highly flexible in seeking business, and their commitment to any one sector and expertise is limited. These firms are profit-driven and pursue low-cost strategies and price competitiveness. They adapt quickly to changing markets to remain competitive. They often rely on the innovations of others, and they could be competitive in radical innovation in fast-moving technologies such as in the software information high-technology sector. Similarly, arm's length controlled firms are also highly dependent on the market, as relations between owners, managers, employees, and business partners are essentially market based. Risk-sharing, commitment, and mutual dependence in employer–employee relations and interfirm relations are quite limited. Employees and business partners have no significant influences on decision-making in these firms. Ultimately, these firms focus on increasing investor returns and rarely develop long-term growth strategies. Given liquid capital markets, fluid labor markets, and market-driven sensibility, such firms tend to have a radical innovation capacity and price competitiveness (Whitley 1999, p. 75–6).

Alliance-controlled firms have a coordinated firm's governance structure, which is exemplified by firms in continental Europe and postwar Japan because these firms make more extensive use of nonmarket modes of coordination to organize their endeavors. These firms are characterized by substantial and long-term risk-sharing and collaboration with their employees, business partners, and banks. Decision-making is constrained by employees, business partners, and banks, which encourages long-term growth goals rather than profitability. Employee involvement and interdependence between business partners enable firms to develop quality competitiveness and incremental innovation (Whitley 1999, p. 76–7).

1.2 Case Analyses on Two Basic Models/Innovation Systems

1.2.1 The "German and Japanese Model" for the Coordinated Firm's Governance Structure

1.2.1.1 The Coordinated Firm's Governance Structure in the German Model

1.2.1.1.1 Ownership and Control of German Firms

Extensive networks of cross-shareholding among German firms that discourage hostile takeovers are distinctive pattern of the ownership structure of German firms, in contrast to the market and volatile pattern of ownership in large American firms (Hall and Soskice 2001, p. 23–4; Vitols 1995a, b, c, d; Hollingsworth 1997, p. 286).

Unlike their counterparts in liberal market economies, top managers in German firms rarely have a capacity for unilateral action. They must secure consensus decision-making, that is, secure agreement for decisions from supervisory boards, including major shareholders, other managers with entrenched positions, employee representatives, and major suppliers and customers. The long-term employment contracts that German firms offer managers lead them to focus heavily on their ability to secure consensus and on the maintenance of their reputations. The managerial compensation in German firms, in which relative to that in firms in liberal market economies less weight is given to stock-option schemes, makes managers focus less on profitability than their counterparts in liberal market economies. Managerial incentives are broadly aligned with those of firms (Hall and Soskice 2001, p. 24).

1.2.1.1.2 Interfirm Coordination

Cross-shareholding and consensus decision-making encourage information sharing and facilitate network monitoring among German firms (Hall and Soskice 2001, p. 24).

Other firms are not only represented on the supervisory boards of firms but are also engaged in joint product development and research. Firms can gain inside information about the operation of other firms within such dense business networks. German firms also cultivate close relationships with major suppliers and clients.

There are also third parties, such as business associations, that are positioned to monitor the firm and penalize it for misleading other firms. Membership of German firms in industry associations also helps these firms gather information about coordinating standard setting, technology transfer, and vocational training (Hall and Soskice 2001, p. 23).

1.2.1.1.3 Employer–Employee Relations and Patterns of Work Organization and Control

German firms make extensive use of long-term labor contracts (Hall and Soskice 2001, p. 26) and have been less likely to lay off workers during economic downturns (Hollingsworth 1997, p. 285). Works councils composed of elected employee representatives are endowed with considerable authority over layoffs and working conditions (Hall and Soskice 2001, p. 25). These works councils participate in organizing working conditions within firms and in ensuring that employment protection laws are obeyed by the management (Hollingsworth 1997, p. 286).

German firms are less hierarchical structures than American firms, with higher involvement of workers in both conceptualizing and executing projects (Hollingsworth 1997, p. 288). Workers and their representatives hold approximately half of the seats on the supervisory boards of German firms. These arrangements have been instrumental in reducing conflict between labor and management and in enhancing flexible production within firms (Hollingsworth 1997, p. 286). German firms rely on a highly skilled labor force that is given substantial work autonomy and is encouraged to share information to generate continuous improvements in product lines (Sorge and Warner 1986; Dore 1986; Hall and Soskice 2001, p. 24).

The German industrial relations system sets wages through industry-level bargains between trade unions and employer associations. By equalizing wages at equivalent skill levels across an industry, this system not only makes it difficult for firms to poach workers, but also ensures that workers are receiving the highest feasible rates of pay in return for a deep commitment to their firms (Hall and Soskice 2001, p. 25).

The key to the German industrial relations system is shaped by the highly developed centralized trade unions and employer and business associations. Association bargaining has played an important role in shaping distributional issues and in influencing the quality and competitiveness of German products. German trade unions and employer associations both have centralized organizational structures. Unions are responsible for collective bargaining and participation through policies of codetermination (Hollingsworth 1997, p. 286).

As works councils provide employees with security against arbitrary layoffs or changes to their working conditions, employees are encouraged to invest in industry-specific skills (Hall and Soskice 2001, p. 25). The job security enjoyed by employees has also encouraged firms to invest in the long-term training of their labor force to adjust to complex and rapidly changing technologies and markets. German firms are constrained by the codetermination system, which results in not only job protection, but also a high-wage system. Thus, it is highly rational for German firms to invest more in the training of their workforce and to develop one of the world's most skilled labor forces and high-quality products to build up Germany's high level of competitiveness in the global economy (Hollingsworth and Streeck 1993).

The German industrial relations system has also led to a highly skilled labor force and high-quality products in another way, that is, via establishing enterprise-based vocational training or apprenticeship programs whereby young workers learn the theoretical principles of related trades and experience a rich practical training (Hollingsworth 1997, p. 287). Such vocational training or apprenticeship programs provide workers with industry-specific skills. Germany relies on industry-wide employer associations and trade unions to supervise its training system. These associations require firms to take on apprentices, monitor their participation, and limit free-riding on the training efforts of others. They also negotiate with the firms on industry-wide skill categories and training protocols in each industrial sector, to ensure both that the training fits the firms' needs and that an apprenticeship will result in lucrative employment for apprentices at the end of the apprenticeship (Hall and Soskice 2001, p. 25).

1.2.1.1.4 The Financing Pattern and Performance Criteria of Firms

German business system provides companies with access to finance that is not entirely dependent on balance sheet financial data or current returns. Investors monitor the performance of companies via dense networks that link the managers within a company to their counterparts in other firms for "inside" information sharing and networking reputation monitoring. This pattern of financing provides German firms with access to financial capital independent of short-term returns, makes German firms exempt from fluctuation of the equity markets, and makes it possible for the firms to invest in projects that will generate returns only in the long run (Hall and Soskice 2001, p. 22–3).

German securities markets have historically been less well developed. Banks have been much more important in supplying capital to firms than the equity and bond markets. Banks have also exercised the stock voting rights of a substantial proportion of outstanding shares of the large companies. Bank officers have served on the supervisory boards of large firms. The long-term relationship between German firms and banks has made firms much more immune to the short-run fluctuations of financial markets than American companies and has encouraged German firms to adopt a long-term development strategy (Cox 1986a, b; Deeg 1992; Dyson 1984; Esser 1990, p. 17–32; Kocka 1980, p. 77–116; Neuberger and Stokes 1974, p. 710–31; Tilly 1976, p. 416–24; Tilly 1982, p. 629–58; Tilly 1986, p. 113–52; Vittas et al. 1978; Zysman 1983, p. 251–65).

On the basis of this pattern of firms' financing, the performance criteria of firms are not based on balance sheets and current returns, but on long-run returns and long-term development.

1.2.1.1.5 Innovation System and Competitive Capacity

A firm's governance structure fosters its particular innovation system and competitive capacity. The German firms' specific governance structure is conducive to an incremental innovation system—the rapid diffusion of the latest technology to the production of traditional products (Junne 1989, p. 249–74). German firms have been successful in applying the latest microelectronic technology to the production of traditional products and to new production processes and have excelled in competing in particular sectors, such as the production of machine tools, automobiles, chemical products, and other traditional industrial products. On the other hand, German firms have been less successful in developing entirely new technologies and industries than in applying the latest technologies to the production of traditional products. Thus, German firms have been less competitive in newer industries, such as computers, semiconductors, and consumer electronics. In addition, the German firms' governance structure is conducive to the development of high-quality products. In the global markets German firms have competed extremely well on the basis of high-performance product segments rather than costs. These characteristics influence the particular product markets in which German firms are highly competitive (Hollingsworth 1997, p. 289–90).

As the discussion suggests, the key to the success of German firms results from the coordinated configuration of their governance structure. All elements of the governance structure complement one another: cross-shareholding and the control structure, interfirm networking and coordination, specific industrial relations, financing pattern, performance and capacity, and incremental innovation. All these elements are intertwined and are the outcomes of a unique path of development of a firm.

1.2.1.2 The Coordinated Firm's Governance Structure in the Japanese Model

The important feature of the Japanese model is the form of the industrial grouping which is established and strengthened by the cross-company pattern of stock ownership and interlocking directorships.

The pattern of intercorporate stockholding encourages long-term business relationships and reinforces ties of interdependence, exchange relations, and reciprocal trust among member firms within the industrial group (Abegglen and Stalk 1985; Aoki 1987, p. 263–88; Aoki 1988; Aoki 1992, p. 142–69; Hollingsworth 1997, p. 280).

Long-term stable relationships have also existed between producers and suppliers, which has facilitated the clustering of firms and cooperation among complementary firms. Japanese trade associations span a variety of suppliers, buyers, and related industries; they have also played an important role in facilitating the clustering of industries (Friedman 1988; Levine 1984, p. 318–56; Miyamoto 1988, p. 1–45; Schneiberg and Rogers Hollingsworth 1990, p. 320–46; Hollingsworth 1997, p. 283).

Japanese firms have developed long-term relations with their employees (Shirai 1983, p. 267–91; Hollingsworth 1997, p. 280). Japanese firms offer long-term job security and have often shifted their employees to other member firms within their group during economic downturns rather than dismissing the workers. Japanese firms have also implemented a seniority-based wage and promotion system, company welfare capitalism, consensus decision-making, employee loyalty, job rotation and flexible labor assignments, and intensive on-the-job training (Aoki 1988; Koike 1983, p. 29–62; O'Brien 1993, p. 43–71; Shigeyoshi 1984; Strath 1993, p. 72–96; Hollingsworth 1997, p. 280–1).

There are linkages between industrial relations and the system of training for management and labor. In Japan, schools provide a set of filters to select the most academically talented, whose academic performance is seen as the key to economic success. Japan's educational system does not provide practical or vocational training. It is the Japanese firms that provide such training. Because of long-term job security, the training is highly firm specific (Hollingsworth 1997, p. 281).

Japanese firms not only provide firm-specific skill but also emphasize job rotation in work teams. Japanese people have long been socialized to integrate the obligations of the group with one's own self-interest (Hollingsworth 1997, p. 281). Japanese firms do not classify jobs with the precision which American firms do, and thereby they emphasize flexibility in internal labor markets (Cole 1979; Koike 1988).

Human resources are considered the most valuable asset of the firm. Decision-making is consensual and participatory. The compensation system combines merit and seniority pay. The profits of the firm are distributed to employees, with a much smaller gap between the salaries of the top executives and lowest starting wages than in the USA (Hollingsworth, p. 282).

These distinctive features structure the Japanese industrial relations and work organization—lifetime employment, seniority-based wage and promotion systems, company welfarism, employee loyalty, consensus decision-making, and participatory work management (Hollingsworth 1997, p. 282). Because Japanese workers pursue their careers within, acquire most of their training from, and receive most of their benefits from a single company, company unions rather than industrial unionism are quite common in Japan (Lincoln and Kalleberg 1990; Lincoln and McBride 1987, p. 289–312; Shirai 1983, p. 267–91).

A further aspect of the governance structure of Japanese firms is their financing pattern. Given that the equity and bond markets are historically poorly developed, it was quite common for Japanese firms to rely on one lead bank for capital. The lead bank not only provides loans to the firm, but also monitors the firm's operations very carefully. The bank also holds equity in the firm, strengthening the bank–firm relationship. Because each Japanese industrial group has a major bank as its main lender and each group is heavily dependent on a single bank, Japanese industrial groups are bank-centered groups (*keiretsu*).

The long-term bank–firm relationship and the institutional arrangement of mutual shareholding and interlocking directorships buffer firms from the fluctuation of stock markets and the uncertainties of labor and product markets. This is also an important reason why Japanese firms can forsake short-term profit maximization in favor of a strategy of long-term goals (Hollingsworth 1997, p. 279–80).

Mainly because of their particular institutional configuration and the firms' governance structure, Japanese firms have been enormously successful in improving upon existing products, but have been less successful in developing new products (Hollingsworth 1997, p. 284), and tend to lack the capacities for radical innovation (Hall and Soskice 2001, p. 35).

The group-based firm's governance structure generates the capacities for cross-sector technology transfer and rapid organizational redeployment which are provided by the *keiretsu* group. On the basis of this, Japanese firms have comparative institutional advantages in the large-scale production of consumer goods, machinery, and electronics (Hall and Soskice 2001, p. 35). They have excelled in producing cars and trucks, small consumer electronic equipment (TV sets, copiers, radios, and video sets), motorcycles, machine tools, watches and clocks, and a number of business-related products, such as small computers, fans, pumps, and tools (Hollingsworth 1997, p. 283).

The Japanese education system emphasizes rote learning rather than creative synthesis and analysis. Japanese universities facilitate the pattern of consensus decision-making, and there is an overall weakness of Japanese universities as research institutions. Thus, Japan has lagged behind in some industries, such as in chemical, biotechnology, and other fields that heavily depend on basic science.

The poorly developed venture capital markets and the coordinated firm's governance structure also do not facilitate Japanese entrepreneurs to bring creative ideas to the market (Hollingsworth 1997, p. 284).

1.2.1.3 Comparison of "Coordination" Between German and Japanese Firms' Coordinated Governance Structures

Although many of the market economies can be classified as liberal or coordinated market economies, and their firms' governance structure can also be classified as a market-based governance structure and a coordinated governance structure, the point of this analysis is not simply to identify these two types, but also to outline an approach that can be used to compare many kinds of firms' governance structures in different market economies. In particular, we place emphasis on the comparison of the variation in the coordinated firms' governance structures in coordinated market economies.

In coordinated market economies, firms' coordinated governance structures resolve many of the coordination problems through strategic interaction. The coordinated firms' governance structures that different coordinated market economies use to achieve coordination may differ to some extent from each other. We use the cases of Germany and Japan to illustrate how nonmarket coordination is achieved in each of the principal spheres of the firms' governance structures (Hall and Soskice 2001, p. 22). We further compare the coordination in these two types of coordinated firms' governance structure.

There is some similarity in the firms' governance structures of Germany and Japan, including cross-shareholding, stable and long-term relationships between firms, long-term commitment between employers and employees, a high level of worker autonomy, a highly trained workforce, the firms' financing pattern, with close ties between large firms and banks, and incremental innovation with high-quality products (Hollingsworth 1997, p. 288).

Despite the similarity in these principal spheres, there are also major differences between the coordination patterns in their firms' governance structures. German firm's governance structure relies primarily on industry-based coordination, while Japanese firm's governance structure fosters group-based coordination. In German firm's governance structure, coordination depends on business associations and trade unions that are organized along sectoral lines, which gives rise to sector-based vocational training schemes that cultivate industry-specific skills, a system of wage coordination that negotiates wages by sectors, and corporate collaboration that is industry-based. By contrast, in Japanese firm's governance structure, coordination is built on *keiretsu*, a group of companies with one major company at its center, and with dense networks cutting across sectors. Workers are encouraged to acquire firm- or group-specific skills. To persuade workers to invest in skills of this specificity, large firms offer lifetime employment to their employees and company unions provide the workforce with a voice in the affairs of the firm (Hall and Soskice 2001, p. 34–5). In Germany, sector-based unions have been highly developed, whereas in Japan the company unions play an important role. In Germany, there is nothing resembling the *keiretsu* structure, which is the basic coordination unit in Japan. German firms tend to focus on the upscale, high-cost segments, whereas Japanese firms tend to focus on markets with low-priced, but high-quality products. In Germany, there is a sector-based public vocational training program, whereas in Japan a limited public vocational training program is practiced. Vocational training in Japan is provided by the firms and the training is high in firm-specific terms (Hollingsworth 1997, p. 288). Thus, although Germany and Japan both clearly have coordinated market economies with coordinated firms' governance structures, Japanese firm's governance structure, which supports group-based coordination conducive to its specific comparative advantages, is somewhat different from the German one, which fosters an industry-based system of coordination and its specific institutional advantages.

1.2.2   The "American and British Models" for the Market-Based Firm's Governance Structure

1.2.2.1   The "American Model" as a Model Case for the Market-Based Firm's Governance Structure with Arm's Length Portfolio Control

Liberal market economies and market-based firm's governance structure can secure levels of overall economic performance as high as those of coordinated market economies and coordinated firm's governance structure, but they do so in a quite different way. In liberal market economies, firm's governance structure relies more heavily on market relations to resolve the coordination problems, while firm's governance structure in coordinated market economies relies more heavily on forms of nonmarket coordination that entail collaboration and strategic interaction to resolve the coordination problems. In each principal sphere of the market-based firm's governance structure, the competitive market is more robust and there is less institutional support for nonmarket forms of coordination (Hall and Soskice 2001, p. 27). Here we use the USA as a case to illustrate how market coordination is achieved in each principal sphere of the firm's governance structure.

1.2.2.1.1   Ownership and Control of American Firms

American firms with a market arm's length control type of ownership encourage strong ownership boundaries because shareholders focus on returns from separate and exclusive ownership in making investment decisions. They also encourage mergers and acquisitions, including the hostile takeovers that become a prospect when the market value of a firm declines (Hall and Soskice 2001, p. 28).

In the American model, shares are widely held and shareholders have little direct say. The shareholders' control is exercised through the market for corporate control. When the firm is poorly managed, shareholders react by selling shares, thereby depressing the stock price and exposing the firm to a hostile takeover. Thus, the management lifts performance and orients toward short-term profit maximization. Legislation prevents the formation of concentrated shareholdings and cross-shareholdings, which would reduce the efficacy of the stock market.

The top management has unilateral control over the firm, including the freedom to hire and fire (Hall and Soskice 2001, p. 29). A firm's governance structure that concentrates authority in the top management makes it easier for the firm to release employees when it faces pressure from financial markets and to impose a new strategy on the firm to take advantage of opportunities from the changing markets (Hall and Soskice 2001, p. 33).

1.2.2.1.2   Employer–Employee Relations and Patterns of Work Organization and Control

American firm's governance structure relies heavily on the market for employers to organize relations with their labor force (Hall and Soskice 2001, p. 29). American management does not develop long-term stable relations between employers and their employees (Hollingsworth 1997, p. 293). The top management has unilateral freedom to hire and fire employees (Hall and Soskice 2001, p. 29). The job mobility from firm to firm is considerable. Workers have narrow job assignments and narrow job skills, so they are easily substitutable. Employers pay employees substantially different rates for different job tasks. There is low worker participation in managerial decisions and a low degree of job security. There is a high degree of distrust and a low degree of communitarian obligations between labor and capital (Hollingsworth 1997, p. 278).

The American industrial relations system is also shaped by the weakly developed business associations and trade unions, which makes it difficult for both employer and employee to engage in collective action (Hollingsworth 1997, p. 292). Firms are under no obligation to establish works councils as representative bodies for employees (Hall and Soskice 2001, p. 29).

American firms with weak associative structures tend to have flexible external labor markets but rigid internal labor markets, and their employment tends to be job-specific, while Japanese and German firms, which are tightly integrated into highly institutionalized systems of business associations, have rigid external labor markets but flexible internal labor markets (Hollingsworth 1997, p. 292–3).

The highly fluid labor markets influence the strategies pursued by both firms and individuals in American firms. The fluid labor markets make it easy for firms to fire or hire employees to take advantage of new opportunities, but make it less attractive for them to pursue long-term employment-based strategies (Hall and Soskice 2001, p. 30). Flexible external job markets make it easy for American workers to leave jobs for other firms; thus, they discourage American employers from investing in worker training and skill development. As a result, American workers have been less broadly trained (Hollingsworth 1997, p. 292). Flexible external job markets encourage individuals to develop career trajectories with a substantial amount of movement among firms. They also encourage individuals to invest in general skills, transferable across firms, rather than company-specific skills (Hall and Soskice 2001, p. 30).

1.2.2.1.3   Interfirm Relations

Market mechanisms and hierarchies work well when firms are embedded in an institutional environment impoverished with collective forms of economic coordination (Hollingsworth 1997, p. 295). Interfirm relations in the American firm's governance structure are based on standard market relationships and enforceable formal contracts. These relations are mediated by rigorous antitrust regulations designed to prevent companies from colluding to control prices or markets.

American firms that engage in close collaboration with other firms run the risk of being sued for damages under antitrust law. These relations are also mediated by contract laws, which rely heavily on the strict interpretation of written contracts. Because the market for corporate governance renders firms sensitive to fluctuations in current profitability, it is difficult for them to make long-term commitments to relational contracts. In addition, it is difficult for extensive relational contracts to exist in liberal market economies which lack the dense business networks or associations (Hall and Soskice 2001, p. 30–1). The relationships among producers and suppliers in the USA have been opportunistic and based on hard-nosed bargaining over prices (Hollingsworth 1997, p. 296). There is a high degree of distrust and instability between the firms and their suppliers and a low degree of cooperation among competitors (Hollingsworth 1997, p. 278).

1.2.2.1.4 The Financing Pattern and Performance Criteria of Firms

The equity markets in the USA were highly institutionalized by the end of World War I. For financing, managers of American firms were only dependent to a low degree on the banking system. The Clayton Antitrust Act in the USA tended to reduce the ability of banks and firms to carry out a long-term strategy of promoting a community of interests among firms. In addition, after the American government forced a separation between commercial and investment banking in 1933, investment banks lost much of their access to capital. As a consequence, for raising capital American firms became dependent on liquid financial markets rather than on banks. Corporate managers became dependent on the strategies of stockholders and bond owners (Hollingsworth 1997, p. 293). To secure finance, American firms are strongly dependent on their valuation in equity markets, where dispersed investors depend on publicly available information to value the company. Thus, the financing pattern of American firms encourages firms to focus on the publicly assessable measures of their performance, that is, current profitability and share price (Hall and Soskice 2001, p. 28–9). The strong emphasis on the performance of firms' share prices on stock exchanges and the rate of return on investment as the key performance indicators encourage American firms to engage in short-term maximization of profits (Hollingsworth 1997, p. 293–6). American firms also resort to acquisitions and mergers to influence quarterly and annual reports, but tend to underinvest in new plants and employee training, none of which belongs to a long-term development strategy (Hollingsworth 1997, p. 296).

The financing pattern of firms in the USA provides an advantage for small new firms to develop. The venture capital markets in America make considerable sums of capital available for risky new firms. Banks are generally reluctant to finance new ventures based on new technologies. In Japan and Germany, where firms rely mainly on banks for capital, there are poorly developed venture capital markets and a few start-up ventures (Laudau and Hatsopoulos 1986, p. 583–606; Reed and Moreno 1986, p. 453–66).

1.2.2.1.5 Innovation System and Competitive Capacity

Because of the highly developed venture capital markets in the USA, American firms have often excelled in the development of new products and industries (Hollingsworth 1997, p. 293–4). There have been dynamic innovative activities involving university scientists as well as large and small firms in the early development of a large number of technologies and products—computers, semiconductors, nuclear power, microwave telecommunications, pharmaceuticals, etc.—and in the development of commercial applications of their creative activities (Hollingsworth 1997, p. 294). But having developed new products and new technologies, American firms have been less successful in improving upon the products than their Japanese and German competitors (Hollingsworth 1997, p. 296). This is because the American labor force tends to lag behind that of their Japanese and German competitors in terms of skills because the American firm's governance structure provides a few incentives for firms to invest in the development of broad skills for their workforce. It is also because of the flexible external labor markets, frequent and unpredictable turnover among key personnel, which results in disruption in research and development plans, serious problems in protecting proprietary information, and high legal costs from litigation over intellectual property rights (Hollingsworth 1997, p. 294). Thus, in the long run, the Japanese firms' strategy may prove to be more successful in building upon the successful technology that the American firms originally developed with their venture capital (Okimoto 1986, p. 541–67).

In contrast to German and Japanese firms, American firms have been more competitive in the production of low-cost standardized products and have been more willing to compromise on quality and to compete in terms of price. The intensive bargaining over price encourages American firms to build up price competitiveness, but it has an adverse effect on their ability to sustain product quality and to achieve a high level of competitiveness in terms of quality. The price-competitive, mass standardized production of the American firms also makes them effective in industrial sectors such as paper products, breakfast cereals, soft drinks, bug spray, floor wax, deodorants, soaps, and shaving cream. American firms are also successful in advertising, entertainment, and leisure industries (Hollingsworth 1997, p. 296).

1.2.2.2 The "British Model" as a Model Case for the Market-Based Firm's Governance Structure with Direct Owner Control

According to Hall and Soskice's *Varieties of Capitalism* approach (Hall and Soskice 2001), both the UK and the USA belong to the liberal market economies, as they have similar institutional environments, institutional arrangements, and coordinating mechanisms. Therefore, both of them share the market-based firms' governance structure model. The main difference between the British type of firm's market-based governance structure and the American type of firm's market-based governance structure lies in the ownership and control dimension. The personal style of

British management differs from the managerial ways of American firms (Chandler 1990, p. 242).

British firms are controlled by individuals or members of founders' families (Chandler 1990, p. 235). The British entrepreneurial or family-controlled enterprises remained personally managed or family-managed—entrepreneurs assembled smaller managerial teams, and they and their heirs continued to play a large role in the processes of middle- and top-management decision-making (Chandler 1990, p. 240, 262). The founders and their families continued to dominate the management of British enterprises (Chandler 1990, p. 235).

There are three types of British enterprises. The first type includes those enterprises managed without the benefit of an extensive managerial hierarchy. Chandler terms this type "personal enterprises." The second type is the "family-controlled enterprises," where the founders and their heirs recruit small managerial teams and set up managerial hierarchies but continue to be the influential stockholders and senior executives in their companies. The third type is the "managerial enterprises," in which the executives in the managerial hierarchy have no connection with the founders or their families and have little or no equity in the company (Chandler 1990, p. 240).

The small number of enterprises with managerial hierarchies and the small size of managerial hierarchies helped to perpetuate a commitment to personal styles of management. In most British enterprises, senior executives had almost daily personal contact with, and thus directly supervised, middle- and lower-level managers. Such enterprises had no detailed organization charts and manuals, which had come into common use in large American firms (Chandler 1990, p. 242). These family firms were reluctant to recruit nonfamily managers and were even slower to bring salaried managers into the top management (Chandler 1990, p. 390). In these British firms, selection to senior positions depended as much on personal ties as on managerial competence. Not only were fewer senior managers placed on boards as internal directors than was the case in American firms, but also external directors were selected as much for personal ties as for managerial competence. As a consequence, the founders and their heirs continue to have a significant influence on top-level decision-making (Chandler 1990, p. 242). Thus, British firms' managerial hierarchies have remained less extensive than those of American firms, making it easier to retain family control at the top of management (Chandler 1990, p. 273).

The management of British companies included "gentlemen"—the sons of the founding fathers—and "players"—the salaried managers. The primary ambition of a player was to become a gentleman (Chandler 1990, p. 292). This undoubtedly reinforces the personal style or culture of British management.

The British bias for personal management is particularly striking when one examines the difference between the USA and Britain in the pattern of industrial growth through merger and acquisition. In both the USA and Britain, many large-scale industrial enterprises were created by mergers, but the patterns of merger in the two economies are different. In the USA, mergers led to the recruitment of centralized, corporate, managerial hierarchies and new organizational capabilities. In Britain, merged firms remained collections of personally run or family-managed firms

(Chandler 1990, p. 286). Holding companies legally controlled their personally managed operating subsidiaries but did not have centralized, corporate, managerial hierarchies for coordinating, monitoring, or resource allocation (Chandler 1990, p. 235). Thus, in the USA, mergers represented augmenting market power through functional and strategic efficiencies, while in Britain, mergers remained no more than a device to maintain market power through contractual cooperation (Chandler 1990, p. 287).

The methods of merger used were much the same in Britain and the USA. A firm would acquire fellow members either by cash purchase or by using newly issued shares of the new company to pay for acquired assets. The normal way of a British merger was to form a holding company, which exchanged its stock for that of each of the constituent firms. The resulting control could be legally maintained. But the legal consolidation in British holding companies did not bring managerial centralization nor did it bring the recruitment of salaried top and middle managers. The directors of the constituent companies remained responsible for the day-to-day production and distribution of their own products as they had been before the merger. The parent company's central office was little more than a meeting place for a board of directors, who, as representatives of the owners of constituent firms, determined output and prices through negotiation. Uniform financial and operating accounting was established to determine output, prices, and profits more accurately (Chandler 1990, p. 288).

The British mergers usually involve numerous firms; their boards include representatives from many constituent firms, which makes them large and unwieldy. Thus, the British pattern of mergers formed loose contractual cooperation (Chandler 1990, p. 288–9). The British industrialists' success in maintaining power through the British pattern of merger, in which contractual cooperation remained, was one reason why the ways of personal management lasted much longer in large industrial enterprises in Britain than in the USA (Chandler 1990, p. 291–2).

British firms had relatively little need to seek the assistance of financial institutions for investment. Banks rarely played any significant role in British firms' investment (Chandler 1990, p. 391). The initial investment came from the founding families (Chandler 1990, p. 391). Expansion of enterprises was financed from retained earnings or, where earnings were paid out in dividends, by issuing debentures or other nonvoting securities (Chandler 1990, p. 266).

In Britain, the goal for family firms appears to have been to provide profits and a steady flow of cash to owners—owners who were also managers (Chandler 1990, p. 390). The profits made by the firms went to the owners. In such personally managed firms, growth was not a primary objective. Owners of firms preferred current income to large-scale, long-term reinvestment in their firms. Private firms held back from expanding investment in production, distribution, research, and development and from recruiting, training, and promoting salaried managers— which were important to the continuing, incremental innovation of new technologies (Chandler 1990, p. 292). There is a good deal of evidence to support the view that in Britain profit and a large income for the family were more of an incentive than the long-term growth of the firm. In the years before World War I, the payout in dividends appeared to have been much greater in British than in American firms, with the ratio of dividends to earnings running as high as 80 or 90%. After the war, many firms wished to expand, and they chose to raise new funds by issuing nonvoting preference stock or debentures rather than to use retained earnings. Many family firms chose to pay dividends rather than to reinvest in research and development (Chandler 1990, p. 390).

In Britain, the large industrial enterprises clustered in a small number of significant industries, as those in the USA and Germany did. Even though the large industrial firms in Britain clustered in much the same broad categories as those in the USA did, within the categories they were concentrated in different subdivisions. A larger proportion of the British firms produced consumer goods, not industrial ones. Many were in the brewing, textile, publishing and printing, and shipbuilding industries (Chandler 1990, p. 239–40). British entrepreneurs were most successful in the production of branded, packaged products—food, drink, tobacco, and consumer chemicals. Most of the largest enterprises clustered in these consumer industries. Here, manufacturing processes were not technologically complex; the production and distribution in these industries required less costly facilities and less complex managerial and technical skills than in other capital-intensive industries; extensive, product-specific distribution facilities and specialized marketing services were not required. British entrepreneurs adopted new production technologies for refining, distilling, milling, and processing food, drink, tobacco, and consumer chemicals. They also devised new ways of packaging and branding products (Chandler 1990, p. 262, 268).

In these industries, mass production did not require the services of technically trained managers, distribution called for little in terms of specialized services and facilities, and thus such evolutionary growth permitted the founding families to continue to manage the enlarged enterprises. British entrepreneurs also built up some firms with managerial teams and competed effectively in certain new, high-volume, capital-intensive industries, such as rubber, glass, explosives, synthetic alkalis, and man-made fibers. But because of the limit of their organizational capacity, they failed to do so in other industries that were even more important to the nation's economy and economic growth, such as machinery, organic chemicals and electrochemicals, and steel, copper, and other metals (Chandler 1990, p. 268).

1.3 Business Model / Innovation System and the Basic Concepts of Institutional Complementarities, Continuity, and Divergence: To Find Where China Is

1.3.1 Institutional Complementarities and the Differences Between Business Models (and Between Innovation Systems)

Two institutions can be said to be complementary if the presence (or efficiency) of one leads to (or increases) the presence (or efficiency) of the other. Of particular importance are complementarities between institutions of different principal spheres within the firm's governance structure. In a business system, a particular type of institution of one principal sphere within the firm's governance structure should tend to develop complementary institutions of other principal spheres as well. For example, long-term employment is more feasible where the firm's financing pattern provides capital on terms that are not sensitive to current profitability. Conversely, fluid labor markets may be more effective in the presence of a firm's financing pattern that focuses on short-term profitability (Hall and Soskice 2001, p. 17–8).

1.3.1.1 Institutional Complementarities Reinforce the Difference Between Firms' Governance Structures (and Between Innovation Systems)

The presence of institutional complementarities reinforces the differences between liberal market economies and coordinated market economies. The principal spheres in a firm's governance structure are complementary to each other, and the logics of institutional complementarities of these spheres are different between liberal and coordinated market economies. For example, the institutional complementarities of two principal spheres (corporate finance and industrial relations) in the firm's governance structure show how different logics of institutional complementarities divide liberal from coordinated market economies. Highly developed stock markets in the corporate-finance sphere tend to have the complementary practice of a low level of employment protection in the industrial-relations sphere. This is the logic of institutional complementarities in liberal market economies, which indicates greater reliance on market modes of coordination in the corporate-finance and industrial-relations spheres. On the other hand, high levels of employment protection tend to have the complementary practice of less reliance on market coordination in corporate finance. This is the logic of institutional complementarities in coordinated market economies, which reflects higher levels of nonmarket coordination in industrial-relations and corporate-finance spheres (Hall and Soskice 2001, p. 18–9).

According to the different logics of institutional complementarities of these two principal spheres, we can place some nations into two different groups of economy—liberal market economies and coordinated market economies; thus, we can see the clear division between the two types. Firms in liberal market economies, such as those of the USA, Britain, Australia, Canada, New Zealand, and Ireland, tend to rely on markets to coordinate their endeavors in corporate financing and industrial relations (Hall and Soskice 2001, p. 19). For example, in the American case, industrial-relations arrangements that allow companies to cut costs in an economic downturn by shedding labor are complementary to the corporate financing pattern that renders a firm's access to capital dependent on its current profitability (Hall and Soskice 2001, p. 32). Firms in coordinated market economies, such as those of Germany, Japan, Switzerland, the Netherlands, Belgium, Sweden, Norway, Denmark, Finland, and Austria, tend to rely on high levels of nonmarket coordination in these spheres (Hall and Soskice 2001, p. 19). For example, in the German case, many firms pursue long-term production strategies that depend on employees with specific skills and high levels of corporate commitment that are secured by offering them long-term employment, industry-based wages, and protective works councils. These practices are complementary with a corporate finance system that provides firms with access to funds on terms that are independent of fluctuations in profitability (Hall and Soskice 2001, p. 27).

1.3.1.2   Institutional Complementarities Generate Disincentives to Radical Change

Firms may attempt to preserve the arrangement in one sphere of the governance structure to protect complementary institutions and hence the whole production regime that is of value to them. For example, facing globalization, many German firms have devoted energy to revising rather than abolishing their cross-shareholding structure and corporate financing system because their production regimes demand their particular ownership structure and corporate financing system. On the basis of these two factors, German firms can offer long-term employment, recruit skilled labor, and sustain worker loyalty and ultimately build their highly competitive particular production regime (Hall and Soskice 2001, p. 64).

Stemming from the internationalization of finance, globalization puts pressure on the institutions of coordinated market economies. Distant investors prefer to supply capital based on transparent balance-sheet criteria. Therefore, firms in coordinated market economies face pressure to revise their accounting standards and deliver the high rates of return associated with "shareholder value," to seek access to these funds. Firms in coordinated market economies will have to deliver high rates of return demanded by distant investors in world financial markets. But this is not inconsistent with their particular firm's governance structure that maximizes comparative institutional advantages. These pressures have actually led many companies to develop a closer relationship with their employees rather than the reverse because employee cooperation becomes more important under these pressures. Germany provides a case in this context. Many German firms have embraced international accounting standards, but the term "shareholder value" has been used mainly as a slogan, and hostile takeovers remain rare because cross-shareholding remains an obstacle against them. The corporate finance system is changing, but it is doing so at a pace that may allow German firms to retain their comparative institutional advantage. Germany firms will deliver to their shareholders a long-term high return but based on their own institutional comparative advantage. They will not abolish their own model to adopt an Anglo-Saxon model, and shareholders will not insist on Anglo-Saxon management model if it cannot deliver a higher return (Hall and Soskice 2001, p. 60–2).

1.3.1.3 Each Type of Firm's Governance Structure/Innovation System Conditions its Specialization in the Production Regime

We have identified the differences between the principal spheres in the market-based firm's governance structure which dominates liberal market economies and those in the coordinated firm's governance structure, which in turn dominates coordinated market economies. In short, firms with coordinated governance structures make more extensive use of nonmarket modes of coordination to organize their endeavors, while firms with market-based governance structures rely mainly on markets to coordinate their endeavors.

On the basis of these findings, an important point to be added here is that a particular firm's governance structure/innovation system provides a firm with advantages for engaging in specific types of activities. A particular mode of coordination in a firm's governance structure/innovation system conditions the efficiency with which the firm can perform certain activities; e.g., the efficiency of producing certain kinds of goods and services. Firms with a particular kind of governance structure/innovation system can perform certain types of activities and produce certain kinds of goods more efficiently than others because of the particular institutional support they receive from that structure, which cannot be secured in other economies. In short, a particular firm's governance structure/innovation system provides firms with a particular comparative institutional advantage, which should give rise to the specialization in the production regime (Hall and Soskice 2001, p. 37–8).

It is not arguing here that one type of firm's governance structure/innovation system is superior to another. The satisfactory levels of long-term economic performance of both liberal and coordinated market economies imply that different business models/innovation systems that are based on different types of firm's governance structure can perform successfully because they can realize their own particular comparative institutional advantage (Hall and Soskice 2001, p. 21). But they can perform more successfully in their own production regime.

1.3.2 An Exceptional Case of Chinese Economy: A Dual-Structured Business Model/Innovation System with a Clear Coordination Boundary in Between

Firstly, an economy has in general one business model and innovation system.

The concept of institutional complementarities implies that only one specific model of firm's governance structure/one type of innovation system exists in an economy because the coordinating mechanism in the model of firm's governance structure and in its corresponding innovation system applies and covers the whole economy, which does not have a clear coordinating boundary and cannot be split and constrained within a certain part of the economy. Thus, in liberal market economies such as the USA and the UK, and in coordinated market economies such as Germany and Japan, only one model of firm's governance structure/one type of innovation system exists.

Secondly, an economy can embrace a dual-structured model/innovation system, only if there is a clear coordination boundary between the two functioning parts.

If it is possible to find a business system with such a specific coordination mechanism, which has clear coordination boundary and only covers a certain part of the economy, then it is also possible for the other part of the economy to develop a different type of coordinating mechanism; thus, two types of firm's governance structure and innovation system can coexist in the economy.

Thirdly, China can build up such a dual-structured model and innovation system.

China provides typical case here. The state sector is a coordination-based business model with an incremental type of innovation system, similar to Germany leading coordinated market economies. But different from Germany leading coordinated market economies, it is the state that plays the coordination role based on its controlling shareholding in the governance structure of corporatized state-controlled enterprises in the Chinese state sector. Such a specific coordination mechanism has a clear coordination boundary because it is based on state controlling shareholding, it can be constrained within the state sector. Outside of the state sector, private enterprises can develop and rely on free market mechanism, upon which a market-based governance structure with a radical innovation system can be built. Because of the clear coordination boundary between the two sectors, the institutional complementarities in each sector are intact and this prevents the interaction-driven convergence between the two sectors. Thus, the case of China does not actually contradict the concept of institutional complementarities. As a specific case, it supports and supplements the concept.

The dual-structured Chinese economy has a very important implication: While the other economies are with only one business model, one type of innovation system and core competitiveness, China has two. The dual strength builds up super innovation power.

1.3.3 Institutional Continuity and Divergence Restrain the Convergence Between Different Business Models (Between Different Innovation Systems)

1.3.3.1 The Assumption of the Economic Convergence Across Different Economies

The economic convergence thesis assumes that firms competing in the same markets tend to become similar in their structure and behavior, and there is only one best solution in organizing a firm's endeavors. Firms must at least emulate if not surpass their most efficient competitors to survive. Whenever innovators discover a new and highly efficient method of production, their competitors are likely to follow. Competition and survival involve discovering and implementing the best techniques and strategies among firms across nations (Chandler 1962, 1977; Chandler and Daems 1980).

In much of this literature, the argument for economic convergence relies heavily on the concept of technology transfer: The greater the technology and productivity gap between leading and following nations, the greater the follower's potential for productivity advances; the follower tends to catch up to the leader owing to technology transfer from leading nations to following nations (Abramowitz 1986; Baumol 1986; Baumol et al. 1989; Baumol and Edward 1989; Maddison 1982; Williamson 1991, p. 56). There was the widely held view that technology transfer would eventually lead to convergence both in the economic models employed by the business systems for coordinating economic activity and in their economic performance (Hollingsworth and Boyer 1997, p. 33).

1.3.3.2 Institutional Continuity and Divergence Restrain the Convergence Effect Between Different Business Models (and Between Different Innovation Systems)

Firstly, if business models/innovation systems are different, performance convergence across different economies cannot easily happen.

The argument for economic convergence across different economies is far from convincing. Because of path dependency and institutional complementarities in different business models, institutional transfer and economic convergence cannot easily occur. It is not easy for a country to alter its economic model toward another kind to approach economic convergence (Hollingsworth 1997).

The key to understanding the degree to which the economic performance of different economies will converge is influenced very much by the extent to which they are based on a similar business model/innovation system, i.e., the firm's governance structure. Firms' governance structures of different economies are complex configurations; therefore, that they cannot easily diffuse across different economies is problematic. Given the strong institutional complementarities of different business models, an easy catch-up by followers would be difficult. The structural advantage taken by a leading economy prevents easy imitation. Followers who try to imitate a leader may finally deliver a different model, which is built on their own economic specificities (Hollingsworth 1997, p. 36). When Germany tried to follow the first British industrial revolution, it moved toward quite a different new model (Gerschenkron 1962; Hollingsworth 1997, p. 36). After World War II, many Japanese firms wanted to follow the American economic development model, but finally got quite a different one (Ohno 1989).

Different business models/innovation systems tend to maximize different performance criteria and result in different types of economic performance. If economies vary in the types of firm's governance structure, there are serious constraints on the degree to which they can converge in their economic performance. In contrast to neoclassical economic theory, in real-world economies, there is no universal performance criterion that all rational economic actors attempt to maximize. Economic history has shown how the varieties of performance criteria are implemented in different economies (Boyer 1990; Gustafsson 1990; Hollingsworth and Streeck 1994; North 1981, 1990; Tolliday and Zeitlin 1991, p. 1–31; Hollingsworth and Boyer 1997, p. 36). For example, profitability is a goal of firms in all market economies, but as it depends on different business models with different firms' governance structures, it may be sought in the short or long term. Business models vary not only in the ways firms approach profits, but also in the degree to which they attempt to maximize (a) the criteria of allocative efficiency versus productive efficiency, (b) social peace and egalitarian distribution versus market-based distribution, (c) quantity versus quality aspects of production, and (d) innovation in developing new products versus innovation in improving upon existing products (Hage 1980).

For example, the German model—with its high wages, high employment stability, highly institutionalized collective forms of coordination, internal mobility of labor, permanent upgrading within existing organizational structures, and strong incentives for process innovations and productivity increases—may perform well in the long run (Buechtemann 1991; Hollingsworth and Streeck 1994), even though its slower adjustments to unexpected disturbances might deliver some losses in the short run on productivity and profit criteria. In contrast, the American model with the market-based firm's governance structure emphasizes short-termism, quickly adjusts to and takes opportunities from changing markets, and delivers gains in the short run on productivity and profit criteria (Hollingsworth and Boyer 1997, p. 37).

Hence, considering these differences in business model/innovation system and economic performance, not all of the sectors in an economy compete and perform equally well. A particular business model/innovation system performs better in certain product markets than in others because the production processes in these sectors fit their own specific institutional structure and can gain from their specific comparative institutional advantage. Most business models succeed in a few industrial sectors, but not very well in most of the others (Hollingsworth and Boyer 1997, p. 38).

Economies have had limited capacity to construct a business model/innovation system in the image of their major competitors. Some firms in lagging economies do attempt to mimic some of the management styles of their successful competitors. When the concept of "the internationalization of Japanese business" was pervasive, firms in both the UK and the USA attempted to mimic Japanese business management (Trevor 1987; Hollingsworth 1997, p. 297). But the firms in the USA and the UK found it very difficult to imitate the practices and performance of their Japanese competitors that appeared to be more effective. Therefore, even though a particular business model/innovation system enhances the competitiveness of firms in certain industrial sectors, it limits their capacity to compete in others (Hollingsworth 1997, p. 279).

Secondly, foreign direct investment and technology transfer from the economy with a different business model/innovation system cannot easily lead to economic convergence between the different economies.

Globalization greatly raises the larger issue of foreign direct investment, technology transfer, joint ventures, and strategic alliances, but is the increasing frequency of this form of coordination truly leading to economic convergence across different economies? Foreign direct investment, technology transfer, joint ventures, and strategic alliances do lead to some convergence in certain management styles, but they do not bring about the convergence of whole business models/innovation systems which are characterized by distinctive firms' governance structures and therefore cannot bring about convergence in economic performance either. Each model is constantly changing and is open to influence from other models. During these processes, many technologies and practices diffuse from one society to another, and there may be a certain convergence in the productive efficiency, but the effectiveness is generally limited, and the direction of change is constrained by the existing business model/innovation system. The same technology may exist in different economies, but how it is employed varies across different economies. Skills, management styles, and modes of innovation are embedded in distinctive business models, and they do not easily diffuse from one economy to another. As a result, variation across different business models/innovation systems remains substantial. In the German and Japanese economies, the institutional arrangements continually support their distinctive coordinated firm's governance structure/innovation system. In contrast, in the American economy, the short-termism of the market mechanism continually supports its market-based firm's governance structure/innovation system (Hollingsworth 1997, p. 298–9).

1.3.4   The Exceptional Case of China: The Concept Supports the Dual Convergence of Dual-Structured Chinese Economy Toward Both the US Leading Liberal Market Economies and Germany Leading Coordinated Market Economies

Firstly, the concept supports the FDI driving conditional convergence between economies with similar models.

The concept of institutional continuity and divergence means a path dependency in running a certain type of business model. It does not support economic convergence between economies with different business models/innovation systems, but it supports the conditional convergence between economies with similar business models/innovation systems. Foreign direct investment and technology transfer realize such a convergence.

Secondly, foreign direct investment from Germany leading coordinated market economies tends to go to the economies with similar business models/innovation systems.

During globalization, there should be much more incentive than at any time before for firms to directly invest in foreign countries with cheaper labor if they also have a commensurate skill and productivity level. Firms in coordinated market economies will not automatically invest abroad only because of low-cost labor. They can get an institutional advantage and core competitiveness from the special institutional arrangements in their home countries. Such a specific institutional infrastructure cannot be secured everywhere, and its competitive advantage is based on quality competitiveness and long-term profitability; therefore, they are not willing to give up this opportunity only for cheaper labor (Hall and Soskice 2001, p. 56–7). But if there is a country with a business model/innovation system similar to that of the firm's home country, the firm may intend to invest there. In contrast, firms in liberal market economies may be more inclined to invest in foreign countries to secure cheaper labor than firms in coordinated market economies because these firms coordinate their endeavors, relying mainly on market mechanisms which developing countries can usually provide. They do not require a special institutional infrastructure, and their core competitiveness is based on price competitiveness and short-term profitability on investment (Hall and Soskice 2001, p. 57).

Thirdly, foreign direct investment and technology transfer based on similar business models/innovation systems imply the economic convergence between the two economies.

According to the concept of institutional continuity and divergence, economic performance convergence across different economies cannot easily happen if the economies follow different business models/innovation systems. Even foreign direct investment and technology transfer cannot bring about economic convergence across these economies. But this concept supports the analysis in this book which shows that foreign direct investment and technology transfer may bring about economic convergence across these economies if their economies are based on similar business models/innovation systems.

Fourthly, the concept therefore supports a dual convergence of the dual-structured Chinese economy toward both advanced liberal market economies and coordinated market economies.

China provides again a typical case under this concept. The Chinese business system has a dual structure. The state sector is coordination-based (i.e., the state coordination through its controlling shareholding), which is similar to the Germany leading coordinated market economies; the private sector is market-based, which is similar to the liberal market economies. This is the ground on which the Chinese dual economic convergence toward these two evolves. Foreign direct investment and technology transfer drive such a dual convergence. The dual-structured Chinese economy supports its dual convergence toward both types of advanced economy, in this way supports its remarkable catching up. It also sparks its own engine for further innovation development.

References

Abegglen, J. C., & Stalk, G. (1985). *Kaisha, the Japanese corporation.* New York: Basic Books.

Abramowitz, M. (1986, June). Catching up, forging ahead, and falling behind. *Journal of Economic History, 46,* 385–406.

Aoki, M. (1987). The Japanese firm in transition. In K. Yamamura & Y. Yasuba (Eds.), *The political economy of Japan* (Vol. 1, pp. 263–288). Stanford, CA: Stanford University Press.

Aoki, M. (1988). *Information, incentive and bargaining in the Japanese economy.* Cambridge: Cambridge University Press.

Aoki, M. (1992). Decentralization-centralization in Japanese organization: A duality principle. In S. Kumon & H. Rosovsky (Eds.), *The political economy of Japan: Culture and social dynamics, III* (pp. 142–169). Stanford, CA: Stanford University Press.

Baumol, W. J. (1986). Productivity growth, convergence, and welfare: What the long-run data show. *American Economic Review, 76*(5), 1072–1085.

Baumol, W. J., Blackman, S. A. B., & Edward, N. W. (1989). *Productivity and American leadership: The long view.* Cambridge: MIT Press.

Baumol, W. J., & Edward, N. W. (1989). Three fundamental productivity concepts: Principles and measurement. In G. R. Feiwel (Ed.), *Joan Robinson and modern economic theory* (pp. 638–659). London: Macmillan.

Boyer, R. (1990, November–December). Economic et Histoire: Vers de nouvelles alliances? *Annales ESC.* (pp. 1397–1426).

Buechtemann, C. F. (1991). Does (de-)regulation matter? Employment protection in West Germany. In E. Matzner & W. Streeck (Eds.), *Beyond Keynesianism, the socio-economics of production and full employment.* Hants, UK: Edward Elgar Publishing.

Chandler, A. D. (1962). *Strategy and structure.* Cambridge: MIT Press.

Chandler, A. D. (1977). *The visible hand: The managerial revolution in American business.* Cambridge: Harvard University Press.

Chandler, A. D. (1990). *Scale and scope.* London: The Belknap Press of Harvard University Press.

Chandler, A. D., & Daems, H. (Eds.). (1980). *Managerial hierarchies: Comparative perspectives on the rise of the modern industrial enterprise.* Cambridge: Harvard University Press.

Cole, R. E. (1979). *Work, mobility, and participation.* Berkeley: University of California Press.

Cox, A. (1986a). State, finance and industry in comparative perspective. In A. Cox (Ed.), *The state, finance, and industry*. New York: St. Martin's.

Cox, A. (1986b). *The state, finance, and industry*. New York: St. Martin's.

Deeg, R. E. (1992). *Banks and the state in Germany: The critical role of subnational institutions in economic governance*. Ph.D dissertation, MIT.

Dore, R. P. (1986). *Flexible rigidities*. Stanford, CA: Stanford University Press.

Dyson, K. (1984). The state, banks, and industry. The West German case. In A. Cox (Ed.), *State, finance and industry*. Brighton: Wheatsheaf.

Esser, J. (1990). Bank power in West Germany revisited. *West European Politics, 13*, 17–32.

Friedman, D. (1988). *The misunderstood miracle: Industrial development and political change in Japan*. Ithaca, NY: Cornell University Press.

Fruin, M. (1992). *The Japanese enterprise system*. Oxford: Oxford University Press.

Gerlach, M. L. (1992). *Alliance capitalism: The social organization of Japanese business*. Berkeley: University of California Press.

Gerschenkron, A. (1962). *Economic backwardness in historical perspective*. Cambridge: Harvard University Press.

Gustafsson, B. (Ed.). (1990). *Power and economic institutions: Reinterpretations in economic history*. Aldershot: Edward Elgar.

Hage, J. (1980). *Theories of organizations: Form, process, and transformation*. New York: John Wiley.

Hall, P. A., & Soskice, D. (2001). *Varieties of capitalism*. New York: Oxford University Press.

Hollingsworth, J. R. (1997). Continuities and changes in social systems of production: The cases of Japan, Germany, and the United States. In J. R. Hollingsworth & R. Boyer (Eds.), *Contemporary capitalism: The embeddedness of institutions*. Cambridge: Cambridge University Press.

Hollingsworth, J. R., & Boyer, R. (1997). Coordination of economic actors and social systems of production. In J. R. Hollingsworth & R. Boyer (Eds.), *Contemporary capitalism: The embeddedness of institutions*. Cambridge: Cambridge University Press.

Hollingsworth, J. R., & Streeck, W. (1993). Performance and control of economic sectors. In J. R. Hollingsworth, P. Schmitter, & W. Streeck (Eds.), *Governing capitalist economies: Performance and control of economic sectors*. New York: Oxford University Press, Chapter 11.

Hollingsworth, J. R., & Streeck, W. (1994). Countries and sectors: Performance, convergence and competitiveness. In J. R. Hollingsworth, P. Schmitter, & W. Streeck (Eds.), *Governing capitalist economies: Performance and control of economic sectors* (pp. 270–300). New York: Oxford University Press.

Junne, G. (1989). Competitiveness and the impact of change: Applications of 'high technologies'. In P. J. Katzenstein (Ed.), *Industry and politics in West Germany* (pp. 249–274). Ithaca: Cornell University Press.

Kocka, J. (1980). The rise of the modern industrial enterprise in Germany. In A. Chandler & H. Daems (Eds.), *Managing hierarchies: Comparative perspectives on the rise of the modern industrial enterprise* (pp. 77–116). Cambridge: Harvard University Press.

Koike, K. (1983). Internal labor markets: Workers in large firms. In T. Shirai (Ed.), *Contemporary industrial relations in Japan* (pp. 29–62). Madison: University of Wisconsin Press.

Koike, K. (1988). *Understanding industrial relations in modern Japan*. London: Macmillan.

Laudau, R., & Hatsopoulos, G. N. (1986). Capital formation in the United States and Japan. In R. Laudau & N. Rosenberg (Eds.), *The positive sum strategy* (pp. 583–606). Washington: National Academy Press.

Lazonick, W. (1991). *Business organization and the myth of the market economy*. Cambridge: Cambridge University Press.

Lazonick, W., & West, J. (1998). Organizational integration and competitive advantage. In G. Dosi et al. (Eds.), *Technology, organization and competitiveness*. Oxford: Oxford University Press.

Levine, S. B. (1984). Employers associations in Japan. In J. P. Windmuller & A. Gladstone (Eds.), *Employers associations and industrial relations: A comparative study* (pp. 318–356). Oxford: Oxford University Press.

Lincoln, J. R., & Kalleberg, A. L. (1990). *Culture, control, and commitment: A study of work organization and work attitudes in the U.S. and Japan*. Cambridge: Cambridge University Press.

Lincoln, J. R., & McBride, K. (1987). Japanese industrial organization in comparative perspective. *Annual Review of Sociology, 13*, 289–312.

Maddison, A. (1982). *Phases of capitalist development*. Oxford: Oxford Universtity Press.

Miyamoto, M. (1988). The development of business association in Prewar Japan. In H. Yamazaki & M. Miyamoto (Eds.), *Trade associations in business history* (pp. 1–45). Tokyo: Tokyo University Press.

Neuberger, H., & Stokes, H. (1974). German banks and German growth, 1883–1913: An empirical view. *Journal of Economic History, 34*, 710–731.

North, D. (1981). *Structure and change in economic history*. New York: Norton.

North, D. (1990). *Insitutions, institutional change and economic performance*. Cambridge: Cambridge University Press.

O'Brien, P. (1993). The steel industry of Japan and the United States. In J. R. Hollingsworth, P. Schmitter, & W. Streeck (Eds.), *Governing capitalist economies: Performance and control of economic sectors* (pp. 43–71). New York: Oxford University Press.

Ohno, T. (1989). *L'esprit toyota*. Paris: Masson.

Okimoto, D. I. (1986). The Japanese challenge in high technology. In R. Laudau & N. Rosenberg (Eds.), *The positive sum strategy* (pp. 541–567). Washington, DC: National Academy Press.

Reed, J. S., & Moreno, G. R. (1986). The role of large banks in financing innovation. In R. Laudau & N. Rosenberg (Eds.), *The positive sum strategy* (pp. 453–466). Washington: National Academy Press.

Sako, M. (1992). *Prices, quality and trust*. Cambridge: Cambridge University Press.

Schneiberg, M., & Rogers Hollingsworth, J. (1990). Can transaction cost economics explain trade associations? In A. M. Aoki, A. B. Gustafsson, & O. E. Williamson (Eds.), *The firm as a nexus of treaties* (pp. 320–346). London: Sage Publications.

Shigeyoshi, T. (Ed.). (1984). *Industrial relations in transition: The case of Japan and the Federal Republic of Germany*. Tokyo: The University of Tokyo Press.

Shirai, T. (Ed.). (1983). *Contemporary industrial relations in Japan* (pp. 267–291). Madison: University of Wisconsin Press.

Sorge, A., & Warner, M. (1986). *Comparative factory organization*. Aldershot: Gower.

Strath, B. (1993). The shipbuilding industries of Germany, Japan, and Sweden. In R. Hollingsworth, P. Schmitter, & W. Streeck (Eds.), *Governing capitalist economies: Performance and control of economic sectors* (pp. 72–96). New York: Oxford University Press.

Tilly, R. (1976). German banks, german growth and econometric history. *Journal of Economic History, 36*, 416–424.

Tilly, R. (1982). Mergers, external growth and finance in the development of large-scale enterprises in Germany, 1880–1913. *Journal of Economic History, 42*, 629–658.

Tilly, R. (1986). German banking, 1850–1994: Development assistance for the strong. *Journal of European Economic History, 15*, 113–152.

Tolliday, S., & Zeitlin, J. (Eds.). (1991). *The power to manage: Employers and industrial relations in comparative historical perspective*. London: Routledge.

Trevor, M. (Ed.). (1987). *The internationalization of Japanese business: European and Japanese perspectives*. Boulder: Westview Press.

Vitols, S. (1995a). *German banks and the modernization of the small firm sector: Long-term finance in comparative perspective*. Discussion Paper, FS-I-95-309. Berlin: Wissenschaftszentrum.

Vitols, S. (1995b). *Inflation versus central bank independence? Banking regulation and financial stability in the U.S. and Germany*. Discussion Paper, FS-I-95-312. Berlin: Wissenschaftszentrum.

Vitols, S. (1995c). *Corporate governance versus economic governance: Banks and industrial restructuring in the U.S and Germany*. Discussion Paper, FS-I-95-311. Berlin: Wissenschaftszentrum.

Vitols, S. (1995d). *Are German banks different?* Discussion Paper, FS-I-95-308. Berlin: Wissenschaftzentrum.

Vittas, D., et al. (1978). *The role of large deposit banks in the financial systems of Germany, France, Italy, the Netherlands, Switzerland, Sweden, Japan, and the United States*. London: Inter-Bank Research Organization.

Whitley, R. (1999). *Divergent capitalisms: The social structuring and change of business systems*. New York: Oxford University Press.

Williamson, J. G. (1991). Productivity and American leadership: A review article. *Journal of Economic Literature, 29*, 51–68.

Williamson, O. E. (1985). *The economic institutions of capitalism*. New York: Free Press.

Zysman, J. (1983). *Governments, markets and growth: Financial systems and the politics of industrial change*. Ithaca, NY: Cornell University Press.

Chapter 2
The Economic Model and Innovation System of Chinese State Sector

Abstract In this chapter, economic model and innovation system in the Chinese state sector are detailed. They operate in the similar way to the Germany leading coordinated market economies (the advanced European countries and Japan). The firms in both business systems have coordinated governance structure and both have coordination-based innovation system. Why do evidences show that the innovation system in the Chinese state sector is superior to the European model? Even though they both are coordination-based models, the coordination types are different from each other: In the Chinese state sector it is state coordination based on its controlling shareholding, while in European model it is institutional coordination. State coordination-based Chinese state strategic innovation appears to be more powerful than institutional coordination-based European Innovation. The success is manifest from the Chinese-made spacecraft and satellites, high speed trains, highly innovated infrastructure networks, and building up of the advanced 5G stations. The chapter focuses on how the economic model and innovation system were built up during the period from the mid-1990s to the middle of the first decade of 21st century.

Keywords Innovation · Chinese innovation · Economic model · Business system · Chinese model · Corporate governance · Competitiveness · State ownership · State-controlled shareholding · State enterprise · Chinese catching-up · High speed railway · High speed train

In this chapter, we will analyze how state-owned enterprises (SOEs) are transformed toward a modern governance structure, i.e., a state-controlled shareholding coordinated firm's governance structure and how the state-controlled shareholding coordinates the technological modernization.

2.1   SOE Reorganization: Keeping the Large and Letting Go of the Small (*zhuada fangxiao*)

Before the mid-1990s, there were two separate parts in China's state industrial sector: one consisted of small and medium-sized SOEs under the supervision of local governments, and the other one consisted of big SOEs under the supervision of the central government. In China's state industrial sector in 1993, although large industrial SOEs accounted for 5% of all enterprises and about two-thirds in profits and taxes and in net value of fixed assets, they had a share of 57% in terms of output, while small and medium-sized industrial SOEs together accounted for 95% of all enterprises, about one-third in profits and taxes as well as in the net value of fixed assets, and 43% in terms of output (see Table 2.1). In a 1995 survey, the State Assets Management Administration reported that there were about 300,000 SOEs. The top 1,000 SOEs accounted for 40% of total assets, 51% of net assets, and 66% of profits (People's Daily 1995).

Most of the small and medium-sized SOEs were under the supervision of county and city governments and were located in competitive industries, like machinery, electronics, textiles, and food processing. Most of the large enterprises were supervised by the central government and were located in the industries that the state views as having strategic value, such as high-technology industries, oil, raw materials, petrochemical, telecommunication, banking, railroad transportation, airlines, and electricity (Cao et al. 1999).

Small firms supervised by local governments had been performing poorly. Reforms of tax, fiscal, monetary, and banking policy in the 1990s hardened the budget constraints of local governments. Local governments and the SOEs under their supervision now had to survive using their own financial resources. At the same time, increased competition, mainly from the nonstate sector, raised pressures on local SOEs. By the mid-1990s, the nonstate sector in China had already become a major force in the economy, and both domestic nonstate firms and foreign firms had become the major source of competition. The SOEs supervised by local governments were in competitive industries, in which nonstate firms entered, while the larger SOEs that were supervised by the central government were in the strategic industries, where there was almost no nonstate firm. Thus, the competition from the nonstate sector had a much greater effect on the local SOEs than on those supervised

Table 2.1   State-owned industrial enterprises by size, 1993

	Number (%)	Output (%)	Employment (%)	Net value of fixed assets (%)	Profits and taxes (%)
Large	4.7	56.7	43.2	62.0	66.7
Medium-sized	12.9	23.6	25.6	18.6	19.4
Small	82.3	19.7	31.1	19.5	13.9

From China Statistical Yearbook (1994, p. 388–391), except employment figures, which are from the State Statistical Bureau by the central government (Cao et al. 1999). Under harder budget constraints and increasing competitive pressures, the performance of many small SOEs deteriorated quickly. In 1994, about 90% of the loss-making SOEs were small ones, while 82% of all SOEs were small ones (Cao et al. 1999; Zhou and Shen 1997; Garnaut et al. 2005a, p. 3; Chiu and Lewis 2006, p. 125). In 1995, 72.5% of local firms were unprofitable, but this was only the case for 24.3% of the big SOEs supervised by the central government (Zhao 1999). Small SOEs also generally carried more debt than big SOEs. In a 1994 survey of the state industrial sector, the debt-to-assets ratio was 71.5% for small SOEs, as compared with an average of 65.6% for all SOEs. The debt-to-equity ratio was 2.49, compared with 1.92 for average SOEs (Zhou and Shen 1997). Increasingly poor performance and highly leveraged debt of small SOEs had become increasingly heavy fiscal burdens for the local governments' budget. These circumstances provided an incentive for local governments to privatize small and medium-sized SOEs, to cut state sector losses, and reduce the flow of bank financing to inefficient small SOEs, while relieving the fiscal burdens of local governments (Cao et al. 1999; Yusuf et al. 2006, p. 217).

SOEs, especially the big ones, have been the key for the state to pursue technological modernization and heavy industry-oriented strategic goals. Most of China's heavy industry and a lot of its technology are in the state industrial sectors. SOEs dominate the heavy industries and the capital-intensive sectors of the economy. They are the major producers in the power, steel, chemicals, and machinery sectors, and in the defense industry. In these heavy industry, capital-intensive, and high-technology sectors, the share of output by SOEs has remained very high over decades. SOEs are at the core of Chinese industry, providing the key productive inputs of iron, steel, power, telecommunications, etc. on which all other sectors rely (Chiu and Lewis 2006, p. 9–56). SOEs have employed a large number of workers and assumed many social responsibilities. The share of employment in SOEs was 65.27% in 1997 and was 53.90% in 2001. SOEs remain the most important financial source of government revenues. SOEs contributed 87% of the total government revenue in 1978 and still 71% in 1995 (Lin and Wei 2006).

In 1994, the Chinese government passed the Corporation Law, which provided the legal framework for the SOE reforms. The Chinese government started to adopt a reform approach toward SOEs, which was officially confirmed at the 15th Party Congress in October 1997, and is characterized with the slogan "Keeping the large and letting go of the small" (*zhuada fangxiao*). This reform strategy was to concentrate state ownership and control on a core of large SOEs in strategic industries, that is, to establish the "strategic core." It was also to withdraw state ownership and control from small and medium-sized SOEs in other "competitive" industries where state intervention is not needed (Lin and Wei 2006; Chiu and Lewis 2006, p. 66–82; Holz and Zhu 2002; OECD 2000, p. 52). The state decided to keep about 1000 large enterprises as state owned or state controlled and to privatize small and medium-sized SOEs. The centerpiece of the "keeping the large" reform strategy is the creation of a strategic core of large SOEs, which involves their corporatization into modern enterprises and the formation of large enterprise groups. Based on the Corporation Law, the government began to corporatize large

SOEs through the introduction of the "modern enterprise institution," which is dominated by the shareholding system. The government also promoted a number of large SOE or state-controlled enterprise groups. By implementing the strategy of "letting go of the small," the government allowed the smaller SOEs to be privatized through selling them to insiders or other parties, leasing, auctioning, merging, and bankruptcy (Chiu and Lewis 2006, p. 66; OECD 2000, p. 51; Smyth et al. 2005a, p. 16; Lin and Wei 2006). According to a national survey in 2005, 86% of all SOEs had been through the "Keeping the large and letting go of the small" reform by the end of 2001, and 70% had been corporatized or privatized (Garnaut et al. 2005b; Yusuf et al. 2006, p. 16).

2.1.1 "Letting Go of the Small" in the Competitive Industries

Following the official decision, local governments quickly embarked on programs to privatize their small and medium-sized SOEs. Of the variable forms of privatization, three forms were the most popular ones. First, stock cooperatives (*gufen hezuozhi*), in which SOEs were sold to and then their shares owned by the employees; second, corporatization (*gongsizhi*) into a limited liability or joint-stock company; and third, outright sale (*chushou*) to outsiders—private domestic or foreign investors. Three modalities accounted for more than half of all privatizations: stock cooperatives had been the most prevalent modality. Stock cooperatives, outright sale to private investors, and corporatization accounted for 35, 11, and 8%, respectively. The other forms of privatization included merging SOEs, leasing of assets, contracting out, and bankruptcy. (Holz and Zhu 2002; Cao et al. 1999; Liu 1997a). Privatization by these modalities had proceeded quite rapidly: as many as 80% of small SOEs had been privatized by the end of 1998 (OECD 2000, p. 52–7).

2.1.2 "Keeping the Large" in the Strategic Industries

"Decisions on issues related to state-owned enterprise reforms and development" issued by the 15th Party Congress held in September 1997 restated the principle that state ownership would continue playing the major role in the Chinese economy. "Keeping the large" was to create the strategic core of large SOEs, and state ownership would retain the dominant position in large SOEs in the strategic industries. State ownership would remain dominant in pillar industries and backbone enterprises in "high-technology sectors"; nonrenewable natural resource, public utility, and infrastructure services sectors; and the military industrial sector. To secure the state strategic goal of technology modernization, state "backbone" enterprises hold a dominant position in high-technology industries. Especially in high-technology areas, the state adopts a driving function to provide financing and to support both basic and applied research (OECD 2000, p. 51–2; Holz and Zhu 2002; Chiu and Lewis 2006, p. 74).

The creation of the strategic core of large SOEs involved their conversion into modern enterprises and the formation of large enterprise groups. Establishing a "modern enterprise system" meant a transformation of the large SOEs into commercially viable entities that would remain under state control. The modern enterprise system is characterized by clearly allocated property rights, clear rights and responsibilities, the separation of government and enterprise, and a scientific management (Holz and Zhu 2002). The shareholding system became the dominant setting to restructure the SOEs and to establish the modern enterprise system. It imposed the governance mechanisms of a joint-stock system and enabled the state to retain ownership of the large SOEs. Two complementary modalities were used to establish the shareholding modern enterprise system: that is, corporatization and ownership diversification.

2.1.2.1 Corporatization

The Chinese SOEs were integrated as a part of the government departments under the prereform central planning system and had had strong ties with the government agencies after the early reforms. The major problem of this arrangement was the ambiguous property rights of the SOEs—the assets of SOEs were subject to the control of a range of government departments but ultimately belonged to no one. "Corporatization" promised to clarify the property rights of the SOEs, to make them separate legal entities and to separate government functions from enterprise operations. "Corporatization" may also transform SOEs into "modern corporate enterprises" with commercial objectives. It introduces governance mechanisms of a shareholding system, which in turn establish accountability of the management to the enterprises' owners (the state) and also initiate a diversified ownership structure. The enactment of the Company Law in 1994 provided the legal framework for the "corporatization." Through "corporatization" SOEs become either limited liability companies or joint-stock limited companies. By the end of 1999, more than 7000 medium-sized and large SOEs had been corporatized. The structure of the shareholders' general meeting, the board of directors, and the supervisory board had been implemented to ensure effective corporate governance (OECD 2000, p. 53). State entities remain the largest shareholders in most corporatized big SOEs, with an average stake of 65% in 2005 in the form of nontradable shares. Many big state-controlled shareholding companies have been listed on stock exchanges (Financial Times 2005; Green 2003).

2.1.2.2 Ownership Diversification

The reform of "ownership diversification" for big SOEs since the early 1990s meant that shareholding among various state entities, such as the central and local governments and the central and local state asset management companies, or other SOEs is encouraged, while nonstate interests in SOEs are allowed. The state directly holds a minimum of 35% of shares of corporatized SOEs. Other entities under state control also hold a similar percentage of shares; however, these shares may not be traded on the stock exchanges. As a result, state ownership has dominated the shareholding companies and only one-third of the companies' shares can be actively traded; nonstate interests in SOEs have been limited to a certain degree. In contrast to the wholesale privatization pursued in European transition economies, China's state ownership still remains more important in the overall economy, despite the reform of "ownership diversification" (OECD 2000, p. 53–4).

The formation of large SOE groups is another important reform approach to create the SOE strategic core. In the early 1990s, authorities began to establish large enterprise groups among the central government-controlled SOEs. The formation of large enterprise groups had been directed by the government through top-down processes and was to achieve the scale, scope, diversity of operations, specialization in production, and coordination among SOEs. Following the 15th Party Congress in 1997, the promotion of a number of large SOE groups became the centerpiece in establishing the strategic core of the SOE industries. The government supports the enterprise groups through credit access and technical upgrading and listing. The enterprise groups are either sector specific or conglomerates, which control companies in several industries. In 1997, the number of these large enterprise groups directly positioned under the central government had grown to 120 (OECD 2000, p. 55), which were known as the "national team." They controlled US $192.7 billion in assets and had total sales of US $112 billion. Table 2.2 shows the general situation of the pilot enterprise group in selected industries in 1999.

Through "Keeping the large and letting go of the small," the number of SOEs fell dramatically, but the state still controls the large and profitable SOEs. In 1997, the 4800 largest industrial SOEs alone accounted for 70.08% of industrial added value. And the large industrial SOEs were the most profitable (Holz and Zhu 2002). The 500 largest SOEs under central government control held 37% of the state's industrial assets, and they accounted for 46% of the taxes and 63% of the profits of the state sector. As Vice Premier Wu Bangguo said in that year, "controlling the [500] largest firms means that we have control of the largest chunk of the state economy" (Zhao 1999). At the beginning of 2000, China's industrial SOEs accounted for 70% of the fixed assets, 69% of the total assets, and 51% of the sales revenues (Broadman 2001). In 2004, state enterprises still accounted for more than half of the total assets and about half of the total output value. Although the number of state enterprises was now fewer, they had become bigger and had grown much faster than nonstate enterprises: 2.5 times versus 1.4 times (Garnaut et al. 2005a, p. 7). Therefore, although the number of SOEs has decreased and the ownership structure has changed, state enterprises are still the main pillar of the Chinese economy, and state-owned and state-controlled large enterprises still monopolize the state strategic industries. Chinese state enterprises play a leading role in the national economy (Zhao 2005, p. 111).

What has been changed through the reforms is that the previous policy of the state owning 100% of the assets and having 100% control over the enterprises has been superseded by a policy of using state capital to control the core enterprises in key

Table 2.2   General situation of the pilot enterprise group in selected industries, 1999

Type of industry	Number of groups	Total assets (billion yuan)	Net assets (billion yuan)	Sales income (billion yuan)	Profit and taxes (billion yuan)	Export income (million US dollars)
Metallurgy	8	35.7	19.2	17.8	2.8	228.0
Energy	11	41.3	20.3	14.7	1.7	30.9
Chemical	7	7.7	2.9	3.5	0.5	25.5
Automobile	6	26.3	9.0	21.9	2.4	42.1
Machinery	14	4.4	1.3	2.5	0.3	26.2
Electronics	10	4.3	1.5	4.3	0.4	103.6
Transportation	8	23.4	8.1	10.3	0.6	256.1
Pharmaceutical	5	3.9	1.3	2.4	0.3	31.4
Construction	3	15.5	3.1	10.7	0.5	48.3
Foreign trade	8	11.9	2.3	13.6	0.3	764.7
Average of 120 groups	13.4	5.4	7.8	0.7	117.3	

The figures refer to enterprise groups controlled by the central government. From Shen (1999) and OECD (2000, p. 56)

sectors and that the state became a shareholder (Chiu and Lewis 2006, p. 75–6). Through industrial restructuring, SOEs concentrate in several strategic industries. Referring to the *Fortune* 2004 listing, "The China 100" are mostly transformed SOEs and are mostly found in oil, steel, chemicals, and other state strategic sectors. Around 30–50 giant state corporations and conglomerates have even been nurtured to become "national champions" (Economist, The 2005).

That the state rids itself of the burden of managing millions of SOEs, and that it rather concentrates on managing fewer large enterprises, can alleviate the problems arising from insufficient information and improve the efficiency of those remaining SOEs. Furthermore, the state can pursue its strategic goals by retaining control over the bigger SOEs. So in a real sense, the industrial restructuring and the reforms of SOEs are not for reducing the state's command over the key sectors of the economy, but for seeking to make the control more effective. After all, the state intends to remain in control in the strategic sectors (Lin et al. 1999; Yusuf et al. 2006, p. 217; Chiu and Lewis 2006, p. 75).

The approach to keep sizable and expanding large enterprises under state ownership control indicates that China's model of development has not reoriented itself to adjust to the orthodox free market model. The state is to retain control over the "commanding heights" of the economy, to direct the path of the overall development, to build up the state strategic innovation system, and to fulfill the strategic goal of technological modernization. At the 16th Party Congress, full privatization continued to be ruled out for the SOE reform. The state made clear that it will not relinquish state control of the "commanding heights" of the economy. It furthermore restated that the essence of public ownership lies in the control rights of the enterprises in the reform process of promoting the shareholding system and the diversification of enterprise ownership (Chiu and Lewis 2006, p. 126).

2.2 The Formation of State-Controlled Shareholding Coordinated Governance Structure of State-Controlled Enterprises and State Strategic Innovation System during the Period from the mid-1990s to the middle of the First Decade of 21st Century

2.2.1 The Corporatization of SOEs Results in High Levels of Surplus

2.2.1.1 The Corporatization of SOEs

In 1993, the Chinese government declared the blueprint to establish a socialist market economy, and promulgated the Company Law. The Company Law provided a legal framework for corporatizing SOEs and for establishing a modern enterprise system. It provided rules for the incorporation of SOEs into limited liability companies and limited liability shareholding companies (joint-stock companies). It also provided the rules regarding the governance structure, the transfer of shares, as well as mergers and bankruptcy (Tenev et al. 2002, p. 16). The limited liability company has a restricted number of shareholders (two to 49 shareholders) with a small equity base (0.5 million yuan), in which equity cannot be transferred. The limited liability shareholding company in contrast has 50 or more shareholders and a large equity base (ten million yuan) and is permitted to be listed on the stock markets to raise capital from the public and to transfer equity in the stock markets. The limited liability shareholding company is the formal equivalent of the Western stock corporation (Chiu and Lewis 2006, p. 118). According to the Company Law, a SOE becomes an independent legal entity after it has been converted into a company, with the state as owner. The SOE acts in a commercial way, adopting management strategies similar to the strategies of an OECD-based shareholding company (Gabriel 2006, p. 112), and is governed by public laws like a private enterprise.

Therefore, since 1998, the category "SOEs," which had included "pure" SOEs, solely state-invested limited liability companies, and state–state joint operations before, has also included all state-controlled shareholding companies (where shareholding companies comprise limited liability companies and stock companies) (Holz and Zhu 2002, p. 74).

2.2.1.2 A Key Priority of the SOE Reforms: The Corporate Governance Reform

In 1999, the Fourth Plenum of the Chinese Communist Party's 15th Central Council further identified corporate governance as "the core" of the modern enterprise system. The establishment of effective corporate governance mechanisms has become a key priority of the SOE reforms. The corporate governance reform ensures that SOEs adopt key features from the OECD model of corporate governance and function effectively in a market environment (Tam 1999; Smyth et al. 2005b, p. 2).

Since the early 1990s, policy-makers in China have increasingly realized that poor SOE performance and weak governance are attributable to the "unclear property rights" and the "lack of separation between the government and the enterprises." Under the old system of the unity of ownership and control by the state, the state imposed noneconomic objectives (e.g., social welfare functions) on SOEs, which made enterprise managers unable to respond efficiently to market forces. Multiple state agencies with conflicting demands supervised the enterprises, and SOEs lacked incentives and sanctions found in private firms. Because of the ambiguity of property rights together with state ownership, there is no clear representative of the state to monitor the performance of managers (Pannier 1996; Estrin 1998; Chiu and Lewis 2006, p. 118; OECD 2000, p. 64–5). In the new environment of the market economy, the Company Law provided means for separating governmental and business functions. It also provided means for separating the state ownership from the state bureaucratic control, clarifying property rights of SOEs, delineating the roles of the state and the enterprises clearly, and freeing managers from bureaucratic interventions in the modern Chinese corporate entity. A regulation, namely, the "Regulation for Changing the Operational Mechanism of Enterprises Owned by the Whole People," issued in 1992, ceded 14 autonomous management rights to SOE managers, including business autonomy, disposal of assets, pricing of output and labor services, use of retained income, investment decisions, export and import, and refusal of request for compulsory contributions from the government.

However, it cannot be assumed that clarifying property rights of SOEs without implementing a corporate governance mechanism was enough for corporatized SOEs to be managed effectively and to improve their performance. In a modern corporation where there is a separation between the ownership and the managerial control of assets, there is an agency problem, that is, managers and employees as the agents of shareholders may have interests that diverge from those of the principals. Without certain checks and balances on managerial behavior, there can be no guarantee that the managers are managing the enterprise's resources in the owner's interests. Corporate governance is concerned with the design of checks and balances to control management behavior and to ensure that the managers are monitored, motivated, and disciplined to act to the best advantage of the owners (Chiu and Lewis 2006, p. 134). Western economists would not argue that managers should be given complete autonomy to improve corporate performance. Rather, managers should be given room to implement their management strategies, while being monitored, up to the point of poor performance, when they may be dismissed.

Chinese policy-makers had held the view that the key to SOE performance is to clarify the property rights, to extend the autonomy of managers, and even to hand over some important rights attaching ownership to managers. The lesson learned from the contract responsibility system was that simply handing over control to managers was not enough to improve the performance of SOEs. Management autonomy cannot be independent of the corporate governance mechanisms to keep the managers in check (Chiu and Lewis 2006, p. 127). Because China is different from OECD countries and other transition countries, the transformation of SOEs in China meant forcing those SOEs remaining under state ownership to act more like private commercial firms. This was carried out through corporatization and the creation of corporate governance to provide the necessary incentives and disciplines. The government is withdrawing from the management of enterprises, while exercising its functions as owner and shareholder through separate entities created for these purposes (OECD 2000, p. 64). If supported by the proper corporate governance, the corporatization of SOEs can be tackled without depleting state assets and undermining the state as owner. In fact, property rights in corporatized SOEs must operate within and can only be effectively protected through a proper corporate governance (Chiu and Lewis 2006, p. 127).

There are two major objectives in the establishment of the effective corporate governance mechanism. The first is to establish mechanisms to exercise the state's ownership rights in corporatized SOEs that are separate from the government's regulatory functions. The second is to establish corporate governance mechanisms, which shall provide incentives and accountability for managers to act in the interest of their owners (OECD 2000, p. 63–5).

2.2.1.3   Separating the State Shareholder Function from the Regulatory Function

In May 2003, China established the State-Owned Assets Supervision and Administration Commission (SASAC) to push forward the reforms and for the restructuring of the SOEs. SASAC acts as a shareholder of state assets to overcome the fragmentation of the state ownership arrangement. See Fig. 2.1.

The state owns assets of enterprises on behalf of the people of China, and the State Council represents the state as the owner of SOE assets. State Council representation is reserved for large SOEs and state-owned holding enterprises. For all other SOEs, the state is represented by governments of provinces, autonomous regions, municipalities, and cities. SASAC is now authorized by the State Council to perform the responsibilities of the "investor" of state-owned assets on behalf of the central government, taking over this role from other state bodies, and being a special ministerial-level institution directly under the State Council. SASAC acts as an investor of SOEs, enjoying owner's equity rights, and assuming legal liabilities under the Corporate Law without intervening directly in the enterprise's day-to-day operations. As an investor, SASAC enjoys ownership rights that are separated from the management of the SOEs. SASAC directly supervises and manages 196 large enterprises that are directly subordinate to the Central Party Commission. State-owned assets supervision and management organizations at provincial and city (region) levels were also established, acting as the investors of lower-level SOEs. SASAC is in charge of guiding and supervising - regional-level state-owned assets management (Chiu and Lewis 2006, p. 122). We can see the functions of SASAC in Box 2.1.

SASAC has the power to appoint and remove the top executives of SOEs under the supervision of the central government, to monitor their performance, to structure the incentive systems for the management of those SOEs, and to supervise

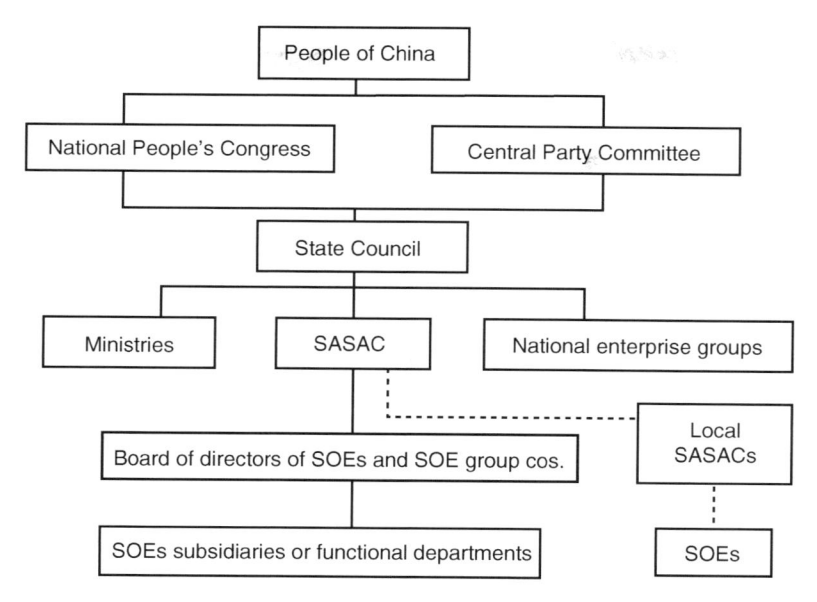

Fig. 2.1 The SASAC model. (from Chiu and Lewis 2006, p. 121, Fig. 4.2c)

the management of regional-level SOEs. The establishment of SASAC and regional-level state-owned assets supervision and management organizations was meant to solve the problem of multiple controllers of state-owned assets. As shown in the following points, it achieves this objective in three ways. First, the interest of the various state bodies within the enterprises is reduced to a common denominator—equity. Second, the new shareholders have only a single way—shareholder voting—to voice their interests. Majority voting rules eliminate conflicting goals. Third, the new shareholders now have a common interest in raising the profitability of their enterprises (Clarke 2003; Chiu and Lewis 2006, p. 110).

> **Box 2.1 Main Responsibilities of State-Owned Assets Supervision and Administration Commission (SASAC) of the State Council**
>
> 1. As authorized by the State Council and in accordance with the Corporate Law of the People's Republic of China and related administrative regulations, SASAC acts as the state-owned assets investor to guide and push the reforms and for the restructuring of the state-owned enterprises. Supervise the maintenance and appreciation of state assets value for those state-invested enterprises, to reinforce the management of the state-owned assets, to promote the establishment of the modern enterprise system of the SOEs and improve enterprise corporate governance, and to drive the strategic adjustment of the state-owned economic structure and layout.

(continued)

Box 2.1 (continued)

2. Dispatch the supervisory board to some large enterprises on behalf of the state and be in charge of daily management of the supervisory board.

3. Appoint, remove, and evaluate the executives of the enterprises through legal procedures and grant rewards and punishments according to their performance. Build corporate leadership selection mechanisms according to the requirements of the socialist market economic system and the modern enterprise system and streamline the motivation and restraint system for the corporate management.

4. Supervise and manage the maintenance and appreciation of state assets via statistics and audit, establish and improve the state-owned assets, maintenance and appreciation target system of state-owned assets, and work out assessment standards. Safeguard the interest and rights of the owners of the state-owned assets.

5. Draft laws, administrative regulations, and related rules on the management of the state-owned assets. Direct and supervise the work of local state-owned assets management according to the law.

6. Undertake other issues assigned by the State Council.

From SASAC website, accessed 29 March 2005

At the provincial and municipal levels, state asset management committees, which act as investors in SOEs and are responsible for preserving and increasing the value of state assets, oversee a number of state holding companies, or, say, state asset management companies that manage the assets of SOEs entrusted to their responsibility. In the case of large SOE groups, their core firms are authorized to carry out the functions of state holding companies for their member firms. Thus, state holding companies are responsible for the exercise of the state's ownership rights and also are accountable to the state asset management committees (OECD 2000, p. 65).

2.2.1.4 Introducing Corporate Governance Mechanisms

Introducing corporate governance mechanisms into corporatized SOEs was meant to strengthen incentives and monitoring mechanisms in these shareholding companies. According to the Company Law, corporate governance for joint-stock limited companies includes the shareholder's general meeting, the board of directors, and the supervisory board (see Box 2.2). Corporate governance is to ensure and strengthen the accountability of the management to the board and the shareholders, the supervision of the board of directors and the senior management by the supervisory board, and the accountability of the directors toward the shareholders (OECD 2000, p. 66).

> **Box 2.2 System of Corporate Governance Under China's Company Law**
>
> Under the Company Law (1993), two types of companies are established, i.e., limited liability company (LLC) and joint-stock limited company (JSC). The Company Law prescribes a system of corporate governance through an organizational structure comprising three main bodies: the shareholders' general meeting, the board of directors, and the board of supervisors.
>
> The shareholders' general meeting is the highest authority within the company. It has the following rights and responsibilities: to decide on the company strategy and on operational business and investment plans; to appoint and dismiss members of the board of directors and representatives of shareholders as members of the supervisory boards; to examine and approve reports by the board of directors and by the supervisory board; to examine and approve the company's proposed annual financial budget and final accounts, the profit distribution plan, and the plan for recovery of losses; and to pass resolutions on the increase or decrease of registered capital, the issuing of bonds, and on merger, division, dissolution, and liquidation. Shareholders' meetings are held once a year. Shareholders are entitled to one vote for each share held.
>
> The board of directors comprises between five and nineteen members, with members elected by the shareholders' meeting. The board of directors is accountable to the shareholders' meeting and empowered with the following rights and responsibilities: to convene the shareholders' meeting and report work to the meeting; to carry out the resolutions and decisions adopted by the shareholders' meeting; to draft proposed operational business and investment plans; to formulate plans for profit distribution, recovery of losses, merger, division, or dissolution of the company; to decide on the company's internal organization and management structure; to appoint, dismiss, and determine the remuneration of the company's general manager, the deputy manager (upon recommendation of the general manager), and the chief financial officer. The meeting of the board of directors is held at least twice a year. The general manager attends the meeting of the board of directors as a non-voting member.
>
> The supervisory board comprises a minimum of three members, including representatives of the shareholders and at least one representative of the company's employees. The employees' representative(s) is (are) to be democratically elected by the employees. The tenure of a supervisory board member is three years, which is renewable upon re-election and re-appointment by the shareholders' meeting. Members of the board of directors, managers, and the chief financial officer are not allowed to serve as members of the supervisory board. The supervisory board is empowered with the following rights and responsibilities: to oversee and examine the financial affairs of the company; to supervise acts of directors and managers; and to request remedies

(continued)

> **Box 2.2** (continued)
> from directors or managers for their acts that have harmed the interests of
> the company. Supervisors attend the meeting of the board of directors as
> non-voting members.
>   From OECD (2000, p. 68)

Shareholders' General Meeting

The shareholders' general meeting is the highest authority within a company in
China. It appoints and dismisses members of the board of directors and members
of the supervisory board.

Board of Directors

Board members are elected by shareholders to look after their interests. The board
hires and fires managers and sets the remuneration package for senior executives.
The board of directors should keep effective control over the company and monitor
the executive management. The directors account for their stewardship to the
shareholders at the annual general meeting. The shareholders appoint auditors to
provide an independent check on the financial statements based on "Western-style"
accounting standards promulgated in 1992 by the Chinese government, which
have become increasingly internationally compatible (Cadbury Committee Report
1992; Chiu and Lewis 2006, p. 147; Smyth et al. 2005a, p. 4).

Supervisory Board

Like Germanic countries, China also applies a two-tier board system in its corporate
governance, with representatives of employees being appointed to the supervisory
board. The supervisory board is designed to oversee and constrain management.
It also allows codetermination between shareholders, managers, and employees.
To understand the function of the supervisory board, we may compare the two-tier
board system in Germanic countries with the one-tier board system in Anglo-Saxon
countries.

   In Germanic countries (Germany, Austria, Switzerland, the Netherlands), shareholders (and others) are encouraged to use their "voice" to influence the management
through the supervisory board, which exists in addition to the executive management
board. Table 2.3 compares the governance functions of the two-tier board and
that of the one-tier board. The functions undertaken by the senior management in
Anglo-Saxon countries devolve to the executive board in the Germanic countries,
while the functions undertaken by the board of directors in the one-tier system
devolve to the supervisory board in the two-tier system (Nietsch 2005).

Table 2.3 Board functions in one-tier and two-tier board systems

Shareholders' annual general meeting
Determines fundamental issues, such as
• Selecting the outside auditing firm
• Selecting the board of directors (single-tier) or the supervisory board of directors (two-tier)

Single-tier	Two-tier
Board of directors	Supervisory board

• Selects, evaluates, and compensates members of senior management (single-tier) or executive board (two-tier)
• Guide corporate strategy
• Oversees corporate performance
• Approves certain important decisions of senior management or executive board body

Senior management	Executive board
Under the direction of the board of direction (single-tier) or supervisory board (two-tier)	
• Executes corporate strategy	
• Manages the operations of the company	

From OECD (1998)

The difference between the two-tier board in China and that in Germanic countries is that in China the shareholders' general meeting appoints the board of directors and the supervisory board, while in Germanic countries the shareholders' general meeting appoints the supervisory board, and the executive board is selected by the supervisory board. Thus, the board of directors is directly accountable to the shareholders' meeting in China, rather than to the supervisory board as is prevalent in Germany (Lin 2000; OECD 2000).

Compensation System

The compensation system reform in Chinese corporate governance has been introduced gradually since the 1990s. The managerial labor market aligns the interests of managers and shareholders through the contractual arrangements, which links management remuneration to the profitability of the firm or the share price value. Performance-enhanced bonuses and stock options are types of management remuneration generally used for these purposes in corporate governance (Prowse 1994; Chiu and Lewis 2006, p. 152). These reflect the major changes in the compensation system compared with the past, and how market forces determine the compensation structure in corporate governance in large listed Chinese companies (China Youth Daily 2003; Zhao 2005, p. 116).

External Control

Corporate control functions in liberal market economies, like those of the USA and the UK. Changes in share prices will trigger takeover threats. This mechanism amounts to corporate control from markets to discipline management. Falling share prices signal the need for managers to improve the performance of firms. Otherwise a hostile takeover might happen to replace the managers. Corporate control provides mechanisms to keep managers under the control of shareholders.

It is difficult for hostile takeovers of Chinese listed companies to happen because of their existing ownership structure. Even though there are some merger and acquisition cases each year, the number in China is insignificant, and the level of industry concentration is low compared with that in the USA. Of 46 industries, only eight had a concentration greater than 40%, with most having a concentration of less than 20% (HSBC (Hong Kong and Shanghai Banking Corporation) 2001; Tenev et al. 2002, p. 115–6).

For external governance in corporatized SOEs, the government as the representative of principal shareholders plays an important role. It is reflected by the fact that the authority appoints operators and managers and exercises external supervision and constraint over the operational activities of managers; for example, to appoint the chief financial supervisor and carry out auditing. A survey conducted in 2000 by the Chinese Entrepreneurs' Survey System showed that government appointment has always been the principal form for choosing and controlling managers and operators of corporatized SOEs, accounting for about 76–80%. Corresponding to such a pattern of external governance exercised by the government, mergers, acquisitions, takeovers, and other components of the market mechanisms play a much less disciplinary role. Studies have demonstrated with substantial evidence that the corporatized SOEs with absolute controlling shares held by the state show less market corporate control, including mergers and acquisitions. Even when control authority is transferred, the transfer is mainly via the contractual transfer and allocation of state shares, not through purchasing on the secondary market (Chen and Huang 2001).

2.2.1.5   The General Process of Corporatization in China

The general process of corporatization in China proceeds is as follows:

- Asset assessment and verification.
- Identification of owners.
- Choice of company form of a limited liability company or a joint-stock company.
- Establishment of the board of directors and the supervisory board.
- Appointment of CEO, deputy CEO, and other senior managers.
- The company begins its business.

In the SOE restructuring, large SOEs are corporatized into limited liability shareholding companies, with a selected few listed on China's two stock exchanges: Shanghai Stock Exchange and Shenzhen Stock Exchange. Until 1999, Chinese companies were selected to be listed according to a system of quota allocation administered by the China Securities Regulatory Commission. The firms that met certain qualifications could apply for listing. Listing was then authorized by a committee to appraise a firm's financial strength, quality, and prospects (Chiu and Lewis 2006, p. 166). After 1999, the Chinese government eliminated the quota system for initial public offerings. Which companies will access the market was from then on based on market principles. The China Securities Regulatory Commission requires the committee assessing initial public offerings to pay attention to corporate governance issues, that is, whether the company's shareholders' meetings, board of directors, and supervisory board have been discharging their duties and exercising their rights independently (Tenev et al. 2002, p. 111). At the beginning of 2005, 1377 enterprises were listed on the two markets, almost all of them were large state-controlled shareholding companies (China Securities Regulatory Commission website, cited by Chiu and Lewis 2006, p. 111). Their market capitalization is about 40% of GDP (Standard and Poor's 2004). The China Securities Regulatory Commission has made efforts to strengthen corporate governance practices among these listed companies (Garnaut et al. 2005b, p. 6), and they have on the whole adopted more modern corporate governance arrangements than other enterprises in China (Chiu and Lewis 2006, p. 165).

2.2.1.6 Classifying Shares of Listed Companies: State Shares Cannot Be Freely Traded

Chinese company shares are classified as A shares, B shares, H shares, and N shares. A shares are designated for domestic investors; B, H, and N shares are designated for overseas investors. A shares are further classified into state shares, legal person shares, and tradable shares. Each type of share accounts for about one-third of all shares. State shares are owned by the state, that is, the central and local governments, which are represented by state asset management companies. State shares can also be held by the parent of the listed company, mostly a SOE. The state is the controlling shareholder, and state shares are not tradable. Legal person shares are held by domestic institutions such as industrial enterprises, security companies, nonbank financial institutions, transportation and power companies, and technology and research institutes. Almost all of the legal person shareholders are SOEs. Legal person shares are not generally tradable but can be transferred to other legal persons. Thus, in the majority of cases, the state is the direct or indirect (through industrial SOEs) controlling shareholder of listed companies. State and legal person shares can only be transferred to domestic institutions if approval is given by the China Securities Regulatory Commission (Tenev et al. 2002, p. 76). The Chinese government ensured that it would not lose control over the listed SOEs by requiring that a proportion of the state's shares could not be sold (Yao 2004). About 30% of all shares are tradable and are owned by domestic individuals and institutions. Thus, listed companies in China have a mixed ownership structure. The state, legal persons, and domestic individual investors constitute the largest groups of stockholders. In 2004, the state held 47% of shares, legal persons held 11% of shares, and domestic investors held 28% of shares. Less than one-third of the shares of listed companies (i.e., those held by individuals) were freely tradable (Chiu and Lewis 2006, p. 111; Tenev et al. 2002, p. 76–7).

2.2.1.7 Effective Corporate Governance Generates More Surpluses to Be Invested in Building up the State Innovation System and in the Rapid Technological Modernization

After realizing the increasingly adverse impact of the weak governance and inefficiency of the SOE sector, the policy-makers saw corporate governance reform as an urgent task in China. The objective of corporate governance reform is to introduce capital market disciplines and to place the managers of SOEs under pressure from shareholders, financiers, and the market. The state as a controlling shareholder invests in enterprises and expects proportional returns from enterprise profits. Other shareholders also expect to receive proportional returns on their investments, and bondholders should be paid interest and principal. To meet these expectations, reformed SOE management was encouraged to adopt Western-style effective corporate governance, to select better managers and to use capital more efficiently. Effective corporate governance ensures that the power to make decisions will be allocated to those people with the best chance of enhancing the performance of the firm. It reorients managerial incentives to engage in more profit-oriented and value-augmenting activities, in line with the owners' interest. It also ensures that reformed SOEs are competitive and can adapt to the changing demands of the market.

The leadership in China encourages the spread of Western corporate governance and expects it to generate more surpluses and to lead to more rapid modernization. The Chinese policy-makers believed that the technologies (hard and soft) that would achieve their strategic goals already existed in the advanced market economies of the OECD. And it was assumed that optimal strategies of Western corporate governance would embody OECD-type technologies. The leadership in China has encouraged the spread of Western corporate governance in reformed SOEs and has encouraged the directors and the managements to implement these operational strategies that were assumed to result in higher levels of surplus (if not profit maximization), to lead to more rapid modernization in the state innovation system, and therefore to meet the state's strategic goals (Gabriel 2006, p. 108). Facing fast expanding international trade and inward foreign direct investment, the need to further improve effective corporate governance in reformed SOEs in China had taken on added significance (Smyth et al. 2005a, p. 3). To compete with the increased competition arising from WTO membership and to attract foreign investment, China's reformed SOEs need to adopt corporate governance mechanisms in line with international practice, to compete successfully in increasingly competitive global markets (OECD 2000, p. 63). After the transformation, the corporate governance in reformed SOEs appears to be akin to that in the firms in OECD economies (Lo and Smith 2005).

Corporatization imposed a limit on state-owner responsibility for reformed SOEs, providing incentives for enterprises to generate more surpluses and freeing up more surpluses to be invested in modernization. The corporatization of SOEs and the corporate governance reform were implemented to separate the state's responsibility for the survival of SOEs from the state-owner's property rights in SOEs. Before the

SOE reforms, there was an implicit contract between the state and the workers, in which the state had unlimited responsibility for the enterprises' survival. After SOEs have been transformed into limited liability companies or shareholding companies, the state would have limited responsibility (up to the actual capital it invests) for reformed enterprises, and the reformed enterprises would have to be responsible for their own profits and losses, to the point of bankruptcy (Lo and Smith 2005). By imposing a limit on state-owner responsibility for enterprises, the state hardened budget constraints on reformed enterprises. It provided an incentive for directors and managers to implement strategies that would generate the higher level of surplus necessary to meet enterprise obligations. Thus, these reforms would improve cash flows from enterprises to the state and reduce subsidies from the state to enterprises and at the same time would free up more surplus to be invested in modernization to meet the state's strategic goals (Gabriel 2006, p. 111).

Being put under the hard budget constraint, enterprise strategies to raise surplus and to adopt technologies are in line with the state's strategic goals. Imposing a limit on state responsibility for enterprises has meant that senior management must rely more heavily on the value-generating potential of their work force to meet the expectations of internal and external occupants of distributive class positions. In reformed SOEs, such a hard budget constraint has provided incentive mechanisms to the management and has motivated managers and workers to generate more surpluses and to invest in new technologies in line with the state's strategic goals (Gabriel 2006, p. 111–2).

Thus, the overall result of the reforms seems to be boosting state revenues (which will be detailed in Sect. 2.2.6), which can be invested in modernization, which leads to more SOE investment in projects that are compatible with state modernization plans (Gabriel 2006, p. 112).

2.2.2 The State as the Controlling Shareholder of State-Controlled Enterprises Has Extraordinary Power to Deploy Investable Funds for Building up the Successful State Strategic Innovation System

The majority of the total shares of reformed SOEs remain under the control of the central government and related holders of legal person shares, which makes the state the primary claimant to the surplus generated within reformed SOEs and furthermore gives the state extraordinary power to deploy investable funds to invest in technological modernization. That the state maintains controlling ownership of key enterprises in the strategic sectors in the pillar industries, and retains a direct surplus appropriation role in the burgeoning market economy, is the "backbone" of the modernization of the Chinese economy (Gabriel 2006, p. 112–49).

Chinese authorities have made it clear that they will not relinquish state control of the "commanding height" of the economy. Even though lots of small and medium-sized SOEs have been privatized, the state still keeps ownership of the larger SOEs, and it wants state ownership to remain a dominant feature of the economy. Corporatization is a useful step in the SOE reforms, which has restructured SOEs as limited liability companies and joint-stock companies and has established scientific corporate governance even without significant ownership changes. State ownership still implies the control rights of enterprises after the corporatization of SOEs and the diversification of enterprise ownership. Corporatization sets a stage for selling shares and separating the state from the enterprise, holds directors responsible for the assets of the state-controlled enterprise, and prevents further asset erosion. It also upgrades the management of the state-controlled enterprises while preserving the state's controlling ownership stake. In practice, this has been sought by classifying the share of corporatized SOEs into several classes. The state as a controlling shareholder is realized by state-owned shares or shares held by other state firms (legal person shares, or, say, *faren gu*), both of which remain subject to restrictions on transfer (Chiu and Lewis 2006, p. 126–31). The State Council and local government leadership delegate ownership control over state-controlled enterprises to state asset management companies. The state, thus acting as controlling shareholder and primary appropriator of surplus, participates in modern corporate governance of corporatized SOEs (Gabriel 2006, p. 106).

2.2.2.1 The State Shareholder as the Controlling Shareholder in Shareholding Companies in China

The ownership structure of shareholding companies in China's state sector is characterized by the prominent role of the state, the negligible role of financial institutions and institutional investors, and the absence of individuals as significant shareholders (Tenev et al. 2002, p. 103). About two-thirds of the value of the issued capital of China's listed companies is held as state-owned shares (by the central government or local governments) and as legal person shares (held by other SOEs, nonbanking financial institutes, and companies in which the state has significant capital ownership). These shares are nontransferable and can only be transferred to domestic institutions if transfer is approved by the China Securities Regulatory Commission (Ho and Hai-Gen 2002; Chiu and Lewis 2006, p. 167). A survey by Tenev et al. (2002) of 257 Shanghai-listed companies found that in 1999 42% of the largest shareholders in the sample held state shares. The state therefore tends to be the controlling shareholder. In 57% of the companies in the sample, the largest shareholder held legal person shares, of which almost all were industrial SOEs. Thus, in more than 95% of the cases, the state directly or indirectly (through SOEs) controls listed companies in China. In about 47% of the companies in the sample, nontradable shares accounted for 70–90% of the total shares. In 41% of the companies in the sample, nontradable shares accounted for 50–69% of the total shares. About 30% of all shares were tradable and mostly held by individuals (Tenev et al. 2002, p. 76–7). A survey by Liu and Sun (2003) of 1105 listed companies found that although only 8.5% of companies were directly controlled by the state, many of the nontradable shares of these companies were held by wholly state-owned holding companies or state-controlled nonlisted holding companies. If indirect control and direct control are combined to one measure, the 2001 numbers show that there was state control of 84% of all the listed companies, and only 16% were not state controlled. The institutions of state control in these cases ranged from central government bureaus to provincial bureaus and many other types of state units (Yusuf et al. 2006, p. 89).

Ownership in China's joint-stock companies is concentrated to a considerable degree. The survey by Tenev et al. (2002) indicates that the three largest shareholders on average held about 58% of the total shares, of which the largest shareholders on average held 47%, and the second and the third ones held 8 and 3%, respectively. In almost 49% of the firms in the sample, the three largest shareholders held 60–80% of all shares. Such a high concentration of ownership combined with the relatively small portion of tradable shares implies that control is contestable in few of China's listed companies.

2.2.2.2 State Shareholders in Control of Corporate Governance in China and the "Backbone" of the State Strategic Innovation System

These ownership features have a direct bearing on the type of corporate governance that is prevalent in China. The most important implication of the dominant role of state ownership in China's shareholding companies is the government and the party's control over management appointments. While the dominant position of controlling shareholders is not unique, in China the role of state shareholders as controlling shareholders that exert direct control over shareholders' meetings and boards of directors is exclusively Chinese (Tenev et al. 2002, p. 104).

Shareholders appoint 76% of the directors of listed companies. State-owned legal person shareholders select 48% of all directors, and state shareholders select 21% of all directors. Thus, the state is directly and indirectly in control of the companies' directorates, selecting nearly 70% of all directors. Like ownership, control is also highly concentrated. The largest shareholder holds less than 50% of all shares but controls more than 50% of board seats. The share of the three largest shareholders is 59% on average, but they appoint 79% of the directors. The marginal value of control diminishes after the largest shareholder has obtained majority control. Table 2.4 compares the size of the largest shareholding with board control. The share of board seats controlled by the largest shareholder is higher than the share of the shareholder's ownership. This situation is only reversed when the largest shareholder has obtained majority control (more than 50%). Thus, holding companies control the boards of listed companies. Only 24% of the total of directors are appointed by nonshareholders, of which the executive directors are mainly recommended by company staff, and are sometimes appointed by the government (Tenev et al. 2002, p. 83–5).

Table 2.4 Discrepancy between size of the largest shareholding and control rights

Largest share (%)	Number of companies in sample	Average size of the largest share (%)	Percentage of directors appointed by largest shareholder
>80	5	87	66
50–80	77	63	62
20–49	78	34	46
<20	11	16	31
Total	171	48	53

From Tenev et al. (2002)

The state agencies as the controlling shareholders exercise effective control. Board chairs exert genuine control over the shareholders' meeting as representatives of the largest shareholder. The controlling shareholder dominates the appointment of the general manager. The board of directors is not independent of the management, and the roles of both the chairman of the board and the general manager are often combined. The executive directors with managerial responsibilities dominate the board, and the general manager acts on behalf of the controlling state shareholder (OECD 2000, p. 71; Tenev et al. 2002, p. 98).

In corporate governance in China, the single majority owner has extraordinary power and the minority owners are weak. In its legislation processes, the entity that is responsible for creating, changing, and enforcing the rules of corporate governance is the majority owner of corporate assets and the primary claimant to the surplus value that is generated by those assets (Gabriel 2006, p. 149–50). Minority shareholders have no effective right to elect boards of directors in the state-dominated shareholding companies. Their sole right is to receive dividends. A few of these firms have appointed some "outside" directors, but these directors appear to have little power over the company's management, which is appointed by the government and the Party as described above (Qian 1999, p. 39; Yusuf et al. 2006, p. 90).

In short, the type of corporate governance in state-controlled shareholding companies in China can best be characterized as insider-dominated corporate governance, which flows from the role of the state as the largest block shareholder (Chiu and Lewis 2006, p. 175).

It is now clear how the state is able to retain a direct surplus appropriation role and how it maintains the "backbone" of modernization of the Chinese economy. While retaining state ownership control, the state decentralizes the appropriation and distribution of surplus value to local governments and directors and managers within various state enterprises. This very organization allows the companies' directors and managers as well as the local governments some "leeway" to use some of the surplus value under their control, to acquire and innovate in favored technologies. In the meantime, decentralization generates market competition. Competition among these enterprises was stimulated to motivate directors and managers to use the surplus value for investment in new technologies, as well as to achieve "professionalism" and competitiveness. New technologies have allowed workers to produce products that have improved quality and marketing characteristics, which are necessary to generate sales in a competitive environment (Gabriel 2006).

It can therefore be concluded that the transition of China's economy toward a market economy that is coordinated by state-controlled shareholding is actually part of a strategy to build up the state strategic innovation system and to achieve technological modernization. The economic transition in China was designed to modernize industry, agriculture, research and development, and the military (*the Four Modernizations*). China continuously underwent processes of adoption in the advanced technologies. This can be identified as the cornerstone of the state's economic development strategy to reach a status equal to that of the USA and the EU in this domain. The strategy of making technological transformation the top priority of the economy has been implemented successfully. Chinese state-controlled enterprises are able to produce and are currently producing a wide range of products with quite sophisticated components for domestic and foreign markets (Gabriel 2006, p. 153–5). The success is manifest in the production of spacecraft and the performance of a spacewalk, the launching of Chinese-made rockets carrying Chinese-made satellites, Three Gorges Dam, the Shanghai magnetic levitation train, high speed train network covering the whole country, high speed railway passing through tall mountains and deep valleys, express ways also across mountains and valleys, World's highest bridges, level 50 bridges, river-canal network, new airports, 4G and 5G intrastructures covering the most remote mountain areas with so far 1.204 billion users connected to 4G and 5G stations, 4G and 5G coverage exceeding 20% more than the rest of the world combined (Dongye 2019), as well as thousands of small-scale incremental innovations in new technologies. The above innovation projects are led by the state-controlled enterprises. They lose money for doing many of these, but they bring huge social benefits to the general people, and they bring kind of long-term profitability. This is called socialism with Chinese characteristics, which is the "backbone" of the state strategic innovation system. The West such as the USA and Europe could not achieve.

2.2.3 Worker Participation in Corporate Governance

The Chinese government has made provisions in the Company Law for employee participation in the corporate governance of SOEs (Chiu and Lewis 2006, p. 168). Chinese workers thereby gain a number of legal rights in corporate governance to protect their interests. Collective contracting governs the employees' interests regarding compensation, firing, social benefits, working conditions, etc. The role of the labor union in collective wage bargaining has been defined (Tenev et al. 2002, p. 41; Garnaut et al. 2005a, p. 143). The workers' congress and trade unions have extensive rights to access consultation and information concerning production plans, the use of public welfare funds, and other matters that could affect employees' interests. In limited liability companies and joint-stock companies that have the government as a controlling shareholder, trade unions have the right to organize workers. They can use this form of organization to oversee and assess the virtues, ability, and achievements of the chair of the board of directors, the general managers, and the high-level management personnel. Managers of the state-controlled enterprises are obligated to report to the employee conference on various business-related expenditures.

In addition to the rights exercised through the workers' congress and the trade unions, employees can be represented on the board of directors and the supervisory board. The Company Law stipulates that a proper proportion of workers' representatives should be elected as board members in limited liability companies, established either with investment from two SOEs, or by two state investment holding companies, or in state-funded companies. Another provision of the Company Law is the proper proportion of workers' representatives on the supervisory board in limited liability companies and joint-stock companies. As these legal regulations show, employees are represented to a significant extent on the board of directors and the supervisory board in the corporatized SOEs in China.

Mandatory worker participation in China's corporate governance, which especially requires employee representation on the supervisory board, is akin to the German corporate model. It also reflects the stakeholder orientation toward corporate governance prevalent in China, which is consistent with the important role of state ownership and the related concept of employees as the masters of enterprises (OECD 2000, p. 66).

An important aspect in the industrial relations system concerns the issue of layoffs. Reformed SOEs may still face significant constraints on dismissals imposed by the government. It is often argued that reformed SOEs do not optimize their labor input. Facing an economic downturn, reformed SOEs would rarely lay off staff according to a fall in the demand for their output. This reflects the fact that reformed SOEs are fulfilling social objectives and how they provide a social safety net for part of the urban workforce, which leads to a lower level of short-term efficiency compared with that in private companies (Dong and Putterman 2002; Yusuf et al. 2006, p. 201; Laurenceson and Chai 2003, p. 40). The data from Meng (2004) indicate that an increase in the capital-to-labor ratio has no impact on state sector employment but significantly reduces employment in the market-oriented private sector. This also has roots in the fact that state firms do not reduce their staff when they implement improved technologies that result in a shift from a low to a high capital-to-labor ratio. In contrast, 10% increase in the capital-to-labor ratio would have reduced employment by 24% in the private sector in 1998 (Meng 2004).

The industrial relations system in state enterprises is likely to concern the wage system as well. As the labor market reform in the state sector accelerated in 1990s, state firms were given autonomy over hiring, firing, and setting wages and bonuses. Wage determination and the incentive-based structure in the state sector became more market oriented. Nevertheless, a seniority-based wage system rather than a pure market-based wage system dominates in the state sector. State sector employees receive state- or firm-provided benefits, such as medical care, housing, and pensions. Private sector employees receive far fewer of these benefits (Garnaut and Song 2004,

p. 149–52). However, wages and major benefits need to be distributed fairly among all the state employees (Garnaut et al. 2001, p. 98). Bonuses also tend to be equally distributed among state employees. In state enterprises the correlation between changes in labor productivity and wages is weaker, the rate of return to education is lower, and the earnings–experience profile is flatter, compared with those in private enterprises. Labor costs in the state sector are therefore found to be higher than in the private sector (Garnaut and Song 2004, p. 149–52).

2.2.4   The State-Controlled Shareholding Coordination-Based SOE Groups

2.2.4.1   The State's Active Role in the Formation of SOE Groups

Throughout much of the 1990s and further on into the first decade in 21 century, the Chinese government authorities attempted to form enterprise groups out of large state-owned firms, to establish the strategic core of SOE industries. Especially enterprises in the state-designated "pillar industries" are viewed as the driving forces of growth and were preferentially selected (OECD 2000, p. 55; Yusuf et al. 2006, p. 219). These groups of large, state-owned firms were deliberately formed by the state through a top-down process directed by government authorities. They resemble Japanese *keiretsu*. Some of these enterprise groups are sector-specific, while others are conglomerates that control enterprises in several industries (Keister 2000, p. 68–9; OECD 2000, p. 55).

This kind of enterprise group in China complies with the standard meaning of a business group (Keister 2000, p. 70). It is involved in production, marketing, transportation, finance, research and development, and other aspects of the production process. These groups are normally very large and their range of activities is quite broad. The single firms in the groups have different primary products and are geographically scattered. While for the most part each member firm keeps separate accounts, the group also keeps some joint accounts for the joint activities; for example, management, joint financing, financial transfer, technology development and dissemination, and research and development activities.

The business group is not a single, legally defined or legally recognized entity. Each member firm of a business group maintains an independent legal status. This arrangement is common among Asian business groups, including Japanese *keiretsu*. The state actively encouraged the groups to form, but the business groups did not report financial information to the state for taxation purposes, and the groups did not have the legal rights and responsibilities of other firms (Keister 2000, p. 70–2).

The structure of these Chinese business groups involves a core firm together with a number of specialized firms, plus several other firms in related lines of business. The core firm is called the "group company," which uses its own departments to manage the member firms to varying degrees. Relations among the member firms are close-knit and expansive, including cross-shareholdings, interlocking directorships, financing relations, trade relations, and joint production. As the ties among firms in the Chinese group strengthen, they become exclusionary, like in the Japanese *keiretsu*. Member firms in Japanese *keiretsu* tend to deal exclusively with each other. Similar to this practice, member firms in Chinese enterprise groups show a tendency to deal primarily or exclusively with suppliers in their group and to sell to other member firms first (Keister 2000, p. 69–71). In Japanese business groups, the emphasis on the norms of reciprocity and trusting relations has produced a level of mutual obligation between member firms. Enterprise groups in China are comparably characterized by reciprocity. Another characteristic of Chinese enterprise groups is the high degree of prestige associated with membership and the high degree of loyalty among their member firms (Keister 2000, p. 92, 115).

The enterprise groups encompass central industries in the Chinese economy. These include the automotive, steel, petroleum, power, transportation, and high-technology industries (Keister 2000, p. 71). Across all these sectors, the number of enterprise groups among the central government-controlled SOEs had grown from 57 in 1991 to 120 in 1997, and up to 147 in the middle of the first decade of 21st century (Chen 2005; OECD 2000, p. 55; Chiu and Lewis 2006, p. 67). Estimates of the proportion of state-owned firms that are members of enterprise groups are difficult to obtain. In 1995, the total assets of SOE groups were 1.12 trillion yuan (US $135.70 billion), one-quarter of the country's total state-owned assets (Kan 1996). Since then, the numbers of enterprise groups and their total assets have continued to grow, and most SOEs are now part of business groups (Yusuf et al. 2006, p. 91).

The Chinese government was actively involved in the establishment and development of SOE groups. Government authorities encouraged group formation, circulated guides for establishing groups in strategic industries, and actively coordinated the formation of these interfirm linkages (Keister 2000, p. 77). The state also played a role in deciding which firms would join which groups, as well as in demanding that a firm should either join or remain associated with a particular group, especially concerning firms in those strategic industries (Keister 2000, p. 92). At the beginning of its establishment, each group was required to be approved by and registered with the government bureau. Through the registration process, the state continued to play an active role in forming and maintaining enterprise groups. The state required the group to have a parent company or a leading firm, as well as a sound management system. This requirement again allowed officials to influence the structure of the group. In requiring the group to have a "sound" management system, the state could indirectly influence the way the group interacted with member firms (Keister 2000, p. 72–3). Additionally, government bureaus advised the groups on long-term and short-term plans, such as production policies, fixed investments, consumption funds, credit practices, and foreign exchange. (Keister 2000, p. 77). The Chinese government furthermore privileged enterprise groups by giving preferential treatment to them in terms of credit access and support for technical upgrading and listing priority (OECD 2000, p. 55).

2.2.4.2 The Ownership, Control, and Organizational Structure of Chinese SOE Groups

The core firms of SOE groups are owned completely or in part by the state, and they in turn own completely or in part the subordinated member firms. The core firm and its member firms are all independent firms, even though they are quite interwoven. Once a SOE enters a group, it is controlled by the core firm in the group. If a firm is listed as a state-owned firm, the state relinquishes its ownership and control rights over the company to the core firm in the group (Dong and Hu 1995; Li 1995). This change in status does not imply that the firm is no longer state owned, but rather that the core firm (a firm that is also state owned) now owns and controls the firm directly. The core firm is generally a large industrial or commercial enterprise that mostly transacts in the business or industry that is the group's primary industry. Because it has ownership ties with them, the core firm is able to influence the other member firms. The core firm's power of influence increases with the extent of its ownership interest. When the core firm's investment in its subsidiaries is great or when it controls the stock of the firms under it, the core firm normally plays a more significant role in the management of the member firms. The whole enterprise group is managed by the board of directors of the core firm that includes representatives from specialized firms, from the core firm's production division, and from other member firms. Workers also may have representatives on the board. The board oversees the management of firms. It plans the group's structure, policies, strategy, and direction. It chooses general managers for the firms, oversees the activities of the managers, and makes financial decisions (Keister 2000, p. 84–93).

For further clarification, Fig. 2.2 depicts the organizational structure of Chinese SOE groups. When a firm enters an enterprise group, its ownership is partially transferred to the core firm in the group; therefore, the owners or stockholders of the core firm are the ultimate authority in the Chinese enterprise groups. However, the term "partial ownership" is used here to describe ownership relations that are similar to the cross-shareholding ownership relations in Japanese *keiretsu*. As the figure illustrates, the core firm's board of directors of Chinese enterprise groups is accountable to the shareholders and oversees the activities of the president of the core firm. The management council or enterprise office of the group is directly subordinate to the president. It forms the management office for the core firm and comprises the vice presidents and general managers of the firms. The enterprise office has some authority over other subsidiaries and is consequently positioned higher than the subsidiaries.

The finance company, the other specialized firms, the other member firms, and the core firm's production units are all directly subordinate to the management council. The finance division or finance company is responsible for the financial activities of the other member firms. Other special divisions or specialized firms are responsible for activities such as the administration of the group, import and export activities, marketing, and research and development. The core firm's production division produces industrial output but does not have its own administrative offices (such

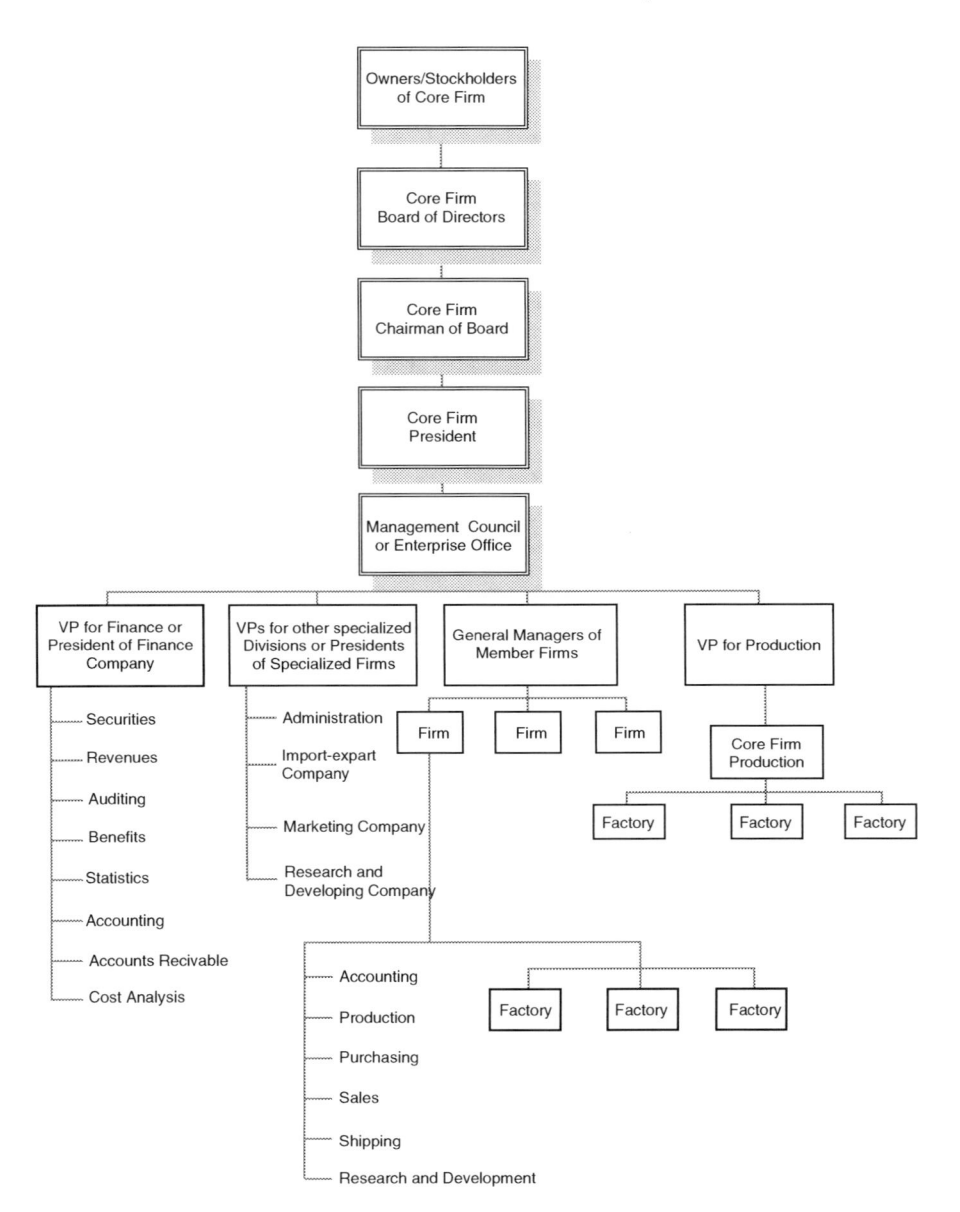

Fig. 2.2 The organizational structure of the Chinese state-owned enterprise group (from Keister 2000, p. 89)

as those for accounting and sales). The enterprise group's administrative offices or specialized firms perform these tasks for the core firm's production unit and for other member firms. In contrast to the core firm, member firms have their own factories, as well as administrative offices, which are responsible for accounting,

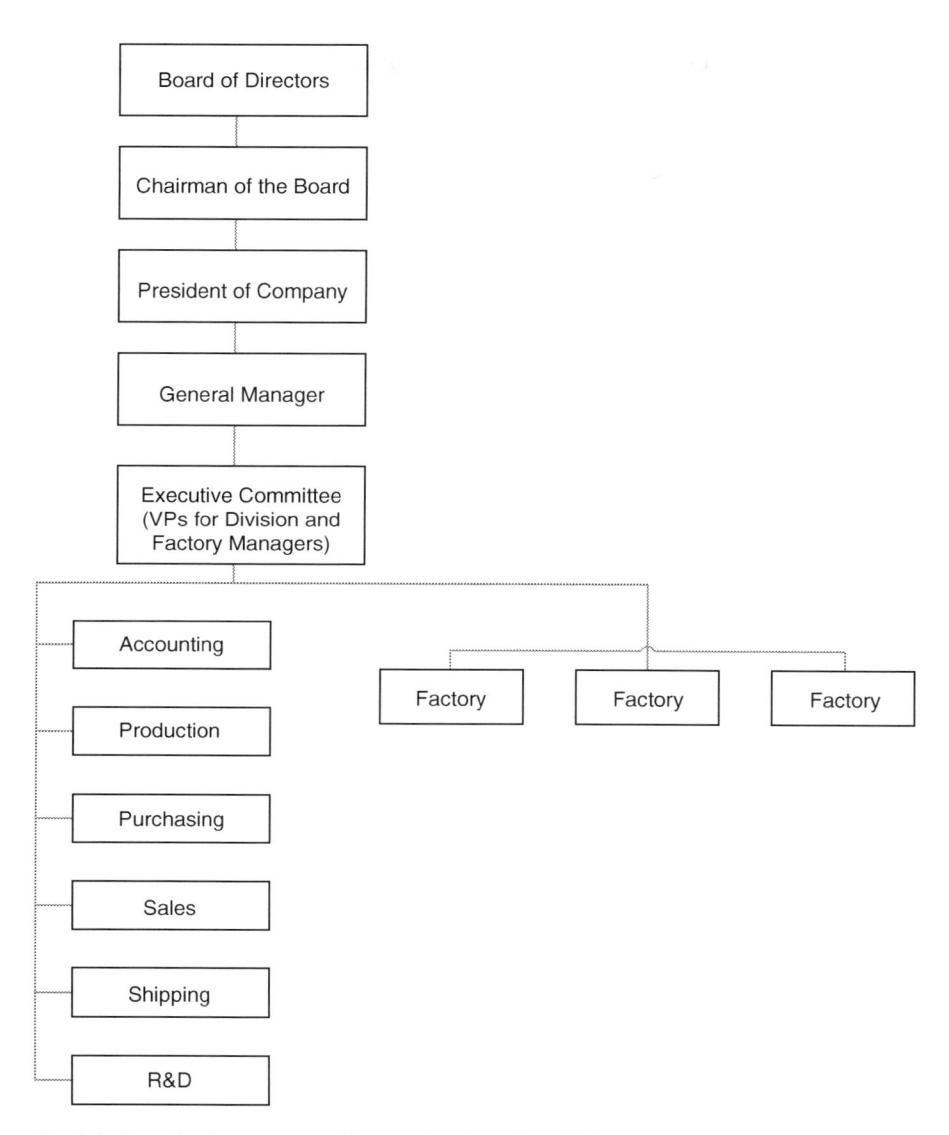

Fig. 2.3 Organization structure of the member firm (from Keister 2000, p. 91)

purchasing, sales, and other administrative activities. Figure 2.3 depicts the general organization of the member firms. The member firm is headed by a board of directors, which oversees the chairman of the board. The president and the general manager of the firm report to the chairman and oversee the firm's executive committee, which comprises the vice presidents for administrative divisions and the managers of the production divisions. The administrative offices coordinate accounting, sales, research and development, and other administrative activities only for the individual member firm, but no tasks that are conducted by the group's administrative offices (Keister 2000, p. 88–91). When an enterprise group lacks a particular specialized firm, the appropriate division of the core firm fulfills the function for the member firms. If a group lacks, for example, a marketing company, the marketing division of the core firm will assist the member firms in marketing matters (Li 1995; Shanghai Association for the Study of Business Groups 1995).

2.2.4.3   Key Players in Chinese SOE Groups

The Core Firm

The core firm manages not only its own divisions but also, to a certain degree, the specialized firms, such as the finance company and other member firms. In many cases, the former administrative bureau has become the core firm. It is also still controlled by the state, especially in the strategic and central industries. The core firm has multiple investors, including the state, legal persons, and individuals. It has the managerial latitude to coordinate other member firms and to expand the group into various industries (Keister 2000, p. 93).

The Finance Company

The Japanese *keiretsu* model has provided a great deal of motivation for Chinese reformers, especially in the financing pattern within a business group. It is common for a bank to be at the center of a Japanese business group *keiretsu*. The Tokyo Stock Exchange is not truly an option for corporate finance. Rather, government-related banks supply funds to the *keiretsu*, and firms find it more efficient to obtain capital from the banks affiliated with the groups. In Japan, firms normally develop a close relationship with a bank, on which they rely for the major part of their financing (Gerlach 1992; Miyashita and Russell 1994; Keister 2000, p. 96–7).

After 1990, the finance companies spread rapidly throughout all industries in China. By the mid-1990s, all of the largest enterprise groups had finance companies (Keister 2000, p. 98). State reformers promoted the formation of finance companies to aid firms in raising funds for growth and expansion and to remove some of the burden from underfunded state-owned banks (Li 1995). Firms that were member firms of enterprise groups had access to an additional source of credit, the finance company. The finance company received deposits primarily from member firms, provided funds for the member firms in the group, aided the firms in making investment, and also acted as a bank to the member firms (Shi 1995; Keister 2000, p. 131). The finance company also enabled member firms to meet research and development needs that might have gone unmet without access to credit (Li 1995). The finance company as a means of "insider lending" permits firms to mitigate informational asymmetries, to reduce transaction costs, and to substitute for the existence of a formal financial system. It fulfills thereby the task of presenting opportunities for funds to be allocated more efficiently within a particular group and giving member firms a degree of control over their access to resources, which might otherwise not be available (Goto 1982; Lamoreaux 1986; Keister 2000, p. 131). Similar to the prospering of Japanese *keiretsu* in their early stages of development, firms (especially core firms) in Chinese enterprise groups with a finance company performed better financially, and were more productive, than firms in an enterprise group without a finance company (Keister 2000, p. 132). Moreover, the finance company itself performed well financially (Li 1995).

The Administrative Company

The administrative company fulfills purchasing, marketing, shipping, and engineering functions that are peripheral to production. It is also responsible for legal matters, human resources, asset management, customer relations, etc. In many cases, the member firms have their own administrative offices, but they normally can relinquish some responsibility to the administrative company in their group and take advantage of economies of scale. Above all, the member firms would not be able to perform these administrative functions but the administrative company can, because the administrative company is professional in this field and has sufficient resources and knowledge about the proper means of performing these tasks (Keister 2000, p. 99–101).

The Research and Development Company: The Access to Advanced Innovations

Chinese enterprise groups had just begun to develop research and development companies by the mid-1990s. The research and development company in an enterprise group centralizes the research and development function and makes available the benefits of technological advances to all members of the group. The research and development company aids member firms in gaining access to advanced technology and innovations. It therefore can improve the competitiveness and performance of the group's member firms (Keister 2000, p. 101, 132).

The finance company, the administrative company, and the research and development company are the most common specialized companies in Chinese SOE groups. The enterprise groups also occasionally have an insurance company, an import–export company, a marketing company, educational and training institutes, and other specialized firms, which play crucial roles in the functioning of the group. The purpose of establishing these specialized firms is to fulfill specific needs that most member firms have in common (Keister 2000, p. 95).

2.2.4.4 Interfirm Relations in Chinese SOE Groups

In addition to connections with the core firm and with the specialized firms discussed in the previous section, member firms are also connected to each other through various types of interfirm relations. Like Japanese *keiretsu*, in which member firms have interfirm relations through cross-shareholding, interlocking directorates, financing arrangements, and production arrangements, member firms in a Chinese SOE group are also interconnected in four basic ways: cross-shareholding, interlocking directorates, debt and financing relations, and production and management relations.

Cross-Shareholding

After the reforms, it became possible for the SOEs to acquire ownership of each other in China (Ni and Zhu 1994). As a consequence, cross-shareholding took place in Chinese SOE groups. When cross-shareholding exists in a group, each firm has a direct interest in the performance of the other. These ties breed mutualism among member firms, by which the member firms feel they have shared interests and are willing to work together. Thus, cross-shareholding results in more joint projects among member firms, increased investment in research and development, and also in more investment in other future projects that would otherwise be too risky (Keister 2000, p. 103).

Interlocking Directorates

That the same individual holds positions on the boards of directors of two or more firms generates interlocking directorate relations among the firms. In the Chinese case, those can be identified as the result of state or core firm appointments (Li 1995; Keister 2000, p. 104). When the state or the core firm assigns representatives to the boards of two member firms, it is often the case that the same individual is assigned to both boards.

Interlocking directorates facilitate information flow among firms and reduce information asymmetries (Haunschild 1993, 1994). Thereby, they also reduce the transaction costs. Given the high level of uncertainty in the Chinese economy, membership in an enterprise group with interlocks indicates increased access to inputs, financing, and the market. Interlocking directorates play an important role in Chinese enterprise groups, and all firms in enterprise groups with interlocking directorates benefit from the director interlocks and perform better financially than firms in enterprise groups without interlocks (Keister 2000, p. 130).

Financing Relations

Member firms in Chinese enterprise groups are moreover related to each other through financing relations. Within an enterprise group, it is common for the core firm to finance the member firms through its finance division or through the group's finance company as discussed in the preceding section. It is also common for member firms to grant loans to each other. This kind of interfirm financing creates another form of tie among firms within an enterprise group, that is, ties through financing relations.

Production and Management Relations

Member firms in Chinese enterprise groups are also connected to each other through production and management relations. Member firms usually develop long-term trading relations with each other, make joint planning and strategy decisions, and jointly complete special projects that they would not be able to complete alone. Member firms, in addition, have administrative linkages through a specialized firm, namely, through the administrative company, which serves all group members (Keister 2000, p. 105–6).

2.2.5 The Financing Pattern of State-Controlled Enterprises Independent of Short-Term Profitability

Except for the financing from the state enterprise groups' financing companies, as mentioned in the preceding part, state enterprises heavily rely on financing from China's banking system. State enterprises also have preferential access to China's stock markets, while majority state shares are not allowed to be freely traded. Therefore, state enterprises are exempted from fluctuations of the stock markets. A "control oriented" instead of an "arm's length" banking system and nonexposure to fluctuations of the stock market depict how state enterprises in China have access to financial capital independent of short-term profitability.

2.2.5.1 The Insider and Bank-Based Financial System in the Chinese State Sector

A distinction is often made between two models of financial systems as to whether they are stock market based or bank based. This is measured according to whether banks or financial markets (i.e., organized markets for securities such as bonds, stocks, futures, and options) play the major role in the allocation of resources and in corporate governance (Allen and Gale 2000; Mayer 1994, p. 189; Whitley 1999).

The first model is labeled the "outsider and stock market-based approach" and is pervasive in the USA and the UK. Firm ownership is diffuse, and individual shareholders are outsiders in the sense that they only have arm's length input into the firm's decision-making through a board of directors. Corporate governance is performed primarily through a market for corporate control. The stock market plays a central role in corporate governance via the takeover mechanism. Banks play a minor role in this model, which is labeled as an arm's length banking system. The second model is labeled the "insider and bank-based model" and is pervasive in Germany and Japan. Here, firm ownership is concentrated in the hands of a few key shareholders that rarely trade their shares. Corporate governance is performed from within the firm by these insiders rather than through a market for corporate control. Banks, rather than stock markets, feature predominantly in the insider and bank-based model. They are important suppliers of external finance and holders of firm equity and hold seats on the firms' supervisory boards. They play a control-oriented role in the corporate governance (Corbett 1994, p. 316; Laurenceson and Chai 2003, p. 88–9).

China's financial system in the state sector remains heavily bank dominated, because the banks and not the stock market provide the main source for business finance. Banks play an effective role in the corporate governance of the state enterprises. Moreover, the ownership of SOEs is concentrated in the hands of a few key shareholders (the state or other SOEs) that rarely trade their shares. Corporate governance is then performed from within the firm by insiders rather than through a market for corporate control. Owing to the abovementioned characteristics, the financial system in the Chinese state sector has more in common with the financial systems of Japan and Germany, than with those in the USA and the UK, where the stock markets and markets for corporate control play the central role (Laurenceson and Chai 2003, p. 88; Chiu and Lewis 2006, p. 207).

Most enterprise financing in China is "indirect" rather than "direct" and hence takes place indirectly through the financial institutions, instead of through raising funds directly from financial markets. Nowadays, the stock market and the bond market provide alternative sources of financing for enterprises in China. However, the stock market and the bond market are small sources of finance relative to bank intermediation (Chiu and Lewis 2006, p. 209). Table 2.5 shows the growth of financing by bank loans, bonds, and equities over the years from 1995 to 2004. Despite what the People's Bank of China (2003) described as a significant buildup of funding in the stock market in 2003, equity issues in reality represented only 3.9% of finance raised by enterprises. The issues of corporate bonds accounted for only 1% of fund raising. Both equity issues and bond issues have declined in relative importance since 1998, when they together constituted 16% of total financing (Chiu and Lewis 2006, p. 206). Until the first decade of 21st century, the financial system was still bank based. Most capital is raised in the form of bank loans (83% in 2004), and only little finance is raised through the equity issue market or the corporate bond market (together about 6% in 2004) (Chiu and Lewis 2006, p. 212).

Table 2.5 New finance raised in Chinese financial markets, 1995–2004

	1995	1998	2001	2002	2003	2004
Total (billion yuan)	1152.0	1395.0	1655.5	2397.6	3515.4	2902.3
(Percentage of total)[a]	(100.0)	(100.0)	(100.0)	(100.0)	(100.0)	(100.0)
Bank loans	1014.0	1152.0	1255.8	1922.8	2993.6	2406.6
(Percentage of total)	(88.0)	(82.6)	(75.9)	(80.2)	(85.1)	(82.9)
Government bonds	22.0	15.0	259.5	346.1	352.5	312.6
(Percentage of total)	(1.9)	(1.1)	(15.7)	(14.4)	(10.0)	(10.8)
Corporate bonds	15.0	84.0	14.7	32.5	33.6	32.7
(Percentage of total)	(1.3)	(6.0)	(0.9)	(1.4)	(1.0)	(1.1)
Stocks	101.0	144.0	125.2	96.2	135.7[b]	150.4[c]
(Percentage of total)	(8.8)	(10.3)	(7.6)	(4.0)	(3.9)	(5.2)

Source: Chiu and Lewis (2006), p. 206
[a]Owing to rounding errors, percentages may not add up to 100
[b]Includes convertible bonds of 18.1 billion yuan
[c]Includes convertible bonds of 20.9 billion yuan

2.2.5.2   China's Banking System Reform

First, China's state-owned banks have become commercial banks with modern corporate governance.

Since 1995, China's state-owned banks have been reformed and have become commercial banks. The objective of a commercial bank in a market economy is to maximize expected profits subject to risk constraint. Commercial banks should therefore allocate loans to those projects that offer the highest expected financial return. They should also diversify their loan portfolios and maintain a strong capital base to effectively manage risk. The performance of a commercial bank can largely be determined by measures of financial return such as profitability and measures of solvency such as capital adequacy (Laurenceson and Chai 2003, p. 46). In the Commercial Banking Law of the People's Republic of China, state commercial banks are required to assume greater responsibility for their own profits and losses and take into account the likelihood of repayment before extending loans. The General Lending Rules, an order of the People's Bank of China in 1995, explicitly states that profitability is to be used as a basic principle to guide lending. As state commercial banks, their operations should remain solvent (Laurenceson and Chai 2003, p. 50). Henceforth, state commercial banks should allocate credit to enterprises on the basis of sound commercial lending principles, rather than on the basis of government mandates (Chiu and Lewis 2006, p. 80).

Commercial banks in China have done a great deal to improve their own corporate governance without fundamentally changing their ownership structure. They have become more transparent by using international accounting standards and reputable external auditors. Banks improve board practices by setting up various committees, such as audit committees and risk management committees, and by appointing independent directors to chair some of these committees. Chinese commercial banks have also made significant progress in improving their corporate governance and financial performance through entering into technical assistance arrangements with reputable international financial institutions, and by attracting strategic investors, including foreign ones. As banks adopt modern corporate governance approaches, their credit decisions are more likely to become sound. A strong capital base will also allow banks to take a long-term approach to their strategic lending decisions (Tenev et al. 2002, p. 67).

Second, China's state-owned banks took significant reform measures in the mid-1990s.

In general, the banking reform program in the mid-1990s consisted of the following major components: the establishment of policy banks and the introduction of a new commercial banking law, which separated policy lending from commercial lending; the relaxation of the credit plan in favor of asset-liability management principles; transforming the People's Bank of China into a real central bank, separated from the Ministry of Finance and policy lending, and recentralizing the People's Bank of China to avoid local government interference; deregulating the banking sector and establishing new banks and various financial institutions that coexist with state commercial banks, which remain the main entities; and solving the problem of nonperforming loans (Laurenceson and Chai 2003, p. 48; Tenev et al. 2002, p. 18, Chiu and Lewis 2006, p. 213).

Since 1995, the four state-owned banks, that is, the Industrial and Commercial Bank of China, the Agriculture Bank of China, the Bank of China, and the Construction Bank of China, which account for approximately 75% of all loans in China, have become state commercial banks (Holz and Zhu 2002). A new Commercial Banking Law was approved in 1995 to regulate commercial banks (Garcia-Herrero et al. 2006). Also in that year, three new policy banks, that is, the China Development Bank, the Import–Export Bank of China, and the Agricultural Development Bank of China, were established to take on the policy loans of the commercial banks (OECD 2000, p. 87). They are designated as the main vehicles for policy-based lending in the future (Tenev et al. 2002, p. 18). After this reform step, policy-related finance is largely separated from commercial lending (Chiu and Lewis 2006, p. 213).

In 1998, the government took a major step in the reform of credit allocation by phasing out the credit quota system that was applied to the four state-owned banks and replacing it with asset-liability management (Tenev et al. 2002, p. 18). The government announced that commercial banks should act on a commercial basis (Chiu and Lewis 2006, p. 207).

Further extensive reform steps have been under way to establish sound lending standards and improve prudential standards. These steps include the use of internal credit rating standards based on enterprise credit history and financial conditions, and the establishment of strict accountability of individual loan officers and their senior managers for containing nonperforming loans (OECD 2000, p. 87). Considerable effort has been made to upgrade accounting skills and standards for assessing credit worthiness and monitoring loan performance. Also remarkable is the development of a national "credit registry" system, similar to those used in Germany, Italy, and several other European countries, which is set up to provide information to potential lenders about the credit history and financial performance of loan applicants. Commercial banks have also been given greater flexibility to vary interest rates from official benchmark levels to better incorporate risk into loan pricing (OECD 2000, p. 88).

A further step was taken in 1999 to cleanse the state banks of nonperforming loans through a debt–share swap (Chiu and Lewis 2006, p. 80). To achieve this goal, four bank asset management companies (BAMCs) were established to take on the nonperforming loans of the four major commercial banks that were incurred before 1996 (OECD 2000, p. 88). Chinese banks had accumulated a huge number of nonperforming loans owing to the credit quota system. As mentioned above, the state set up four BAMCs, one for each state commercial bank, and supplied them with money through the Ministry of Finance, the People's Bank of China, and nontradable bonds. Then, BAMCs provided money to the firms, and the firms paid their loans back to the banks. BAMCs also provided nontradable bonds to the big four state commercial banks in exchange for nonperforming loans (Chiu and Lewis 2006, p. 77, 235). In total, the BAMCs were authorized to acquire 1.2 trillion yuan of nonperforming loans, amounting to nearly 18% of the total loans of the four state commercial banks (OECD 2000, p. 88). Subsequently, the firms' debts were turned into shares held by the BAMCs on behalf of the state. Banks appeared to be in a healthier condition after getting rid of the bad loans in exchange for debt claims issued by the BAMCs, while the SOEs were less highly geared (Chiu and Lewis 2006, p. 77, 235). The establishment of separate entities to deal with nonperforming loans allows more flexible means to work out the loans and is consistent with "best practices" that emerged from international experiences (OECD 2000, p. 88). The transfer of old bad loans to the BAMCs in 1999 and 2000 was to create a clean balance sheet from which the state commercial banks could start out anew with purely commercial lending (Holz and Zhu 2002).

The government also started to deregulate the banking sector and to lower the barriers to entry. This resulted in the establishment of new banks. Nonstate commercial banks and various financial institutions, even foreign banks, entered China's market (Tenev et al. 2002, p. 18). The old monobank system was replaced with a multitiered one (Garcia-Herrero et al. 2006), in which, however, state commercial banks remain the main entities (Chiu and Lewis 2006, p. 213).

The People's Bank of China still lies at the heart of the financial system, but its role has greatly changed. Its commercial banking activities have been transferred to the four state commercial banks, whereas policy lending is now undertaken by the three policy banks. Bank supervision responsibilities, which the People's Bank of China assumed with the growth of an array of shareholding, city and regional banks, along with other financial institutions, were removed and vested with the newly established China Banking Regulatory Commission in 2003. It is the China Banking Regulatory Commission that now oversees the reforms and regulation of the banking sector, allowing the People's Bank of China to focus on monetary policy. While the State Council is ultimately responsible for key monetary policy decisions, the 1995 act guaranteed the People's Bank of China a high degree of independence from other levels of government, including provincial governments and central government ministries. The People's Bank of China has used this independence to change from direct to indirect controls. In 1998, it ended its controls on loan limit ceiling. The People's Bank of China utilizes a combination of central bank loans, rediscounting, open market operations, interest rates, exchange rates, and lending policy to control the macroeconomy. The monetary policy targets are both stability of the exchange rate and GDP growth (Chiu and Lewis 2006, p. 202–3).

In 1998, the People's Bank of China underwent significant restructuring that was aimed at reducing provincial and local government intervention in credit allocation and monetary policy. The People's Bank of China replaced 31 provincial branches with nine regional branches. The old provincial branch system had been based on administrative jurisdictions, in which the provincial governments had a strong influence over the decisions made by the subordinate provincial branches. The move from a provincial branch system to a regional branch system was expected to minimize such influence and improve the central bank's independence (Tenev et al. 2002, p. 18).

Taken as a whole, the financial reform measures that were adopted represent important progress toward establishing sound commercial lending standards and financial discipline. There is widespread agreement that banking loan standards and credit quality have indeed improved significantly since 1996 in China (OECD 2000, p. 88).

2.2.5.3   China's Statist Banking System Concentrates Financing on State Enterprises

One of the distinctive features of the Chinese financial system is that all domestic financial institutions are either state owned or state controlled (OECD 2000, p. 80).

Table 2.6 sets out the various classes of financial institutions as of the end of 2003 and their shares of banking assets. The numbers illustrate that the financial system in China is fundamentally statist, with all levels of the banking system being state dominated. Starting at the top, the three policy banks and the four state commercial banks together have a 62% share of banking assets. The three policy banks are 100% owned by the state. The four large and nationwide state commercial banks were fully state owned until the strategic foreign investments in 2005 in the Bank of China, the Construction Bank of China, and the Industrial and Commercial Bank of China, and they remain majority state owned. The next tier consists of the smaller regional joint-stock commercial banks and of the main banks of the SOEs, which are owned either by the local government or by SOEs and issue nearly 20% of loans. There are then the credit cooperatives, postal savings banks, and nonbank financial institutions (financial companies, trust and investment companies, and leasing companies), which all have predominantly shareholding ties with the central state or the local government or are controlled by SOEs. Urban credit cooperatives in 1995 were compelled to forge shareholding links with municipal governments, which became the largest shareholders. City commercial banks were formed by amalgamating the urban cooperatives. Financial companies are amalgams of financial institutions and state enterprises, with equity raised from state enterprises in the group. They

Table 2.6   Chinese banking institutions, end of 2003

	Number of institutions	Assets (100 million yuan)	Percentage of total assets
Policy banks[a]	3	21,247.0	7.7
State-owned commercial banks[b]	4	151,940.6	55.0
Joint-stock commercial banks[c]	11	38,169.7	13.8
City commercial banks[d]	99	14,621.7	5.3
Rural commercial banks	NA	384.8	0.1
Urban credit cooperatives[e]	3240	1468.3	0.5
Rural credit cooperatives[e]	41,500	26,509.2	9.6
Nonbank financial institutions[f]	NA	9100.0	3.3
Postal savings institutions[g]	21,000	8984.4	3.3
Foreign-funded financial institutions	180	3969.0	1.4
	Total	276,394.5	100.0

NA not available

Source: Chiu and Lewis (2006), p. 205

[a]China Development Bank, Import–Export Bank of China, and Agricultural Development Bank of China

[b]Industrial and Commercial Bank of China, Agricultural Bank of China, Bank of China, Construction Bank of China

[c]Bank of Communications, CITIC Industrial Bank, China Everbright Bank, Huaxia Bank, Shenzhen Development Bank Corporation Ltd., Guangdong Development Bank Corporation Ltd., China Merchants Bank, Shanghai Pudong Development Bank Corporation Ltd., China Minsheng Banking Corporation Ltd., Industrial Bank Corporation Ltd., and Evergrowing Bank Corporation Ltd.

[d]Numbers as at end of 2001

[e]Numbers as at end of 1999

[f]Nonbanking financial institutions as a category include finance companies, trust and investment companies, and financial leasing companies

[g]Number of branches as at 1995. Assets refer to deposits collected and deposited with the People's Bank of China

are owned by the parent companies, which are again state enterprises. Trust and investment companies mobilize financial resources for investment projects. Among 386 trust and investment companies in 1995, 11 belong to central government departments, 170 belong to the specialized state banks, and 205 belong to local governments. Financial leasing companies finance the rental and leasing of equipment to enterprises, the capital of which is held by state-controlled shareholding companies. Postal savings institutions are operated by the Ministry of Post and Telecommunications. They collect deposits and transfer them to the People's Bank of China that pays interest on the funds. Only the 180 foreign banks can be said to be truly nonstate owned. They were restricted from taking local deposits until the end of 2003 and relied mainly on deposits from joint ventures or foreign firms operating in China. Their share of assets was only 1.4% in 2003 (Chiu and Lewis 2006, p. 204–12).

Another distinctive feature of China's statist banking system is the concentration of financing on state enterprises. State policy banks and state commercial banks have been committed to lending to the state sector, and their core business continued to be funding the state sector (Chiu and Lewis 2006, p. 204–7). Until 2000, about 80% of loans of state banks went to the state sector, and the share of state banks in total lending by all financial institutions was about 77% (see Table 2.7).

In the middle of the first decade of 21 century, State enterprises received three-quarters of state banks' short-term loans and about 60% of the state banks' medium-term to long-term loans for fixed assets (Chiu and Lewis 2006, p. 207–13). Still in recent years, the great bulk of bank lending has gone to the state sector.

2.2.5.4 State Commercial Banks Pursue Developmental Objectives by Lending Predominantly to the State Sector

Being under state ownership control, the state commercial bank is akin to a development bank. The objective of a development bank is to maximize the development impact of lending, subject to the necessary condition that its operations remain solvent (Bhatt 1982, p. 61; Laurenceson and Chai 2003, p. 49). The objectives that Chinese state commercial banks follow are outlined in two pieces of legislation: the 1986 Interim Banking Control Regulations of the People's Republic of China (IBCR), and the 1995 Commercial Banking Law of the People's Republic of China (CBL). IBCR states that the activities of all financial institutions "shall be aimed at the economic development, the stabilization of currency, and the promotion of beneficial social and economic results" (ACFB (Almanac of China's Finance and Banking) (Various years) n.d., English edition, p. 177; Laurenceson and Chai 2003, p. 49). The CBL specifies that profitability is not to be the sole criterion state commercial banks are to consider. It states, "A commercial bank shall conduct its loan business in accordance with the need for the development of the national economy and social progress, and under the guidance of the state industrial policy." Therefore, the objectives of state commercial banks are now a combination of development and commercial goals, or likewise a combination of developmental returns and financial returns on lending (Laurenceson and Chai 2003, p. 50).

State commercial banks attach greater importance to the development impact of their lending than to financial returns. Consequently, the particular criteria that state commercial banks use to evaluate potential borrowers have a direct relationship to the development objectives of the country. Thus, testing the development impact of state commercial bank lending is a necessary addition to evaluating the performance of state commercial banks (Laurenceson and Chai 2003, p. 50).

According to the findings of Laurenceson and Chai (2001, 2003, p. 53) and Liu and Li (2001), the investment funded through state commercial bank loans has been productive, and the development impact of state commercial bank lending has been great. One channel through which state commercial banks may have positively influenced economic development is by selecting relatively productive state

Table 2.7 State bank lending

	1978	1980	1985	1990	1995	1996	1997	1998	1999	2000
Total loans (billion yuan)	185.00	214.43	620.62	1516.66	3939.36	4743.47	5931.75	6844.21	7369.58	7639.375
Growth over previous year (%)	–	–	–	–	–	20.41	25.05	15.38	7.68	3.66
Total lending to state-owned enterprises (billion yuan)	168.46	215.60	528.79	1289.82	3307.66	4004.66	4907.67	5666.75	5989.05	6044.784
Growth over previous year (%)	–	–	–	–	–	21.07	22.05	15.47	5.69	9.31
Lending to state-owned enterprises for investment in fixed assets (billion yuan)	0.00	5.55	70.53	224.57	1002.56	1203.42	1472.46	1974.43	2279.17	2640.609
Growth over previous year (%)	–	–	–	–	–	20.03	22.36	34.09	15.43	15.86
Share of total lending (%)										
State-owned enterprises	91.06	89.30	80.90	85.04	83.96	84.42	82.74	82.80	81.27	79.13
Agriculture	6.25	7.29	6.71	6.84	4.88	4.99	5.16	5.17	4.95	3.54
Urban collective enterprises	2.69	3.23	5.00	5.38	2.71	2.53	–	–	–	–
Individual-owned industry and commerce	0.00	0.00	0.17	0.10	0.09	0.11	0.27	0.30	0.41	0.46
Foreign-funded enterprises	–	–	–	–	2.28	2.57	2.89	3.25	3.63	3.51
Others	0.00	0.17	2.91	2.63	6.08	5.37	8.93	8.48	9.74	13.36
Total loans by all financial institutions (billion yuan)	–	–	–	1768.07	5053.80	6115.28	7491.41	8652.41	9373.43	9937.107
Share of state banks in total lending (%)	–	–	–	85.78	77.95	77.57	79.18	79.10	78.62	76.88

State banks comprise the People's Bank of China (until 1983 it was a commercial bank as well as the central bank, since then it has been the central bank only), the four state commercial banks (Industrial and Commercial Bank of China [since 1985], Agricultural Bank of China [since 1980], Bank of China [since 1980], Construction Bank of China [since 1985]), Bank of Communications (since 1990), CITIC Industrial Bank (since 1990), and the three development banks (State Development Bank, China Import–Export Bank, and Agricultural Development Bank of China) since 1995

Lending to state-owned enterprises comprises lending to industrial production enterprises, material supply enterprises, commercial enterprises, construction enterprises, and lending for investment purposes. Beginning with the 1998 data, "investment in fixed assets loans" have been relabeled "medium-term and long-term loans," while all other loans, apart from a small category of "other loans," are now labeled "short-term loans"

Lending to agriculture since 1998 is the sum of lending to "agriculture" and (a newly published category) "township and village enterprises." Lending to agriculture is in part or perhaps even predominantly lending to state-owned agriculture

(continued)

All financial institutions comprise the People's Bank of China, the three development banks, the four state commercial banks, other commercial banks, urban commercial banks, urban credit cooperatives, rural credit cooperatives, post offices, financial trust and investment companies, finance companies, and financial leasing companies

From China Financial Statistics 1952–1996 (China Financial Statistics 1952–1996 1997), p. 12–4; China Financial Yearbook 1997, 1998, 1999, 2000, Beijing: The People's Bank of China n.d., p. 464, 471; China Financial Yearbook 1997, 1998, 1999, 2000, Beijing: The People's Bank of China n.d., p. 508–9; China Financial Yearbook 1997, 1998, 1999, 2000, Beijing: The People's Bank of China n.d., p. 384–5; China Financial Yearbook 1997, 1998, 1999, 2000, Beijing: The People's Bank of China n.d., p. 401–2; and Zhongguo jinrong (The Journal of Finance of China), no. 2 (2001), p. 47–8 enterprises for their lending programs and by promoting the productivity of state enterprises through their effective role in the corporate governance of the state enterprises. There have been improvements in areas such as accounting and disclosure standards that have made it easier for state commercial banks to identify productive state enterprises. Cull and Xu (2000) and Lee (1997) found a positive relationship between bank credit and firm productivity. Bank loans, as the chief source of external finance, have placed financial institutions in a strong position to exert corporate governance over state enterprises (Laurenceson and Chai 2003, p. 54).

The second channel through which state commercial banks may have positively impacted on economic development is by directing credits to certain state strategic industries, and thereby correcting market failure. During the financial liberalization in the early stage of reform, state commercial banks began to channel credit toward areas of the economy where short-term profitability was available. As a result, investment in several key industries with long-term development potential and strategic value fell significantly, and they became bottlenecks to development. To correct this short-sighted investment structure, the state tightened its grip on state commercial bank lending and directed the credits toward the state strategic industries (Laurenceson and Chai 2003, p. 55), based on state-controlled shareholding coordination.

The third channel through which state commercial banks may have promoted economic development in China is by lending predominantly to the state sector; inflationary pressures and the scope for moral hazard to occur in lending have been moderated. When the economic reform began to erode the traditional tax revenue base—the remitted profits of SOEs—the government was forced to borrow from the state banking system to meet current expenditures. This implies that there exists little room for noninflationary bank lending to the private sector. The fact that Chinese state commercial bank lending to private firms has been limited could partly explain the superior performance of China in the area of price stability, compared with other transitional economies (Laurenceson and Chai 2003, p. 55).

The final channel through which state commercial banks may have positively influenced economic development is their continued support of the state sector, through which many positive externalities have been conferred on the private sector. One example here is that state sector development has provided a stable environment, in which the private sector can flourish; state enterprises have also constructed an infrastructure and facilitated private sector economic activity (Laurenceson and Chai 2003, p. 56).

2.2.5.5 The Main Banks in China Participate in the Corporate Governance of State Enterprises

The main bank (*zhuban yinhang*) relationship, resembling that in Japan, has been promoted by the Chinese government since 1996 to transform state enterprises into efficient and modern corporations. The idea was to promote a key monitoring role for the main banks to participate in the corporate governance of state enterprises and to develop a stable bank-centered financial environment for these enterprises to make them more efficient modern corporations (Tam 2000; Chiu and Lewis 2006, p. 170).

According to China's Ninth 5-year plan, a main bank relationship should be established between a state bank and a state enterprise. This was supposed to provide the participating main bank with a more comprehensive ability to monitor the performance of the state enterprise. According to the *Interim Regulations for the Administration of the Main Bank*, the state enterprise should allow the main bank to monitor the firm's major business and financial activities and to further facilitate this process. The main bank could audit all dealings between the firm and other banking institutions. Moreover, it was enabled to implement any punitive credit measures on behalf of itself and other banks against the firm, if the firm was found to be evading its obligations as a debtor. However, when the state enterprise cannot meet its "reasonable" credit needs, the main bank should help by allocating loans as the lead lender. The participating enterprise has access to credit facilities of the main bank to meet most of its borrowing needs and also enjoys preferential treatment in obtaining financial services from the main bank, such as settlements and the provision of information and advice (Chiu and Lewis 2006, p. 170–1).

As mentioned above, the Chinese version of a main bank system resembles the main bank system in Japan (and the *Hausbank* system in Germany), which is labeled as a "control-oriented" banking system and described as "corporate governance by intervention." The Japanese–German model of the banking system is different from the Anglo-Saxon model of the banking system, which is labeled as an "arm's length" banking system, and is described as "corporate governance by objective" (Aoki and Kim 1995). Banks in arm's length banking systems neither need to interfere with the corporate management directly nor need to monitor enterprises too closely, because they are paid according to a formal contract and their loans are backed by collateral, or security, including the enterprises' physical assets.

The "arm's length" banking system does not fit into the institutional environment in China and faces two obstacles. The first obstacle persists because of ill-defined property rights, which makes it unlikely that a market for enterprises' physical assets will exist. The second obstacle is due to moral hazard, because enterprises may not provide full information on the risks involved, or which might make them unwilling to repay loans. Thus, reliance on collateral or security to ensure the repayment of loans is not possible. In these circumstances, the banks would provide finance only on the basis of certain strict conditions being met, including the exertion of control over the corporate management, particularly in the case of poor performance. The banking system in China is therefore likely to evolve into a control-oriented system, similar to the Japanese–German model.

In the "control-oriented" banking system, mutual trust might be enhanced. If an enterprise is assured of a long-term relationship with a bank, which is prepared to share some risk in the case of financial distress, the enterprise has an incentive to provide full information. Banks may agree to a long-term main bank relationship and may be willing to share some risk with enterprises if they are assured of participation in enterprise governance and of their right to make changes to the management (Chiu and Lewis 2006, p. 171–2).

2.2.5.6   Access of State Enterprises to Stock Market Financing: Majority State-Owned Shares Are Not Allowed to Be Freely Traded

China's financial system is fundamentally statist. This is not only so for the banking system but also holds for the stock market, since most securities firms are state controlled (Chiu and Lewis 2006, p. 212), and state enterprises typically enjoy preferred access to equity and bond market financing.

Treasury and fiscal bonds have been issued by the Ministry of Finance, capital construction bonds have been issued by the State Planning Commission, and enterprise bonds have been issued by various ministries. Many corporate bonds are also issued by the state banks or by the state enterprises. They are then placed directly with various state institutions, obviating the need for secondary market trading. Some of these bonds are a refinancing of loans from the state banks to the state enterprises. Nonstate firms have played a minor role in this market. This is also true for the stock market, which has served as a funding market for the state enterprises. "The Securities market is essentially a state securities market conceived and designed to support corporatized SOEs" (Huang 2003, p. 128; Chiu and Lewis 2006, p. 209). A strict quota system was implemented by the central government on the number of firms to be listed, and state enterprises have had priority to be listed (Chiu and Lewis 2006, p. 209). Private enterprises have been largely prohibited from either listing or assuming majority control of listed firms through market takeover (OECD 2000, p. 82). As of January 2005, there were 1,377 listed companies on the stock markets, very few of them being private firms (Huang 2003, p. 128; Chiu and Lewis 2006, p. 209). Thus, the stock market has been an insignificant source of financing for private enterprises (Laurenceson and Chai 2003, p. 91).

China's stock markets consist of the primary market, where firms make their initial offering, and the secondary market, where the stocks are traded. There are various types of shares in China, including state shares (owned by the state), legal person shares (owned by corporate or other institutional units with legal person status, and which are mainly state owned), individual shares (owned by individual Chinese citizens, known as A shares), and domestically listed foreign-held shares (available to foreigners, known as B shares). State-owned shares include shares directly owned by state agencies and shares owned by legal persons. The trading of directly state-owned shares on the secondary market is prohibited and the trading of legal person shares is mostly confined to other legal persons. Therefore, state-owned shares, which constitute nearly two-thirds of all shares, are effectively removed from active secondary trading (OECD 2000, p. 82). That makes state enterprises exempted from fluctuations of the stock markets and ensures their insider-dominated corporate governance.

In China most listed companies have been transformed from SOEs. The Chinese government insists that listed companies, which are transformed SOEs, must still be subsidiaries of a state-owned holding company, with the state-owned holding company retaining the founder's stock. Table 2.8 shows the equity structure of stocks listed on Chinese stock markets from 1992 to 2004. Outstanding features of the table are the extent of the founder's stock, the dominance of state ownership,

Table 2.8 Equity structure of stocks listed on China's stock markets, 1992–2004 (percentage of total shares)

Share type	1992	1997	2000	2003	2004
I. Shares not yet in circulation	69.25	65.44	64.28	64.46	63.54
1. Founder's stock	58.59	55.50	57.11	59.23	58.43
a. State share	41.38	31.52	38.90	47.39	46.83
b. Domestic legal person shares	13.14	22.64	16.94	10.88	10.61
c. Foreign legal person shares	4.07	1.34	1.22	0.95	0.99
2. Fund-raising legal person shares	9.42	6.72	5.65	4.82	4.82
3. Internal employee shares	1.23	2.04	0.64	0.17	0.13
4. Other (transferred allotment)	0.00	1.18	0.65	0.23	0.16
II. Shares in circulation	30.75	34.56	35.72	35.27	36.04
1. Domestically listed renminbi shares (A shares)	15.87	22.79	28.44	26.67	27.87
2. Domestically listed foreign capital shares (B shares)	14.88	6.04	4.00	2.72	2.75
3. Overseas-listed foreign capital shares (H shares)	0.00	5.74	3.28	5.87	5.42

From China Securities and Futures Statistical Yearbook 2000 and China Securities Regulatory Commission website, accessed in April 2004, 2005

and the relatively low proportion of shares that are traded publicly (Chiu and Lewis 2006, p. 209–10).

Because only a third of the share capital (about 35% of total shares) is traded, while majority state-owned shares are not allowed to be freely traded (Chiu and Lewis 2006, p. 209–11), state enterprises are exempted from fluctuations of the stock markets. In addition, as we analyzed in the preceding part, the type of corporate governance in the state-controlled shareholding companies in China is insider dominated, resulting from the role of the state as the largest block shareholder.

2.2.6 Good Performance and Successful Long-Term Innovation Strategies of State-Controlled Enterprises

2.2.6.1 The Performance of State-Controlled Enterprises Has Been Significantly Improved by the Reforms

The reform efforts in the state sectors have been fruitful. They have introduced a number of efficiency-enhancing elements into the state sectors. Establishing shareholder meetings and boards of directors and less involvement by the state leads to efficiency gains. The reformed SOEs are actively upgrading their production technologies and processes (Yusuf et al. 2006, p. 209).

The overall performance of the reformed SOEs has been significantly improved since 1998. Table 2.9 illustrates the main financial indicators of industrial SOEs and the relative important position of SOEs in the Chinese economy from 1999 to 2004.

Table 2.9 Number of state-owned enterprises (*SOEs*) in China's industrial sector and related financial data, 1999–2004

Year	Number of enterprises	Total assets (billion yuan)	Total profits (billion yuan)	SOEs as percentage of all enterprises	SOE assets as percentage of total assets	Average asset size of SOEs (million yuan)	SOE profits as percentage of total profits	Return on assets of SOEs (%)
1999	154,882	11,238	220	37	68	134	44	1.3
2000	158,749	12,398	426	34	67	155	56	2.9
2001	168,799	13,418	466	28	65	184	50	2.7
2002	178,876	14,479	562	24	62	210	47	2.9
2003	193,483	16,707	815	19	57	260	46	4.0
2004	212,648	18,984	913	15	53	317	49	4.5

Data for 2004 are until October 2004. From Garnaut et al. (2005b, p. 8)

From 1999 to 2004, the total profit increased from 220 billion yuan to 913 billion yuan. The return on assets increased from 1.3 to 4.5%.

According to the statistics from the Ministry of Finance, state enterprises in China achieved sales revenues of 13.7 trillion yuan in 2006, an increase of 19.5% over that in 2005. The profit achieved was 1.1 trillion yuan, an increase of 19.7%.[1] In 2007, the total profit of state enterprises reached a record of 1.62 trillion yuan, and their sales revenue grew to 18 trillion yuan.[2]

Owing to industrial restructuring, the total number of state enterprises decreased. However, because the state enterprise profit has continually and dramatically increased, the state-owned assets and the state-controlled assets have increased accordingly. During the period 1998–2003, state-owned assets continually increased, with an average annual rate of 8%.[3] In 2006, state-owned assets amounted to 29 trillion yuan and had increased by 45.7% since 2003, with an average annual increase rate of 13.4%.[4] In 2007, state-owned assets increased by 23.1% over 2006.[5]

According to the *Fortune* 2004 listing of "The China 100," it was apparent that the ranking is dominated by transformed SOEs. For example, Petra China is 90% owned by China National Petroleum Corporation, which is 100% state owned. Other examples of state ownership of successful large enterprises are Sinopec (84%), China Mobile (75%), China Life (73%), CNOOC (71%), and Baoshan Iron and Steel (61%). Around 30–50 large state enterprises had been nurtured to become "national champions" and "globally competitive" multinationals before 2010 (*Fortune*, 6 September 2004; Chiu and Lewis 2006, p. 78).

The good performance of large-scale state enterprises has been crucial for China's growth (Nolan 1996, 2001; Nolan and Yeung 2001a, b; Nolan and Wang 1999; Nolan and Zhang 2002; Lo 1997, 1999b; Smyth 1997, 2000; Lo and Smith 2005, p. 12). The large-scale industrial state enterprises normally stay in upstream industries. They form the core of and retain their vital position in the economy. The rapid growth in upstream industries, through supplying producer goods and establishing substantial linkages, has fueled growth in downstream industries (Nolan 1996).

---

[1]Profit in state-owned enterprises exceeded RMBI.1 trillion for 2006, online: http://findarticles.com/p/articles/mi_hb048/is_200702/ai_n18815017. [30 11 2007].

[2]China's state-owned enterprises post 32% rise in profits (24.01.2008), online: http://english.people.com.cn/90001/90776/90884/6344066.html. [24.01.2008].

[3]*Guoyou jingji kongzhili buduan zengqiang* (17.11.2004), *in Shanghai zhengjuan bao* (newspaper), online: http://finance.sina.com.cn/roll/20041117/080141914t.shtml. [30.11.2007].

[4]SOE competitiveness has enhanced (16.10.2007), online: http://cn.chinagate.com.cn/enterprises/2007-10/16/content_9065723.htm [24.01.2008].

[5]SOEs realized profit of 1.62 trillion yuan in 2007 and made a new historical record (24.01.2008), online: http://cn.chinagate.com.cn/enterprises/2007-10/16/content_9065723.htm [24.01.2008].

2.2.6.2   The Relatively High Portion of State Ownership Has a Positive and Significant Impact on Firm Performance

The research on the performance of Chinese corporatized SOEs by Sun et al. (2002) found that neither too much nor too little state ownership is beneficial for a firm's efficiency and that state ownership (whether in the form of state shares or legal person shares) has a positive and significant impact on firm performance. The benefit of state ownership is generated as the state shows commitment to the firm by:

- Retaining a relatively high portion of the firm's equity,
- Coordinating and monitoring based on the state ownership, and
- Formulating enterprise-supporting policies.

It may be beneficial for a reformed SOE to maintain a certain degree of state ownership rather than to change completely from the state-owned to private status (Garnaut and Song 2004a, p. 166). Sun et al. (2002) do not differentiate between state shares and legal person shares and combine both in the category of state ownership. Figure 2.4 compares the three performance indicators ("profitability"— return to assets, "unit cost"—the percentage of the material and operational cost over the revenue, and "labor productivity"—the revenue contributed by a worker) of sample firms with different ownership patterns (wholly state-owned, state-controlled, and privately controlled firms), which were investigated by Garnaut et al. (2005a, p. 159). State-controlled firms appear to be the best performers in the sample, followed by privately controlled and wholly state-owned firms.

Especially the outside state ownership has a strong positive impact on the performance of the firm, and it helps a firm improve its profitability and labor productivity. Outside state ownership exists in legal person shareholding companies, in which the attribute of the fundamental property right of legal person stocks is state ownership. The holders of legal person stocks are more effective than the holders of state shares in the corporate internal governance. This is so because legal person stocks have more characteristics of personalization of "economic persons" compared with state-owned stocks, and the shareholder representatives of legal person stocks will be more able to assume the risk in partaking in making decisions than the representatives of the shareholder of state shares—government officials (Chen and Dong 2000; Shi 2000; Xu and Wang 2000; Chen and Huang 2001). The advantages of outside versus inside state ownership are also based on the power of outsiders to modify the implicit contracts within the firm that entrench managers and employees. Outsiders find it easier to introduce changes that affect managerial practices. An outside SOE may not be able to establish work discipline among its own employees, but it may have more leverage to do so with the employees in the new firm. Thus, outside state shareholding shows a positive and statistically significant association with profitability, labor productivity, and overall performance (Garnaut et al. 2005b, p. 168–174). A study with substantial evidence also indicates that in the competitive areas the performance of the legal person-controlled listed companies is higher than that of the state-controlled listed companies (Chen and

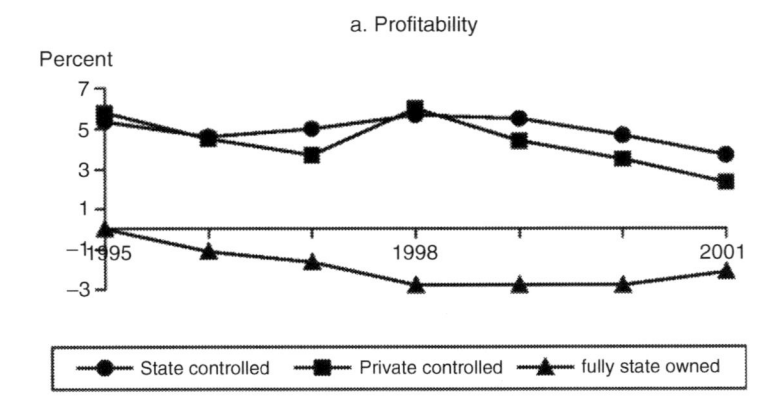

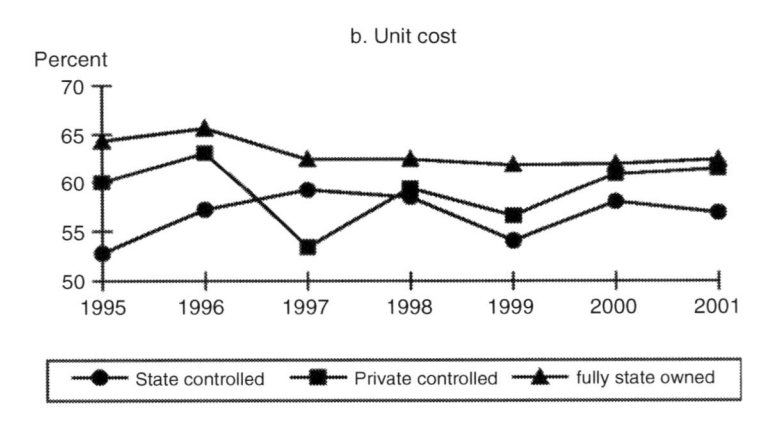

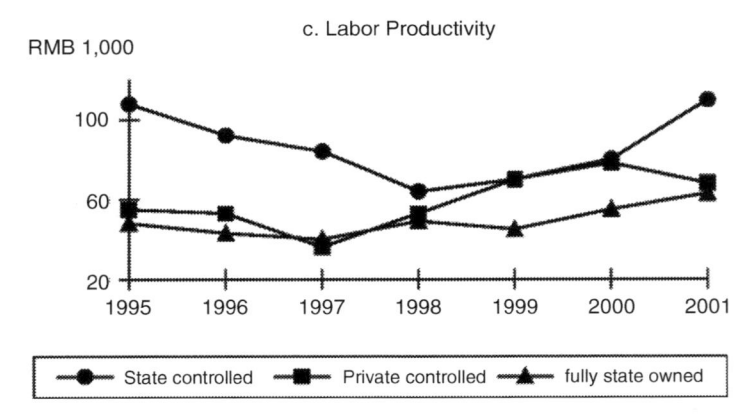

Fig. 2.4 Comparison of private- and state-controlled firms on three performance dimensions, 1995–2001 (from Garnaut et al. 2005b, p. 161)

Dong 2000; Shi 2000; Xu and Wang 2000; Chen and Huang 2001). The finding that outside state ownership has an important positive impact on the performance of a firm has important implications for our understanding of state ownership. With a relatively high degree of autonomy to participate in the market, China's SOEs can be effective agents of change and find it easier to put reforms into effect in other state enterprises. The state as the ultimate owner can also use agents effectively to monitor other agents, which contrasts with the conventional view that SOEs fail because public ownership provides an inadequate incentive structure within the firm. In the Chinese context, outside state ownership may bring more advantages to firms relative to outside private ownership (Garnaut et al. 2005b, p. 168–174).

2.2.6.3 The Objectives of State-Controlled Enterprises: Long-Term Profitability and Long-Term Strategies for Economic Development and Innovative Enhancement

Profitability is only one of the objectives of the reformed SOEs. The state has used state-controlled enterprises to attain a variety of goals, such as the promotion of economic development, technological transformation in key areas, establishment of a social security system, and employment (Yusuf et al. 2006, p. 90; Laurenceson and Chai 2003, p. 5). For pursuing the state's strategic goals, state-controlled enterprises have a higher capital intensity than private enterprises; thus, the profitability of state-controlled enterprises seems to be hurt twice by the higher ratio of equity to sales revenue. For a given amount of sales revenue, state-controlled enterprises incur higher financial charges (because they have more liabilities), as well as a larger volume of depreciation. Financial charges and depreciation are subtracted from the sales revenue, which lowers the residual profit. Alternatively, the ratio of profit to equity is lower because of the larger volume of equity, given a certain amount of profit (Holz 2002). State-controlled enterprises have essentially constituted China's social security system by providing benefits to workers such as pensions, subsidized housing, and medical care (Hu 1996, p. 126–9). The provision of such services will increase costs and so reduce the profitability of state-controlled enterprises. The state retains the ownership over strategic industries to minimize urban job losses from industrial restructuring. This means a conflict with short-term profit maximization from the shareholder's point of view (Yusuf et al. 2006, p. 235). Thus, the objectives of state-controlled enterprises are fundamentally different from those of private firms in China and from those of firms in a liberal market economy, which are solely attempting to maximize profits. Financial profitability alone can therefore not be the sole criterion for evaluating the performance of state-controlled enterprises (Gabriel 2006, p. 112; Laurenceson and Chai 2003, p. 5–44; Chiu and Lewis 2006, p. 125). Long-term growth and long-term strategies for pursuing economic development and innovative enhancement but not short-term profit maximization are the objectives of state-controlled enterprises.

2.2.6.4 The State-Controlled Shareholding-Coordinated Firms' Governance Structure of State-Controlled Enterprises Pursues Long-Term State Strategic Goals

A state-controlled shareholding company in China is usually headed by a holding company. The holding company is again usually controlled and majority owned by a state asset management committee. State holding companies tend to be heavily influenced by their upper-level state asset management committees, which are the representatives of the state, and act as investors of state assets. The holding companies and the asset management committees become the channel for the government. Thus, the shareholding companies are majority owned by the holding companies directly and are indirectly controlled by the government. The ultimate controller might motivate state shareholding companies to pursue a long-term strategic goal different from short-term profit maximization, which is in line with the state's strategic goals (Watanabe 2002; OECD 2000, p. 70).

The effective control of limited liability companies and limited liability shareholding companies, which is based on state dominant ownership, involves selecting the top management and influencing the composition of the board of directors. This kind of state-controlled shareholding-coordinated governance structure supports long-term strategies rather than short-term profit maximization.

2.2.6.5 The Governance Structure of the Reformed SOEs Is Stakeholder Oriented: Focusing on Productive Efficiency and Incremental Innovation Rather Than on Allocative Efficiency and Short-Term Profit Maximization

The corporate governance of modern SOEs is a stakeholder accountability system, which has a rigid institutional arrangement appearing antithetical to the principles of the market, and hence is prone to cause allocative inefficiency. However, the corporate governance of reformed SOEs in particular, and the corporate governance system of stakeholder accountability in general, should rather be assessed against broader criteria of economic development, than just the allocative efficiency alone. There are a range of arguments that suggest that the corporate governance system of stakeholder accountability does have its distinctive advantages vis-à-vis shareholder accountability (Aoki 1986, 1990, 1995, 1996; Amsden 1991; Lo 1999a; Lo and Smith 2005, p. 22). The possible sacrifice of allocative efficiency under the long-term-oriented system could be compensated by gains in productive efficiency. In other words, the long-term commitment of major stakeholders of enterprises offers potential for collective learning, intensive horizontal cooperation, and continuous incremental innovations, which are important sources of productive efficiency and could not be materialized under a shareholder accountability system (Lo and Smith 2005, p. 22).

In the corporate governance of Chinese state-controlled enterprises, the management focuses on long-term growth and incremental innovation, which is similar to the orientation of the managements of Japanese firms. Nolan and Yeung (2001a, p. 463) found that the senior management "worked for growth within their industries, rather than for the short-term profit maximization." Most of the large Chinese state-controlled enterprises and enterprise groups plow back a large proportion of retained earnings to finance further expansion and modernization. For example, in the mid-1990s, 60% of retained earnings in Shougang was devoted to technological modernization and to improving production capabilities (Steinfeld 1998, p. 196; Lo and Smith 2005, p. 22). This is similar to the stakeholder accountability arrangements in the typical Japanese firm. In these Japanese firms, most of the capital is retained within the firm to finance further expansion; hence, the dividend-to-profit ratio is much lower than in liberal market economies.

Chinese state-controlled enterprises have used a high proportion of retained profits to import technologies, adapt them to local conditions, and promote incremental innovation. This has been well documented in a number of large Chinese state-controlled enterprises. For example, the giant Shougang made large purchases of equipment from Europe and the USA and then updated and adapted it to local conditions (Nolan and Yeung 2001a, p. 446–7; Steinfeld 1998, p. 201–2). This is also similar to what Japanese enterprises have done. After the Second World War, Japanese enterprises mainly imported technologies from the USA and Europe and made improvements through incremental innovation (Lo and Smith 2005, p. 23).

In terms of rigid institutions, which are a characteristic of the stakeholder arrangement, Chinese state-controlled enterprises are also similar to Japanese enterprises. The rigid institutions in Japan are reflected by the main bank system, that is, the close relationship between the main bank and the Japanese firm. Because the risk bearing and the control functions of the main bank are asymmetric and the Japanese firm benefits from some degree of soft budget constraint, the rigidities in the main bank system seem like an allocative inefficiency. However, there is an important offsetting feature of the Japanese firm, which is that the major stakeholders—like banks, shareholders, and workers—make a long-term commitment to the firm. This promotes productive efficiency through cushioning the firm from the full rigors of the financial and labor markets and through collective learning, intensive horizontal cooperation, and continuous incremental technical innovations. This is similar to the large SOEs in China, suggesting that a trade-off exists between allocative efficiency and productive efficiency. The rigidities characteristic of China's reformed SOEs, in terms of close government ties, low labor mobility, long-term relationships with their stakeholders, and the lack of exit options for failed firms, though detrimental to allocative efficiency, might have been conductive for the productive efficiency (Lo 1997, 1999b; Lo and Smith 2005, p. 23).

The preceding discussion can be generalized to suggest a trade-off between stakeholder accountability and shareholder accountability. The corporate governance system of shareholder accountability is based on the market mechanism. It centers on the notion of information. The relative efficiency attribute of this model is allocative efficiency or economies of scale. This model is reflected in the stylized Anglo-American firms. The corporate governance system of stakeholder accountability is founded on the coordinated institutional arrangements. It centers on the notion of knowledge, which is generated through collective learning. The relative efficiency attribute of this model is productive efficiency or economies of scope. This model is reflected in the stylized Japanese and German firms (Lo and Smith 2005, p. 21–25). The corporate governance of Chinese state-controlled enterprises is also a stakeholder-oriented corporate governance structure, in which the possible sacrifice of allocative efficiency, generated from rigid institutions under the long-term-oriented system, can be compensated by gains in productive efficiency, incremental innovations, and technological transformation.

2.2.7 The Corporate Governance and Innovation System of State-Controlled Enterprises Resemble the German–Japanese "Insider" Model

2.2.7.1 "Insider" Corporate Governance (German–Japanese Model) and "Outsider" Corporate Governance (American Model)

OECD (Organisation for Economic Co-operation and Development) (1995) suggested that existing systems of corporate governance can be classified into two opposing models: an outsider model and an insider model.

The outsider model is prevalent in the USA and other Anglo-Saxon countries. In the outsider model, shares are widely held and shareholders have little direct say. The shareholder's control is exercised through the market for corporate control. When the firm is poorly managed, investors react by selling shares, thereby depressing the stock price and exposing the firm to a hostile takeover. To prevent this from happening, the management lifts the performance and strives for short-term profit maximization. Such a mechanism in the outside model supposes an ample disclosure of information and a good information flow, as well as liquid stock markets, and widely held shares. The outsider model breaks down when shares are held by a few owners only.

The outsider model is actually a type of shareholder-oriented corporate governance. The representation on boards has remained restricted to the shareholders, the disclosure of accounting information to shareholders is mandatory, while the use of insider information in stock transactions is prohibited. Legislation prevents the formation of concentrated shareholdings and cross-shareholdings between large companies, which would reduce the efficacy of the stock market. In some countries, including the USA, banks are also prevented from holding large blocks of shares.

The relationships with workers are market based. Long-term job security is low, labor market competition is high, and group cohesiveness is being eroded. Worker participation arrangements are largely absent, and employees have few formal mechanisms to counter the management.

Concerning the contractual arrangements with suppliers, the outsider model is characterized by formal contracts, which can be enforced by law. These contracts tend to be on a short-term arm's length basis. The formal contracts also specify the items supplied and the responsibilities of the contracting parties in detail (Chiu and Lewis 2006, p. 141–2).

The alternative "insider" model is prevalent in Japan, Germany, and other Germanic countries (Austria, Switzerland, the Netherlands). It is actually a stakeholder-oriented corporate governance model that recognizes more diverse groups of "stakeholders" than simply shareholders. These include workers, banks, nonfinancial companies with close ties to the company, and the government. Insider systems are also characterized by a concentrated shareholding and by a cross-shareholding among companies. The external corporate control in the insider model is weak (Chiu and Lewis 2006, p. 142). The insider model has evolved differently in Germany and Japan, and this will be illustrated in the following.

The German Model

In the enterprises of the Germanic countries, the two-tiered board system separates the executive and supervisory responsibilities. All directors, executives, as well as nonexecutives are appointed by the controlling shareholders. The executive board encompasses the top-level management team, while the supervisory board includes outside experts, such as bankers, executives from other corporations (e.g., interlocking directorships), and employee representatives. The supervisory boards are legally obliged to watch over the corporate enterprise as a whole, rather than only over the interests of the shareholders. Hence, the governance function in enterprises in the Germanic countries has a broader setting than in those of Anglo-Saxon countries.

Creditors, especially banks, play a prominent role in corporate governance in Germany. The German universal banks grant loans to firms and also own part of their equity. Financial companies and nonfinancial companies own large blocks of shares of firms.

The shareholdings are concentrated. Block shareholders monitor firms through representation on the supervisory boards (Vitols 2005). Cross-holdings among companies are fairly common. Cross-holdings of large blocks of equity provide a means to monitor actions by associated firms, and they are an effective instrument to reinforce long-term relationships between companies. The supervisory boards of German firms consist in part of members of the management board of other companies. This network is also effective in disseminating information and preventing opportunistic behavior.

Cross-holdings of shares, bank control of voting rights at general meetings, and legislation concerning the number of votes required to replace the management at general meetings made hostile takeovers unknown in Germany until very recently.

In Germany, contractual arrangements with suppliers (contractual governance) are characterized by relational contracts. Personal reputation plays an important role. This is different from the outsider model of contractual governance that is characterized by formal and complete contracts.

In the German model, the employees are treated as one group of stakeholders, and codetermination laws underpin the work governance. These laws require half of the supervisory board members to be employee representatives. According to those laws, the functions of the supervisory board are to control and to monitor the management, to appoint and dismiss members of the management board, to fix their salaries, to approve major decisions of the management board, and to appoint auditors (Gomme 2005). Thus, workers are guaranteed a significant voice in the process of corporate decision-making in Germany. The labor contracts are relational and long-term oriented. Long-term job security and institutions providing protection of employee rights support worker participation in the corporate governance (Chiu and Lewis 2006, p. 143–5).

The Japanese Model

Industrial structures in Japan are characterized by industrial groups, the *keiretsu*. Most large groups contain manufacturing firms and a number of banks and insurance companies, which provide the member firms with credit as well as with equity capital. These industrial groups are centered around a leading bank, forming the main bank system. The bank executives are appointed to managerial positions and to boards of other member firms. Banks are the primary suppliers of external funding for firms. Although a firm can obtain loans from a number of banks, the main bank is normally the largest lender. The banks own significant portions of the equity of the firms to which they lend, and they play an important role in their corporate governance. The commitments between bank and member firms or between member firms in the *keiretsu* are for the long term.

Another feature of *keiretsu* is cross-shareholdings among member firms with close trading ties. The cross-shareholdings are also accompanied by interlocking directorships. Because of these mutual relationships and commitments, the consensus decision-making structure is a distinctive feature of the *keiretsu*.

The contractual governance in Japanese *keiretsu* is highly informal, implicit, and long-term oriented. Compared with the Anglo-Saxon contractual arrangements that are based on formal contracts, and with the German ones that are based on relational contacts, the Japanese type is based on strong internal relationships and trust between group members.

The implicit, informal contracting extends to the work governance in Japanese *keiretsu*. Work governance is built on consensus management (decisions are made at the top but are shared at all levels), lifetime employment, and large bonuses according to the performance of the firm (Chiu and Lewis 2006, p. 145–6).

2.2.7.2 The Modern Corporate Governance and Innovation System of State-Controlled Enterprises in China Resemble the "Insider" Corporate Governance (German–Japanese Model)

The German–Japanese model is in many ways the one that Chinese authorities would find the most congenial. The Chinese reformers have certainly considered the German–Japanese "insider" model of corporate governance (Chiu and Lewis 2006, p. 170–1). Thus, the inspiration for the Company Law in China came largely from the civil law tradition of continental Europe, Germany in particular, and from Japan (Jordan 1998; Lin 2000).

First, the Chinese state enterprise group system is similar to the Japanese *keiretsu* structure.

These similarities are in terms of the formation of enterprise groups and concerning the financing pattern within a group. The firms in Chinese SOE groups are interconnected through cross-shareholding, interlocking directorates, financing arrangements, and production and trade relations, like those in Japanese *keiretsu*.

The Chinese reformers were also motivated by the financing pattern within Japanese business groups, regarding the bank placed at their center. The Chinese state reformers promoted the formation of finance companies within all of the largest state enterprise groups to aid member firms in raising funds for growth and to remove some of the burden from the underfunded state-controlled banks.

Second, Chinese corporations resemble the Germanic ones as regards the supervisory board and employee representation.

As in enterprises in Germanic countries, the Chinese corporation has a two-tiered board structure, which consists of an executive board and a supervisory board. There are also similarities between Chinese corporations and the Germanic system in terms of the supervisory board structure. The Company Law in China has provisions that allow employee participation in the corporate governance of state-controlled enterprises through their representation on the supervisory board as in Germany. The mandatory employee representation on the supervisory board reflects both countries' stakeholder orientation in corporate governance.

Third, concentrated shareholding, cross-shareholding, and interlocking directorship in the Chinese state-controlled enterprises resemble the German–Japanese models.

Similar to the German–Japanese models, concentrated shareholding, cross-shareholding, and interlocking directorship are also features of the corporate governance of the Chinese state-controlled enterprises. This kind of corporate configuration generates mutual relationships, mutual commitments, and a consensus decision-making structure. It also makes hostile takeovers among enterprises unlikely to happen in these countries.

Fourth, work governance in the corporate governance of Chinese state-controlled enterprises is similar to the German–Japanese models.

As in the German–Japanese models, worker participation is encouraged in corporate governance of the Chinese state-controlled enterprises and employees are treated as one group of stakeholders. The workers have a role in the corporate decision-making process, and such consensus management is supported by long-term labor contracts.

Fifth, "voice" instead of "exit" is the form of corporate control in the corporate model of Chinese state-controlled enterprises as in the German–Japanese models.

Albert Hirschman depicted the corporate control choice as "voice," i.e., directly influencing the management, or "exit," i.e., disposing of poorly performing shares. In the USA and the UK, small shareholders use exit, with takeovers as the ultimate disciplinary means over the management. In Germany and Japan, voice becomes the tool, with banks and other firms as stakeholders enforcing accountability via complex links (Chiu and Lewis 2006, p. 175). In China, exit of state-controlled enterprises is uncommon (Chiu and Lewis 2006, p. 176), because the existing ownership and control structure of Chinese listed companies makes hostile takeovers unlikely (Tenev et al. 2002, p. 115). The controlling shareholders as well as the stakeholders, such as the government, other firms, and employees, normally use voice to discipline the management and lift performance.

Sixth, the "control-oriented" banking system used in China is similar to the German–Japanese models.

Aoki and Kim (1995) draw a distinction between two types of banking systems: the "arm's length" and the "control-oriented" ones. The "control-oriented" banking system is similar to the German–Japanese model, and the "arm's length" banking system is the typical American model. The Chinese main bank system, resembling the Japanese main bank system, is also a "control-oriented" banking system. The main banks play an important role in the corporate governance of Chinese state enterprises.

Seventh, the contractual governance in the Chinese state enterprise group is similar to the Japanese *keiretsu* model.

In terms of contractual governance, the Chinese model is built on the strong internal relationships and trust between the member firms in an enterprise group, and the commitment and arrangement are long-term oriented, as in the Japanese *keiretsu* model.

Finally, the "stakeholder"-oriented corporate governance and the related incremental innovation system in the Chinese state enterprises resemble the German–Japanese model.

The corporate governance of Chinese state-controlled enterprises aims for stakeholder accountability arrangements, productive efficiency, incremental innovation, long-term profitability, and long-term economic development, all of which resemble features of the German–Japanese model. It is quite different from the American model, which focuses on shareholder accountability arrangements, short-term profit maximization, allocative efficiency, and radical innovation.

The governance structure and innovation system of the Chinese state-controlled enterprises tend to be characterized by a complex web of compromises and balances among the main stakeholders, each having a long-term commitment to the enterprise. The state, as the most important stakeholder, focuses on the enterprises' long-term strategies, related to the economic development and technological transformation. The banks as important stakeholders, being the main source of external financing for industrial enterprises, continue to provide credit to the enterprises, even during the period of secular decline in industrial profitability. The workers as a group of stakeholders have a strong collective voice in influencing the decisions of the enterprises over surplus distribution as well as in their bargaining positions (Lo and Smith 2005, p. 21).

2.2.8 The Different Types of Coordination Between Chinese State-Controlled Enterprises and the Firms in Coordinated Market Economies

The coordinated firm's governance structure of Chinese state-controlled enterprises is in general similar to the coordinated firm's governance structure in coordinated market economies. What differentiates China's model from the model of coordinated market economies are (1) the identity of the controlling shareholders and (2) the primary coordinating mechanism.

The ownership structure of Chinese corporatized SOEs is concentrated at levels similar to those of the firms in coordinated market economies, like those in most of Western Europe. But the controlling shareholders in Chinese state-controlled enterprises are the state or SOEs (Tenev et al. 2002, p. 82).

The main mechanisms with which the firms arrange their activities differ also between the different types of governance structures of firms. In the American model, the firms' governance primarily relies on the market mechanisms. We therefore name this kind of governance structure "market-based firm's governance structure." In the German–Japanese models, the firms' governance more heavily relies on coordinating mechanisms based on institutional nonmarket arrangements, such as association or network-based cross-shareholding, network monitoring, information sharing, collaboration between firms, and employer–employee interdependence. We therefore name this kind of governance structure "institutional coordinated firm's governance structure." In the model of the Chinese state-controlled enterprises, the primary coordinating mechanism on which corporate governance is based is "state coordination through state controlling shareholding." We therefore name it "state-controlled shareholding-coordinated firm's governance structure."

The state-controlled shareholding coordinating mechanism can only play a role within the state sector; thus, the state-controlled shareholding-coordinated firm's governance structure is confined to the state sector. The coordinating mechanism in coordinated market economies, which is based on nonstate institutional arrangements, plays the coordinating role for the whole economy. The institutional coordinated firm's governance structure therefore extends to the whole economy.

It is easier for economic transformation to happen if it is—like in China—led by the state, based on state-controlled shareholding coordination, than if it proceeds in extensive institutional coordination arrangements—like in Germany, Japan, and other countries with coordinated market economies.

2.3   Innovation Highlight and Chapter Conclusion

It can therefore be concluded that the transition of China's economy toward a market economy that is coordinated by state-controlled shareholding is actually part of a strategy to build up the state strategic innovation system and to achieve technological modernization. Chinese state sector continuously undergoes processes of developing the advanced technologies.

Even though Chinese state strategic development model and its related innovation system in the state sector work quite similar to the coordination-based European model, but the coordination type in the Chinese state sector is different from European model. It is the state coordination based on its controlling shareholding, while in Germany and many other European countries it is institutional coordination. State coordination-based Chinese state strategic innovation appears more powerful than institutional coordination-based European Innovation.

The strategy of making technological transformation the top priority of the economy has been implemented quite successfully. In this chapter, we just show the great success that led by the Chinese state sector. Chinese state-controlled enterprises are able to produce and are currently producing a wide range of products with quite sophisticated components for domestic and foreign markets (Gabriel 2006, p. 153–5). The success is manifest in the production of spacecraft and the performance of a spacewalk, the launching of Chinese-made rockets carrying Chinese-made satellites, Three Gorges Dam, the Shanghai magnetic levitation train, high speed railway network covering the whole country, high speed train passing through tall mountains and deep valleys, express ways also across mountains and valleys, World's highest bridges, level 50 bridges, river-canal network, new airports, 4G and 5G intrastructures covering the most remote mountain areas with so far 1.204 billion users connected to 4G and 5G stations, 4G and 5G coverage exceeding 20% more than the rest of the world combined (Dongye 2019), as well as thousands of small-scale incremental innovations in new technologies. The above innovation projects are led by the state-controlled enterprises based on state-controlled shareholding coordinated firm's governance structure and the state strategic innovation system. State-controlled enterprises focus on long-term profitability, or they lose money for doing many of these, but they bring huge social benefits to the general people. This is called socialism with Chinese characteristics, which is the "backbone" of the state strategic innovation system. The West such as the USA and Europe could not achieve.

In the meantime, based on the state-controlled shareholding coordination China has the strong capability to control crises (e.g., the corona virus crisis) and also the strong stability to avoid global economic crises (e.g., the 2008 global financial crisis).

References

ACFB (Almanac of China's Finance and Banking) (Various years). (n.d.). English (EE) and Chinese (CE) editions, Beijing: People's China Publishing House.

Allen, F., & Gale, D. (2000). *Comparing financial systems*. Cambridge, MA: MIT Press.

Amsden, A. (1991). Diffusion of development: The late industrializing model and greater Asia. *American Economic Review, 81*(2), 282–286.

Aoki, M. (1986). Horizontal vs. vertical information structure of the firm. *American Economic Review, 76*, 971–983.

Aoki, M. (1990). Toward an economic model of the Japanese firm. *Journal of Economic Literature, 28*, 1–27.

Aoki, M. (1995). An evolving diversity of organizational mode and its implications for transitional economies. *Journal of the Japanese and International Economies, 9*, 330–353.

Aoki, M. (1996). Towards a comparative institutional analysis: Motivations and some tentative theorising. *Japanese Economic Review, 47*, 1–19.

Aoki, M., & Kim, H. K. (Eds.). (1995). *Corporate governance in transiton economies-insider control and the role of banks*. Washington, DC: World Bank.

Bhatt, V. (1982). On a development bank's selection criteria for industrial projects. In W. Diamond & V. Raghavan (Eds.), *Aspects of development bank management* (pp. 60–79). Baltimore: Johns Hopkins University Press.

Broadman, H. (2001). The business(es) of the Chinese state. *World Economy, 24*(7), 849–875.

Cadbury Committee Report. (1992). *The financial aspects of corporate governance*. London: Gee & Company.

Cao, Y., Qian, Y., & Weingast, B. R. (1999). From federalism, Chinese style to privatization, Chinese style. *Economics of Transition, 7*(1), 103–131.

Chen, J., & Huang, Q. (2001). Comparison of governance structure of Chinese enterprises with different types of ownership, *China & World Economy*, 6. Retrieved May 11, 2007, from http://www.iwep.org.cn

Chen, J. (2005). *Corporate governance in China*. London: Routledge Curzon.

Chen, X., & Dong, J. (2000). Movement of equity toward multi-factors, corporate performance and industrial competition. *Economic Research*, 8.

China Financial Statistics 1952–1996. (1997). Beijing: China Fiscal Economy Press.

China Financial Yearbook 1997, 1998, 1999, 2000, Beijing: The People's Bank of China.

China Statistical Yearbook, Beijing, State Statistical Bureau.

China Youth Daily. (2003, July). Shenzhen municipal government sets up compensation system for state-owned firms. *China Youth Daily*, 15.

Chiu, B., & Lewis, M. K. (2006). *Reforming China's state-owned enterprises and banks*. Cheltenham: Edward Elgar Press.

Clarke, D.C. (2003). *Corporate governance in China: An overview* (Working Paper). University of Washington School of Law.

Corbett, J. (1994). An overview of the Japanese financial system. In N. Dimsdale & M. Prevezer (Eds.), *Capital markets and corporate governance* (pp. 306–324). Oxford: Clarendon Press.

Cull, R., & Xu, C. (2000). Bureaucrats, state banks, and the efficiency of credit allocation: The experience of Chinese state-owned enterprises. *Journal of Comparative Economics, 28*(1), 1–31.

Dong, J., & Hu, J. (1995). Mergers and acquisitions in China. *Federal Reserve Bank of Atlanta Economic Review, 80*, 15–29.

Dong, X.-Y., & Putterman, L. (2002). China's state-owned enterprises in the first reform decade: An analysis of a declining monopsony. *Economics of Planning, 35*, 109–139.

Dongye, J. (2019). *China daily 05-21-2019*.

Economist, The. (2005, January 8). China's corporate champions. *The Economist* (pp. 57–59).

Estrin, S. (1998). State ownership, corporate governance and privatisation. In *Corporate governance, state-owned enterprises and privatisation*. Paris: OECD.

Financial Times. (2005, June 20). *Big names join China stock market reform*.

Gabriel, S. J. (2006). *Chinese capitalism and the modernist vision*. London: Routledge.

Garnaut, R., & Song, L. (Eds.). (2004a). *China's third economic transformation: The rise of the private economy*. London: RoutledgeCurzon.

Garnaut, R., Song, L., Tenev, S., & Yang, Y. (2005a). *China restructures: Letting the small go in China's state enterprises sector*. Washington, DC: World Bank and International Finance Corporation.

Garnaut, R., Song, L., Tenev, S., & Yang, Y. (2005b). *China's ownership transformation: Process, outcome, prospects*. Washington, DC: The International Finance Corporation and the World Bank.

Garnaut, R., Song, L., Yang, Y., & Wang, X. (2001). *Private enterprise in China*. Canberra, ACT; Beijing: Asia Pacific Press, The Australian National University; Peking University.

Gerlach, M. L. (1992). *Alliance capitalism: The social organization of Japanese business*. Berkeley: University of California Press.

Gomme, G. (2005). Corporate governance in Germany and the German corporate governance code. *Corporate Governance: An International Review, 13*(3), 362–367.

Goto, A. (1982). Business groups in a market economy. *European Economic Review, 19*, 53–70.

Green, S. (2003). *China's stock market: A guide to its progress, player, and prospects*. London: Profile Books.

Haunschild, P. R. (1993). Interorganizational imitation: The impact of interlocks on corporate acquisition activity. *Administrative Science Quarterly, 38*, 564–592.

Haunschild, P. R. (1994). How much is that company worth? Interorganizational relationships, uncertainty, and acquisition premiums. *Administrative Science Quarterly, 39*, 391–411.

Herrero, A. G., Gavila, S., & Santabarbara, D. (2006). China's banking reform: An assessment of its evolution and possible impact. *CESifo Economic Studies, 52*(2), 304–363.

Ho, S. S. M., & Hai-Gen, X. (2002). Corporate governance in the People's Republic of China. In L. C. Keong (Ed.), *Corporate governance: An Asia-Pacific critique* (pp. 269–302). Hong Kong: Sweet and Maxwell.

Holz, C. A. (2002). Long live China's state-owned enterprise: Deflating the myth of poor financial performance. *Journal of Asian Economics, 13*, 493–529.

Holz, A. C., & Zhu, T. (2002). Chapter 8. Assessment of the current state of China's economic reforms. *The Chinese Economy, 35*(3), 71–109.

HSBC (Hong Kong and Shanghai Banking Corporation). (2001). Beijing: China Strategy Research, China Economic Forum.

Hu, X. (1996). Reducing state owned enterprises social burdens and establishing a social insurance system. In H. Broadman (Ed.), *Policy options for reform in China's state owned enterprises* (pp. 125–148). Washington, DC: World Bank.

Huang, Y. (2003). *Selling China. Foreign direct investment during the reform era*. Cambridge: Cambridge University Press.

Jordan, C. (1998, August). *An international survey of companies law in the commonwealth, North American, Asian and Europe*. Mimeo.

Kan, R. (1996, April 29). Finance firms seek role. *China Daily* (p. 1). Beijing: People's Republic of China.

Keister, L. A. (2000). *Chinese business groups: The structure and impact of interfirm relations during economic development*. New York: Oxford University Press.

Lamoreaux, N. (1986). Banks, kinships, and economic development: The New England case. *Journal of Economic History, 46*, 647–667.

Laurenceson, J., & Chai, J. C. H. (2001). State banks and economic development in China. *Journal of International Development, 13*, 211–225.

Laurenceson, J., & Chai, J. C. H. (2003). *Financial reform and economic development in China*. Cheltenham: Edward Elgar Press.

Lee, Y. (1997). Bank loans, self financing, and grants in China's SOEs: Optimal policy under incomplete information. *Journal of Comparative Economics, 24*(2), 140–160.

Li, Z. (1995). *Modern Chinese business groups (Zhongguo Xiandai Qiye Jituan)*. Beijing: Zhongguo Shangye Ban.

Lin, C. (2000, January). *Corporate governance in China*. Paper presented at the OECD/DRC conference on Corporate Governance of State-Owned Enterprises in China, Beijing.

Lin, J. Y., Cai, F., & Li, Z. (1999). Fair competition and China's state-owned enterprises reform. *MOST: Economic Policy in Transitional Economies, 9*(1), 61–74.

Lin, S., & Wei, R. (2006). Determinants of the profitability of China's regional SOEs. *China Economic Review, 17*, 120–141.

Liu, G. S., & Sun, P. (2003). *Identifying ultimate controlling shareholders in Chinese public corporations: An empirical survey* (Asia Programme Working Paper No. 2). London: The Royal Institute of International Affairs.

Liu, G. (1997a, March). Some issues concerning medium and small enterprise reform. *Zhongguo Gongye Jingji (China Industrial Economy)*.

Liu, T., & Li, K. W. (2001). Impact of liberalization of financial resources in China's economic growth: Evidence from provinces. *Journal of Asian Economics, 12*, 245–262.

Lo, D. (1997). *Market and institutional regulation in Chinese industrialisation 1978–1994*. London: Macmillan.

Lo, D. (1999a). The East Asian phenomenon: The consensus, the dissent and the significance of the present crisis. *Capital & Class, 67*, 1–24.

Lo, D. (1999b). Reappraising the performance of China's state-owned industrial enterprises, 1980–1996. *Cambridge Journal of Economics, 23*(6), 693–718.

Lo, D., & Smith, R. (2005). Industrial restructuring and corporate governance in China's large-scale state-owned enterprises. In R. Smyth, O. K. Tam, M. Warner, & C. J. Zhu (Eds.), *China's business reforms: Institutional challenges in a globalized economy* (pp. 11–26). London: RoutledgeCurzon.

Mayer, C. (1994). Stock-markets, financial institutions, and corporate governance. In N. Dimsdale & M. Prevezer (Eds.), *Capital markets and corporate governance* (pp. 179–194). Oxford: Clarendon Press.

Meng, X. (2004). Private sector development and labor market reform. In R. Garnaut & L. Song (Eds.), *China's third economic transformation: The rise of the private economy*. London: RoutledgeCurzon.

Miyashita, K., & Russell, D. W. (1994). *Keiretsu: Inside the hidden Japanese conglomerates*. New York: McGraw-Hill.

Ni, J., & Zhu, Z. (1994). A study on the ownership transfer of the state-owned enterprises. *Economic Research, 10*, 42–47.

Nietsch, M. (2005). Corporate governance and company law reform: A German perspective. *Corporate Governance: An International Review, 13*(3), 368–376.

Nolan, P. (1996). Large firms and industrial reform in former planned economies: The Case of china. *Cambridge Journal of Economics, 20*(1), 1–29.

Nolan, P. (2001). *China and the global business revolution*. Basingstoke: Palgrave.

Nolan, P., & Wang, X. (1999). Beyond privatization: Institutional innovation and growth in China's large state-owned enterprises. *World Development, 27*(1), 169–200.

Nolan, P., & Yeung, G. (2001a). Big business with Chinese characteristics: Two paths to growth of the firm in China under reform. *Cambridge Journal of Economics, 25*, 443–465.

Nolan, P., & Yeung, G. (2001b). Large firms and catch-up in a transitional economy: The case of Shougang Group in China. *Economics of Planning, 34*, 159–178.

Nolan, P., & Zhang, J. (2002). The challenge of globalization for large Chinese firms. *World Development, 30*(12), 2089–2107.

OECD (Organisation for Economic Co-operation and Development). (1995). Financial markets and corporate governance. *Financial Market Trends, 62*, 13–35.

OECD. (2000). *Reform China's enterprises*. Paris: Author.

Pannier, D. (ed.) (1996). *Corporate governance of public enterprises in transitional economies*. World Bank Technical Paper No. 323.

People's Bank of China. (2003). *China Monetary Policy Report*. Beijing: Monetary Policy Analysis Group of the People's Bank of China.

People's Daily. (1995) (in Chinese), August 14.

Prowse, S. (1994, May). *Corporate governance in an international perspective: A survey of corporate governance mechanisms among large firms in the United States, the United Kingdom, Japan and Germany*. BIS economic papers no. 41.

Qian, Y. (1999, April 29). *The institutional foundations of China's market transition*. Paper presented at the Annual World Bank Conference on Development Economics, Washington, DC.

Shanghai Association for the Study of Business Groups. (1995). *The Shanghai business groups (Shanghai Qiye Jituan Fenghua Lu)*. Shanghai: Shanghai Kexue Jishu Chubanshe.

Shen, Z. (1999, November). *New development of enterprise groups in China*. Paper presented at the conference on The Emergence and the Structuring of Corporate Groups in P.R. of China: An International Perspective, The University of Hong Kong.

Shi, D. (2000). *Equity structure, corporate governance and efficiency performance, economic research*.

Shi, J. (1995). *Modern (Chinese) banking (Xiandai Yinhang)*. Beijing: Jingji Guanli Chubanshe.

Smyth, R. (1997). A (re)interpretation of recent developments in the reform of state-owned enterprises. *China Report, 33*(4), 507–525.

Smyth, R. (2000). Should China be promoting large-scale enterprises and enterprise groups? *World Development, 28*(4), 721–737.

Smyth, R., et al. (2005a). Institutional challenges for China's business reforms in a globalised economy. In R. Smyth, O. K. Tam, M. Warner, & C. J. Zhu (Eds.), *China's business reforms: Institutional challenges in a globalized economy* (pp. 1–10). London: RoutledgeCurzon.

Smyth, R., Tam, O. K., Warner, M., & Zhu, C. J. (Eds.). (2005b). *China's business reforms: Institutional challenges in a globalized economy*. London: RoutledgeCurzon.

Song, L. (2004). Emerging private enterprise in China: Transitional paths and implications. In R. Garnaut & L. Song (Eds.), *China's third economic transformation: The rise of the private economy* (pp. 29–47). London: RoutledgeCurson.

Standard & Poor's. (2004, December), Emerging stock markets review: Performance, valuations, and constituents, *Emerging Markets Database*.

Steinfeld, E. (1998). *Forging reform in China: The fate of state-owned industry*. Cambridge: Cambridge University Press.

Sun, Q., Tong, W., & Tong, J. (2002). How does government ownership affect firm performance? Evidence from China's privatization experience. *Journal of Business Finance and Accounting, 29*(1), 1–27.

Tam, O. K. (1999). *The development of corporate governance in China*. Cheltenham: Edward Elgar.

Tam, O. K. (2000). Models of corporate governance for Chinese companies. *Corporate Governance, 8*, 52–64.

Tenev, S., Zhang, C., & Brefort, L. (2002). *Corporate governance and enterprise reform in China: Building the institutions of modern markets*. Washington, DC: World Bank and the Institutional Finance Corporation.

Vitols, S. (2005). Changes in Germany's bank-based financial system: Implications for corporate governance. *Corporate Governance: An International Review, 13*(3), 386–396.

Watanabe, M. (2002). Holding company risk in China: A final step of state-owned enterprises reform and an emerging problem of corporate governance. *China Economic Review, 13*, 373–381.

Whitley, R. (1999). *Divergent capitalisms: The social structuring and change of business systems*. New York: Oxford University Press.

Xu, X.-n., & Wang, Y. (2000). Ownership structure & corporate governance in Chinese listed companies. In L.-n. Zuo (Ed.), *Corporate governance structure: Practice in China & experience in U.S.* Beijing: Publishing House of Renmin University of China.

Yao, Y. (2004). Privatizing the small SOEs. In R. Garnaut & L. Song (Eds.), *China's third economic transformation: The rise of the private economy* (pp. 91–101). London: RoutledgeCurzon.

Yusuf, S., Nabeshima, K., & Perkins, D. H. (2006). *Privatizing China's state-owned enterprises*. Washington, DC: Stanford University Press and the World Bank.

Zhao, S. (2005). Changing structure of Chinese enterprises and human resource managemnet practices in China. In R. Smyth, O. K. Tam, M. Warner, & C. J. Zhu (Eds.), *China's business reforms: Institutional challenges in a globalized economy* (pp. 106–123). London: RoutledgeCurzon.

Zhao, X. (1999). *Competition, public choice and institutional change*, CCER (Working Paper No. C1999025). Beijing University.

Zhongguo jinrong (The Journal of Finance of China), no. 2. (2001, February) (pp. 47–48) (in Chinese).

Zhou, F., & Shen, Y. (1997). 'Letting go small SOEs' is good for enhancing the quality of the state assets. In *Realistic choice: Preliminary summery of the practice of reforming small state-owned enterprise, China reform and development report*. Shanghai: Far East Publishing House.

Chapter 3
The Economic Model and Innovation System of Chinese Private Sector

Abstract The business model and innovation system in the Chinese private sector are defined. They operate in a similar way to the US leading liberal market economies (the advanced English speaking countries). The firms in both business systems have a market-based firm's governance structure and market-oriented innovation system. Such an innovation system supports IT industry, artificial intelligence, and other high technology development in the Chinese private sector. The success is manifest in the development of 5G, AI, ICT, e-commerce, Fintech, Internet of Things, smart logistics, smart city, and so on. The chapter focuses on how the business model and innovation system were built up during the period from the mid-1990s to the middle of the first decade of 21st century.

Keywords Innovation · Chinese innovation · Economic model · Chinese model · Business system · Corporate governance · Competitiveness · Family firm · Private firm · Personal network · Chinese catching-up · IT industry · AI · High technology development

3.1 The Development and the Sectoral Distribution of the Private Sector during the Period from the mid-1990s to the middle of the First Decade of 21st Century

3.1.1 Development of the Private Sector

The Chinese Communist Party's policies and formal legal institutions regarding private entrepreneurs have gone through stages of strict prohibition, accommodation, and encouragement. The private sector was suppressed in China during the period of central planning (1957–1978). It has reemerged since the era of reforms started in the late 1970s and it has grown quickly in the past few decades (Garnaut et al. 2001, p. xi).

C. LIAO, *The Governance Structures of Chinese Firms*, Innovation, Technology, and Knowledge Management, https://doi.org/10.1007/978-3-030-52218-6_3

A spontaneous boost in the development of China's private enterprise was triggered by a series of economic reforms at the end of 1978. In the agricultural reform, the introduction of the household responsibility system heightened the income of farmers and enhanced their productivity and created a labor surplus (Lin 1992; McMillan and Naughton 1996). The state's recognition of the legitimacy of private businesses strongly encouraged farmers to engage in small-scale and nonagricultural activities. Some households then specialized in nonagricultural activities and became "specialized households" (*zhuanyehu*). These were in fact private businesses. The private enterprise boom had begun in rural areas (Song 2004; IFC (International Finance Corporation) 2000, p. 9).

In the cities, the government faced the problem of youth unemployment after a large number of urban youths who had been sent to the countryside during the Cultural Revolution returned home. The urban unemployment pressure motivated the reform leaders to break the old taboo against private business. Self-employment was encouraged as a means to curb the problem. The returnees were allowed to employ themselves as small business owners (Song 2004).

As a result, sole industrial and commercial proprietorships (*geti gongshanghu* or *getihu*) flourished in the 1980s. The government was cautious about the development of *getihu*. They were seen as only supplementary to state enterprises and collective enterprises, and certain limits were set on their development (Song 2004).

Many individual or family-based *getihu* developed and expanded rapidly, some grew large and started to hire laborers. *Getihu* started to become private enterprises. In 1988, in response to the development of the *getihu*, the State Council issued the Tentative Stipulations on Private Enterprises to govern the registration and the management of private firms. The Tentative Stipulations on Private Enterprises defined a private firm as "a for-profit organization that is owned by individuals and employs more than eight people." Firms that hired fewer than eight workers could still be registered as *getihu*.

The changes in legislation to accommodate the development of private firms have encouraged the emergence of a new type of private enterprise: those transferred from the collectives and township and village enterprises (TVEs). This led to a rapid increase in the number of private enterprises (Song 2004).

In 1993, the 14th Party Congress called for the transformation of the Chinese economy to a market economy. The development of the private sector was enhanced by the decision of the 14th Party Congress to privatize small and medium-sized state-owned enterprises (SOEs) (Song 2004). The private sector has served as an appropriate model for these privatized small and medium-sized SOEs (Garnaut et al. 2001, p. 15). The emergence of private enterprises derived from SOEs has substantially increased the private component of the Chinese economy. By the end of 1990s, about 80% of small and medium-sized SOEs had been privatized (Song 2004; Garnaut et al. 2001, p. 20).

Recognizing the contribution private enterprise had made to the economy, the Communist Party's 15th National Congress in 1997 "elevated the role of the private sector to one of parity with the state sector." Private enterprises formally shook off their "supplementary" status and became an important component of China's

Table 3.1 Main indicators of the development of private industrial enterprises

Year	Number of enterprises (1000 units)	Gross industrial output (100 million yuan)	Annual average number of employed persons (10,000 persons)
1991	107.8	93.70	18.39
1992	139.6	116.00	23.18
1993	237.9	260.10	37.26
1994	432.2	551.70	64.83
1995	654.5	1005.30	95.60
1996	819.3	1592.30	117.11
1997	960.7	1983.70	134.93
1998	1066.7	2082.87	160.80
1999	1460.1	3244.56	229.06
2000	2212.8	5220.36	346.42
2001	3621.8	8760.89	541.52
2002	4917.6	12,950.86	732.90
2003	6760.7	20,980.23	1027.61
2004	11,935.7	35,141.25	1515.43
2005	12,382	47,778.20	1692.06

From *Yearbook of China's Industrial and Commerce Administrative Management*, 1992–1998; *China Statistical Yearbook*, 1992–1998, State Statistical Bureau, Beijing

economy. In 1999, the National People's Congress passed an amendment to the constitution to recognize the status of the private sector (Garnaut et al. 2001, p. 15; Peng 2004). The Constitutional Amendment of 1999 that ensured the status of the private sector as an important component of the Chinese market economy and furthermore guaranteed the legal protection of private property rights was an important step toward creating a protected private sphere in China (IFC (International Finance Corporation) 2000, p. 35). In 2001, President Jiang Zemin announced that the Chinese Communist Party should recruit private entrepreneurs because they represent advanced productive forces (Peng 2004). In 2004, private assets and capital were finally legalized and protected by the country's constitution (Wang 2004a; Ralston et al. 2006).

China's private sector has experienced dynamic growth—in the number of enterprises, output, and employment (see Table 3.1). The number of formally registered private firms increased from 139,000 in 1992 to 12.4 million in 2005, and formally registered private firms accounted for most of the growth in the private sector (Garnaut and Song 2004, p. 7). The industrial output of formally registered private enterprises grew rapidly over the first two decades of reform to reach 4.8 trillion yuan by 2005. In 1991, China's private sector employed 180,000 people; the number had increased to 16.9 million in 2005.

In 1998, the share of the private sector in the national output was 33% (Garnaut and Song 2004, p. 6). By the middle of the first decade of the 21st century, the private sector accounts for about 40% of the national industrial output (Chiu and Lewis 2006, p. 56).

In 1981, the formally registered private enterprises employed only about 2% of the nonagricultural labor force. By 1997, the private sector's share of industrial employment had risen to more than 18%.[1] By the mid of the first decade of the 21 century, one-third of the employees in urban areas are working for private enterprises (Zhao 2005).

The revival of the private sector from the late 1970s on has followed different routes. These have mainly included a spontaneous eruption of individually operated private firms in urban and rural areas, the emergence of private enterprises from collectives and TVEs, and the transformation of small and medium-sized SOEs into private enterprises (Song 2004). Following the changes in the laws, newly established privately owned enterprises have emerged, while many of the private enterprises were transformed collectives, TVEs, and SOEs. However, China emphasized de novo private firms instead of transforming the ownership of existing companies (IFC (International Finance Corporation) 2000, p. 14). Therefore, privatization in China was not achieved primarily by converting SOEs and collectives into privately owned enterprises. Rather, it was achieved by allowing new firms to choose the private ownership structure (Li et al. 2004).

3.1.2 The Sectoral Distribution of Private Sector and State Sector

The Chinese private sector emerged on the fringes of the state economy (IFC (International Finance Corporation) 2000, p. 14). As we analyzed at the beginning of Chap. 2, large state enterprises which are supervised by the central government dominate the state strategic industries and form the state sector, whereas small and medium-sized state enterprises which are supervised by the local government and which were found in competitive industries had been privatized. The state sector with the strategic industries, and the private sector with the competitive industries, therefore have formed a dual business system in China (Krug and Polos 2004; Cao et al. 1999).

The sectors in which state ownership is dominant are not open to private investment, and the legal restrictions keep private enterprises out of the industries that are dominated by state-controlled enterprises (Garnaut et al. 2001, p. xxi; IFC (International Finance Corporation) 2000, p. 30). The central government stipulates that 15 types of industries should exclude the entry of private firms (see Box 3.1). These industries can be divided into three main categories: (1) industries using very scarce resources; (2) industries that are vital to the national economy; and (3) industries whose products involve certain public hazards.

---

[1] *Yearbook of China's Industrial and Commerce Administrative Management,* 1992–1998; Statistical Yearbook of China, 1982–1998.

> **Box 3.1 Businesses with Restricted Entry for Private Firms**
> In the following list of 15 types of businesses, for those marked with an asterisk, the entry of private firms is excluded by the government in Beijing.
>
> 1. Production and selling of gold and silver products
> 2. Taxis*
> 3. Primary real estate market (in Beijing, private firms can engage in the primary real estate market by obtaining a license from the government)
> 4. Radio and audio products*
> 5. Safety products, rubber products
> 6. Pressure containers
> 7. Inflammable products*
> 8. Radio transmission equipment*
> 9. Anesthetic, psychiatric, and radiate medicines
> 10. Recycling production
> 11. Air guns and hunting rifles
> 12. Antiques designated by the government
> 13. Important raw materials
> 14. Copper, steel, iron, and platinum
> 15. Polyethylene products
>
> From IFC (International Finance Corporation) (2000, Box 4.1, p. 37)

There are other laws that also restrict the entry of private enterprises into certain industries. One list sets out extensive industry-related restrictions for the establishment of private enterprises in 30 industries plus 17 products that belong to other industries, including banking, railways, freeways, telecommunications, and wholesale networks for a large number of goods. Another list is said to "restrict" private capital in 20 industries, including automobile, manufacturing, and chemical fibers (IFC (International Finance Corporation) 2000, p. 37).

State enterprises concentrate in industries with high capital intensity, while private firms stay clear of those industries. In terms of net fixed assets relative to sales revenue, the higher the ratio of net fixed assets relative to sales revenue, the larger the market share of the state enterprises; the higher the ratio, the smaller the market share of the private firms. Thus, private firms appear to stay clear of those industries in which a large volume of fixed assets is required relative to sales revenue, while state enterprises dominate those industries. This can be interpreted by assuming that the market share of the state enterprises would have been eroded by new entrants if the fixed asset requirement were low. With no or very few new entrants in the mature state sector, state enterprises provide the bulk of industrial output in those fixed asset intensive industries where private firms do not wish to, are unable to, or are not allowed to tread (Holz 2002). Furthermore, state enterprises are large enterprises with relatively high capital intensity under the state-controlled shareholding-coordinated institutional arrangement. Many of these enterprises have large positive externalities through research and development, learning by doing, and their impact on the development of a local infrastructure. Private entrepreneurs that focus on profitability might choose to eschew these industries if they cannot internalize such positive externalities (Holz and Zhu 2002).

State enterprises concentrate in industries with high sales taxes, while private firms avoid participating in those industries. The higher the rates of sales taxes in a particular industry, the larger the market share of state enterprises in this industry, and the smaller the private firm market share in this industry. Private firm production is taking place primarily in those industries which face the lowest sales taxes, while the state enterprise allocation of industrial production does not depend on sales taxes in any way. It is actually determined by state-controlled shareholding coordination for the high market share of state enterprises to be in the industries in which they pay high sales taxes (Holz 2002).

Another means for keeping the division of industries dominated by state enterprises and those dominated by private firms is the fact that state enterprises have preferential access to bank credit, land, and resources. Also, state enterprises have been able to exploit their political patronage to obtain contacts. As a result, private entrepreneurs have tended to seek niches where the competition from state enterprises is a limited threat, such as new products (software) or rapidly changing markets (fashions, toys), where state enterprises find it difficult to compete (IFC (International Finance Corporation) 2000, p. 30).

According to an empirical survey (Asian Development Bank 2003, p. 16–7), private firms are comparatively concentrated, with 43% of the sample found in only seven (of 55) industry classifications in which there are quite a few or no state enterprises: retailing, metal manufacture, industrial machinery and equipment manufacture, food services, other services, textiles, and garment manufacture. The survey also identified some industries in which state enterprises dominate with either a few or no private ventures, for example, tobacco manufacturing, petroleum processing, and legal services. The reasons for the lack of private business in industries such as the ones cited are a prohibition on the entry of private firms, extremely high capital requirements for production, and a dearth of the required professional technical support among the private firms.

Because private firms and state enterprises are concentrated in different industries—the private sector dominates the competitive industries, while the state sector dominates the state strategic industries—research has found little head-to-head competition between private enterprises and state enterprises. Cao et al. (1999) found in their study that before the reform of SOEs, there was furious competition between private firms and local-government-supervised SOEs, which were in competitive industries which the private firms had entered. But since the privatization of these local small and medium-sized SOEs, the competition effect has been kept within the private sector, while the competition between the private sector and the state sector is low. In the survey by IFC (International Finance Corporation) (2000), only 12% of the CEOs of private firms interviewed thought that state firms were their competitors; 81% saw other private firms as their main competitors. The survey by Garnaut et al. (2001, p. 46) also found that the competitors of private firms were overwhelmingly other private firms: 46% said their competitors were small private firms, 35% said they were large private firms, only 12% said state firms were their competitors. In the survey by the Asian Development Bank (2003, p. 17), the majority of private firms viewed other private firms as their main competitors; only 15% found themselves to be competing with SOEs. The low degree of competition between private firms and state enterprises indicates that private firms are restricted from entering the state strategic industries that have been dominated by state enterprises (Garnaut et al. 2001, p. 47).

Therefore, the Chinese state sector and the Chinese private sector are restrained in different industries and constitute different markets with low competition between them (Garnaut et al. 2001, p. 49).

3.2 The Formation of Governance Structure and Innovation System of Chinese Private Firms during the Period from the mid-1990s to the middle of the First Decade of the 21st Century

The Chinese economy is characterized by the coexistence of the state sector business system on the one hand and the private sector business system on the other hand. In the state sector business system, the firm's governance structure continues in large part to be coordinated by the state through a state controlling shareholding, while in the competitive private sector business system the firm's governance structure is mainly based on the market mechanism.

According to the five main dimensions for defining the firm's governance structure and its related innovation system as described in Chap. 1, we can define the governance structure and innovation system of Chinese private firms as a market-based governance structure with a radical innovation system.

3.2.1 Ownership and Control of Chinese Private Firms

3.2.1.1 Chinese Private Firms Are Generally Firms Under the Owner's Direct Control, the Majority of Which Are Family-Managed Businesses

In June 1988, the State Council issued the Tentative Stipulations on Private Enterprises to govern the registration of private firms. It defined a private firm (*siying qiyie*) as "a for-profit organization that is owned by individuals and employs more than eight people." Chinese private firms are founded by individuals or groups of individuals (Child and Pleister 2004) and are generally firms under the owner's direct control, including family and individual-based business, business founded by groups of similar sentimental ties (such as friends or groups of people who know each other well) (Song 2004; Jacobs et al. 2004; Gregory et al. 2000, p. 13), and other types of direct owner-controlled firms. A majority of the Chinese private enterprises are family-managed business (IFC (International Finance Corporation) 2000, p. 23; Ralston et al. 2006).

Family ties can also be seen as a metaphor for the general closeness of ties in China. Therefore, based on the closeness of ties, in the family firms, the inner circle or key positions of family management can include not only family members but also friends or other fellows. Management in a partnership or a business that is owned by groups of individuals who are friends is in this style also similar to a family-based management (Hamilton 1990, p. 146–7).

Schlevogt (2001) examined the shareholder structure of Chinese private enterprises to analyze whether Chinese private enterprises indeed attached greater importance to the family. The results of his study show that most Chinese private firms (87%) are family controlled, of which 60% are fully family owned and 27% are majority-family-owned enterprises. His findings also confirmed that the family-based ownership pattern of Chinese management that was found in other Southeast Asian enterprises (Wong 1985; Heller 1991) is readopted in private firms in China (Schlevogt 2001).

A survey of the governance structure of private companies in China shows the basic characteristic of the equity of such companies: private stocks account for 92%, the share of personal stocks of proprietors is 66%, the share of stocks of brothers bearing the same name is 14%, the share of stocks of brothers bearing different names is 3%, the sum of the stocks of proprietors and their family members, relatives, and friends amounts to 83%. Collective stocks account for about 3%, legal persons' stocks make up about 3%, and township governments hold about 2% of stocks. Obviously, private companies in China show the typical characteristic of family-dominated enterprises (Guo 2000; Chen and Huang 2001).

According to another survey (Jacobs et al. 2004, p. 178) of the Chinese private sector, more than half of the respondents' firms are individual and family-based firms or friendship-based firms, and almost all firms are under the owner's direct control.

The listed private companies in China are characterized by a high degree of centralization of the principal shareholder's equity, and they have traits of the family-oriented governance pattern (Chen and Huang 2001).

3.2.1.2 Ownership and Control of Chinese Private Firms Are Highly Concentrated and Centralized in the Hands of the Owner-Managers

The tentative stipulations on private enterprises further define three types of private firms according to their specific organizational forms: sole ownership enterprises, partnership enterprises, and limited liability companies (Garnaut et al. p. 13; Chen and Huang 2001). Owners of the first two kinds of firms accept unlimited liability, and owners of the last kind of firms accept limited liability. For an owner who does not want to have a partner, it would be better to register the firm as a sole ownership. Sole ownership makes management easier. If the firm is not large, this is a big advantage. A limited liability company offers a firm several advantages, such as the protection of personal wealth, a better firm image, and a better internal management structure with legal backup; thus, it is the preferred organizational form for larger firms (Garnaut et al. 2001, p. 23, p. 91–2). In China, many firms with a single owner try to find a partner so they can qualify as a limited liability company. In many cases, sole proprietors find a family member to be a partner. For example, in some cities, such as Shunde, a spouse is permitted to act as a partner, and that way a firm can set up a limited liability company without having the sole owner's family lose control of the firm. In other cities, such as Beijing, a spouse is not qualified to be a partner. In such cases, some firms try to find a sleeping partner, that is, to find a nominal partner and offer a nominal share, so the sole owners would not lose control of the firms (IFC (International Finance Corporation) 2000, p. 21). The Law of Corporation stipulates that a manufacturing firm has to have more than 500,000 yuan of initial capital to qualify as a limited liability company. Therefore, the existence of many partnership firms might be explained by the fact that the initial capital value of these firms could not reach the minimum capital required for a limited liability company (Garnaut et al. 2001, p. 91).

To become larger, to build business, to expand the management team, and to obtain external financing, some limited liability companies further develop into limited liability shareholding companies. In cities like Wenzhou and Shunde, private companies have made rapid progress in the transition to limited liability shareholding companies (Garnaut et al. 2001, p. 90; IFC (International Finance Corporation) 2000, p. 60). Box 3.2 shows an example of such firms.

Box 3.2   Changing Ownership and Internal Governance in Private Firms

In Wenzhou city, private enterprises have developed quickly and dominate the local economy. Most private firms are owned by an individual or a family and are also managed by the owners. However, many firms that have grown large are changing ownership and internal governance structures.

TZ, a private firm established in 1990, became fairly large after just 9 years of growth, with more than 200 million yuan (US $24 million) of total capital and more than 3,000 employees. It had undergone three episodes of internal restructuring.

In 1994, it converted from a solely owned small private firm to a company. Several senior managers became owners. In 1997, it changed into a shareholding company, issuing 50% of its shares to the 50 middle-level managers. In 1999, it bought the largest parts of the shares of ten member firms and made itself the shareholding company of these firms. Thus, it was able to integrate these small factories into a large one.

(continued)

Box 3.2 (continued)
These changes enabled the company to recruit experienced managers from outside to improve its management, to reduce the management costs, and also to expand its size. In these 2 years its total capital expanded 6 times, and its sales expanded 4 times. Its share of the domestic market and its exports increased. Technical innovation in the company also accelerated. The company now allocates 1–2% of its total revenue to research and development of new products.
From IFC (International Finance Corporation) (2000, p. 61)

Table 3.2 shows the ownership structure of private firms in 1991, 1994, and 1997. From 1991 to 1997, the number of private firms in China increased 7.9 times; the number of limited liability companies grew most rapidly, increasing 65.3 times. The number of sole ownership enterprises increased 5.4 times; the number of partnership enterprises increased 2.2 times. Thus, limited liability companies had the smallest share in 1991, but became the predominant form of ownership structure in 1997 (Garnaut et al. 2001, p. 23). In 1992, the ratios of sole ownership enterprises, partnership enterprises, and limited liability companies were 55.3, 32.0, and 12.7%, respectively. In 1997 and 1998, the ratio of sole ownership enterprises among private enterprises dropped to 40.3 and 36.8% that of partnership enterprises dropped to 13.6 and 11.5%, while that of limited liability companies rose to 46.1 and 51.8% (Chen and Huang 2001, p. 6). By June 1999 there were 700,000 limited liability companies, constituting an increase of 33.7% from June 1998 and those accounted for about 55% of private firms in China (Garnaut and Song 2004a, p. 5).

The rapidly increasing share of limited liability companies compared with the declining shares of sole ownerships and partnerships (see Fig. 3.1) clearly reflects an increased acceptance of modern corporate structures by private enterprises in China (Song 2004, p. 43).

Notwithstanding this trend, the ownership of private firms in China is still very concentrated. According to a survey by the Asian Development Bank (2003, p. 16) on the ownership structure of the private limited liability companies, the largest individual shareholders on average held 59% of their companies' shares. Thus, in private limited liability companies with modern corporate structures, ownership may remain highly concentrated (Child and Pleister 2004, p. 196).

Table 3.2 Ownership structure of private firms

	1991		1994		1997	
	Firms	Share (%)	Firms	Share (%)	Firms	Share (%)
Sole ownership	60,613	56.2	100,621	47.6	387,534	40.3
Partnership	40,552	37.6	37,532	17.8	130,668	13.6
Limited liability	6678	6.2	103,235	48.8	442,554	46.1
Total	107,843	100.0	211,388	100.0	960,726	100.0

From Yearbook of China Industrial and Commerce Administrative Management, 1992–1998

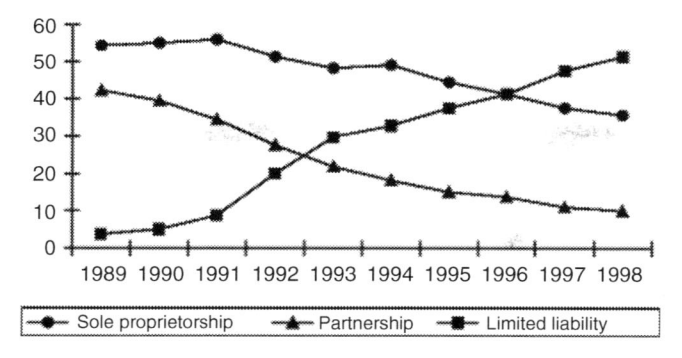

Fig. 3.1 Changing pattern of organizational structure, 1989–1998 (percent) (From Wang 2000a, p. 41)

The concentration of ownership is also reflected in the internal governance control structure (Asian Development Bank 2003, p. 16). Owner-managers have almost exclusive control over the direction of the firms. Overall delegation in the firms is weak. According to Child and Pleister (2004, p. 196–8), a different organizational form of a private firm affected the form that its chief internal agency took. In most sole proprietorships, managerial meetings were the primary agency acting on behalf of the owner. In such cases, the managers were themselves owners. Among the partnerships, the primary agency was distributed almost equally between managerial meetings and a board of directors. In limited liability companies, boards of directors were most often the internal agency. The larger private firms with over 500 employees were more likely to have boards of directors than management meetings as the internal agency.

The composition of the board of directors and managers has the characteristics of a closure and of being family-oriented. According to the third national survey of private companies conducted in 1998, 50.5% of the spouses of the proprietors of private firms and 20.3% of their grown-up children were engaged in managerial work (Chen and Huang 2001). According to a 1999 study of 1900 medium-sized and large private enterprises by the Chinese Academy of Social Sciences and the National Association of Industry and Commerce, 48% of the family members of the entrepreneur were engaged in the management of the enterprises, including 51% of the spouses and 20% of the adult children. The study by the All-China Federation of Industry and Commerce found that 98% of private firms were family-managed (IFC (International Finance Corporation) 2000, p. 23).

Some nonfamily members who have served the company for a long time and who are trusted by the owners can also be promoted to management positions and involved in the inner circle of management. The closeness of the inner circle of management strengthens the control of owners and lessens the possibility of a challenge to their authority (Tsang 2001; Hamilton 1990, p. 146). Private firms address the question of managerial incentives not only by hiring family members or hiring nonfamily member on the basis of the closeness of ties, but also by giving the

Table 3.3 Pattern of top decision-making in firms (percentage of valid data)

	Percentage of important decisions made by		
	Manager	Board of directors	Others
By ownership of firms			
Sole proprietor	26.9	65.5	7.7
Partnership	20.1	67.6	12.4
Company	22.3	71.0	6.7
Publicly listed	–	100.0	–
By size of firms			
<51	22.5	67.6	10.0
51–100	30.4	61.3	8.3
101–500	24.4	67.8	7.8
>500	10.1	83.4	6.5
By age of firms			
<3 years	23.5	67.4	9.1
3–5 years	29.1	65.1	5.8
5–10 years	21.2	70.7	8.1
>10 years	16.4	76.0	7.6

From Garnaut et al. (2001, p. 93)

outsider-managers shares in the ownership and internalizing outsider-managers to become owner-managers (IFC (International Finance Corporation) 2000, p. 23).

In terms of the decision-making structure in private firms, according to the survey by the Asian Development Bank (2003), the highest decision-making bodies are the president of the company or the chairman of the board (36%), the board of directors (33%), major shareholders (14%), or shareholders' meetings (13%) (Asian Development Bank 2003, p. 16). The studies by Garnaut et al. (2001) and Child and Pleister (2004) also show that among private firms in China top decision-making is concentrated in the hands of the owners (see Table 3.3).

In the sole proprietorships, 66% of important decisions were made by boards, which are constituted of close associates and friends. In limited liability companies, the important decisions were often made by boards (71.0%). The boards of the larger private firms with over 500 employees made a substantially higher percentage of important decisions than those of smaller firms. In firms that had been operating for more than 10 years, the boards rather than the managers tended to make the important decisions. There is growing differentiation over time between executive decision-making by the management meeting and policy decision-making by the boards. Even though decision-making shifted somewhat toward managers when the management meetings were the internal agency, top decision-making in private firms tended to be in the hands of owners (see Table 3.4).

Thus, the internal decision-making structure of private firms shows that the board of directors controls the important decisions in a firm. Corporations do not delegate more power to managers. Even in the publicly listed firms, the board of directors

Table 3.4 Internal agency and balance of decision-making

Internal agency	Percentage of important decisions made by owners minus percentage made by managers
Board of directors	56.2
Management meeting or board	48.6
Management meeting	32.6

From Child and Pleister (2004, p. 197)

controls all the important decisions. The decisions controlled by managers may actually also be controlled by the owners because these managers may well be owners themselves. This is consistent with what was found in the study—most of the CEOs were themselves owners. Therefore, delegation in the private firms is weak (Garnaut et al. 2001, p. 92–3; Child and Pleister 2004).

According to the survey by the Asian Development Bank (2003), the firms' major decision-makers are in nine cases out of ten the major shareholders. This means that the firms are still run by the owners themselves, delegating less power to professional managers (Asian Development Bank 2003, p. 16). Despite the existence of the board of directors and the shareholder's meeting, individual entrepreneurs continue to play a dominant role in making decisions.[2]

Thus, notwithstanding the trend that the limited liability company seems to be the organizational form on which Chinese private firms are converging (Asian Development Bank 2003, p. 16), and that many large private companies have introduced a modern corporate structure with the shareholder's meeting, the board of directors, the supervisory board, and the general managers, ownership and control are highly concentrated and centralized, the internal systems of coordination and control are highly personal, and the characteristics of family control remain evident (Chen and Huang 2001; Tsang 2001).

3.2.1.3   The Chinese Private Business Management Model Significantly Differs from the State Enterprise Management Model

The overseas Chinese private business management model described in previous studies of overseas Chinese business has been readopted by the newly established Chinese private enterprises in mainland China. This model puts a strong emphasis on owner direct control and family-based management. Chinese private enterprises significantly differ from state enterprises in terms of such a business management model. This difference also indicates that, in the business management model of the Chinese private sector, there is a greater institutional influence from traditional

---

[2]Forms of Making Important Decisions and Ordinary Decisions on Management by Private Companies Surveyed in 1997, Report on Development of Chinese Private Companies 1978–1998, Beijing: Social Science Documentation Publishing House, 1999.

Chinese culture (Confucianism), which puts emphasis on respect for seniority, authority, and personal power (Schlevogt 2001), than in the state sector. This is because the Chinese state sector is strongly influenced by state-controlled shareholding coordination, while the private sector is not.

There are two distinctive characteristics of the Chinese private enterprise management model: a high centralization of power and a low degree of bureaucracy. The power lies in the hands of one autocratic entrepreneur, who is usually the founder and owner (Redding and Wong 1986; Kao 1993; Schlevogt 1998, 2001; Turpin 1998). Chinese private enterprises are controlled by the owner-managers. In contrast, state enterprises are relatively decentralized compared with private enterprises (Child and Lu 1990, p. 334; Child 1994, p. 94–5; Schlevogt 2001).

There is a low degree of bureaucracy in Chinese private enterprises. The degree of formalization, specialization of control systems, and integration is also very low (Redding 1990; Weidenbaum 1996, p. 149–50; Schlevogt 2001). There is a distinctive lack of a formal organizational hierarchy (Leung 1995; Schlevogt 2001). The owner-manager tends to exert personal control instead of using formal rules. A low degree of specialization is also a distinctive trait of Chinese private enterprises. Written instructions are limited in number, as staff departments do not generate such written instructions for specialization and standardization. The low degree of integration is reflected in the fact that private enterprises use significantly fewer integrative devices, such as liaison personnel, committees, and interdepartmental bargaining (Schlevogt 2001). In contrast, Chinese state enterprises are more bureaucratic and emphasize the high degree of "structuredness" of formal organizations (Weihrich 1990; Krone et al. 1992; Schlevogt 2001). State enterprises emphasize a formal organizational hierarchy and make more use of formal control devices than private enterprises. Thus, the Chinese private enterprise management model is characterized by a strong centralization and a low degree of bureaucracy, which is composed of low degrees of formalization, specialization, use of control systems, and integration. Table 3.5 compares these management profiles between private and state enterprises.

Table 3.5 Comparison of management characteristics between private and state enterprises

Aspect	Private enterprises	State enterprises
Centralization	Higher	Lower
Formalization	Lower	Higher
Specialization	Lower	Higher
Control	Lower	Higher
Integration	Lower	Higher

From Schlevogt (2001, p. 5)

3.2.2 Employer–Employee Relations

3.2.2.1 Proprietorial Prerogative and Market-Oriented Employment Relations in Chinese Private Firms

The employment relations in Chinese private firms often tend to be informal. Owner-managers play a dominant role in determining how the business is to be run and what employment terms and conditions are to be offered to their workers (Cooke 2005). Workers either do not participate in the decision-making of the private firms or have a limited say, even in questions concerning benefits. The decisions on issues of wages and benefits are largely made and controlled by the owner (Child and Pleister 2004; Garnaut et al. 2001, p. 98). Employees tend to accept terms and conditions as a given fact instead of as an outcome of bargaining. The limited role of employees in a private firm is also related to their weak collective bargaining power. Collective workplace representation is often lacking (Cooke 2005; Garnaut et al. 2001, p. 98).

The employment system in Chinese private firms is flexible and market-oriented (Meng 2004, p. 156). Private enterprises often do not draw up written employment contracts with their employees. Verbal agreements between employers and their employees at the recruitment stage lay down a few basic terms and conditions instead. Those firms that offer contracts tend to offer short-term contracts with their employees. Enforcement of employment standards by the Labor Bureau is minimal for private firms. The Labor Bureau does not intervene in workshop practices (Child and Pleister 2004; Cooke 2005; Meng 2004, p. 156).

The labor turnover rate is high in private firms, which indicates the hire–fire mode in private sector employment. A vast majority of workers have worked for their employers on short-term contracts. While some individuals chose to quit their jobs, many were fired by their employers (Cooke 2005).

A high turnover rate is a factor that discourages firms from investing in training, which in turn reduces the quality of the labor force. The annual turnover rate in the sample firms in the study by Garnaut et al. (2001) was between 15 and 20%. Because of such a high turnover rate, the training of workers is unattractive for private firms.

Employee wages, bonus, and benefits are based on market determination. A survey by Cooke (2005) found that employers in Chinese private firms determined unilaterally the wage levels of their employees on the basis of the market rate. Private firms freely reward employees in line with performance (Child and Pleister 2004). The rewards sensitively relate to the individuals' productivity and are greatly influenced by the market-based incentive system (Meng 2004). Most employers adopted some sort of profit-related pay scheme, giving a certain percentage of profit as a bonus to motivate employees to increase the performance level. Profit-related bonuses generally made up 30–50% of the worker's total wage income. This also means that a high level of market risk is shared by individual workers (Cooke 2005). The study by Meng (2004) found that the rate of return on each level of education is much higher in the private sector than in the state sector. A university graduate in the private sector earns approximately 92% more than a worker with primary school education. The difference is around 50% in the state sector. The earnings profiles for tenure and job experience appear to be an inverse-U shape in the private sector but continually increase in the state sector, which shows that the earnings determination in the private sector is more market-oriented.

The workers in private firms work for long hours, one main reason for which is the cost of the operation. The vast majority of workers worked well beyond 40 h a week, with a low level of rest and a few holidays given to the workers. Most owners did not allow their workers to take their days off during holidays when their business was at its busiest period. Sixty-two percent of owners admitted that they would ask their employees to work overtime on short notice (Cooke 2005).

Employment welfare benefits and employment protection are inadequate in Chinese private firms. In general, they offer far fewer employment welfare benefits and less employment protection, such as pensions, health insurance, and housing, to their employees than state enterprises do. The majority of state enterprise employees receive medical care and pensions, while most private firm employees do not receive anything comparable (Meng 2004; Cooke 2005).

Labor costs in private firms are lower than in the state enterprises. Comparing the annual and hourly wages between private firm employees and state enterprise employees, those in private firms are 16% higher than those in state enterprises on average. If the long working hours of employees in private firms are taken into account, the difference falls to 1.7%. If the fact that private firm employees not only work longer hours but also receive far fewer benefits is taken into account, the labor costs in private firms are found to be lower than those in state enterprises (Meng 2004).

Political affiliation does not affect earnings in the private firms, but it does in the state enterprises. This also indicates that non-market-related factors have little bearing on wage determination in the private firms (Meng 2004).

Labor demand is also determined by the market. The data from Garnaut et al. (2001) show a much higher output elasticity and price elasticity of demand for labor in the private sector compared with the state sector. Hence, the labor demand curve for the private sector is much steeper than that for the state sector. The data from Meng (2004) show that an increase in the capital-to-labor ratio has no impact on state sector employment, but it significantly reduces employment in the private sector.

A clear distinction has been made in the labor force of private firms between locals (and externally recruited university graduates) and rural migrants. Employees of the first group generally hold better positions, enjoy better wages and benefits, and stay with the firm longer. Rural migrants are treated as a secondary labor force, with less favorable jobs, lower wages, and almost no other benefits. They even have a higher turnover rate (Child and Pleister 2004; Garnaut et al. 2001, p. 98).

In China's private sector, effective labor unions and other collective mechanisms to articulate labor interests are absent (Child and Pleister 2004; Cooke 2005). As a result of the long-term underdevelopment of associations, a few workers' associations exist in the Chinese private sector. The only official channel which workers can use to protect their labor rights is the local labor authorities. In any case, neither the employers nor the workers would choose the labor authorities as their favorite mechanism for resolving their disputes (Cooke 2005).

Collective bargaining is weak because of a low percentage of unionized workers. In the survey by Garnaut et al. (2001, p. 98), only 173 firms (27%) provided a usable questionnaire entry, of which the average percentage of unionized workers was 60%. However, the firms that did not provide answers to the survey might well have no unionized workers at all. The data from Cooke (2005) reveal that quite a few workers in the surveyed firms were trade union members or belonged to other worker's associations as their representing body. Workers not represented by unions tended to "have little bargaining power in an economic climate of rising unemployment and underemployment" (Levine 1997, p. 12). Collective bargaining in the Chinese private sector is apparently difficult to organize owing to the absence of a collective mechanism (Cooke 2005).

3.2.2.2 Employment Relations in Chinese Private Firms Are Different from Those in Chinese State Enterprises, but Are Similar to Those in Small Firms in Liberal Market Economies

The findings by Cooke (2005) show that the employment relations in Chinese private firms are significantly different from those found in the Chinese state enterprises (Child 1994; Cooke 2000, 2002; Ding and Warner 1999; Wang 2000a; Warner and Ng 1998), with the former being more disadvantageous for workers. By comparison, there is a much greater level of formality of employment relations in Chinese state enterprises, and the quality of employment tends to be higher for the workers when judged by the owner–employee relations, working hours, and employment protection (Cooke 2005).

This study also shows that there appear to be considerable similarities between Chinese private firms and those in liberal market economies, such as the UK, in terms of owner characteristics and management style. Both systems are characterized by proprietorial prerogative and procedural informality in the employment relations. As has been observed (Ram 1994, p. 6), workers in small firms in the UK "rarely questioned the employer's right to manage and the primacy of profitability." This proprietorial prerogative also holds true for Chinese private business. Chinese private business management is likewise characterized by a strong power core, which is exercised by the owner-manager. In both systems there is a low level of awareness and adherence to employment regulations (Keasey and Watson 1993; Rainnie 1989; Scott et al. 1989; Stokes 1998). The policy of employment relations is often not formulated in an explicit self-conscious manner. Informal routinization shapes in large part the day-to-day running of the business. There is little evidence of preplanning of the labor relations in order to avoid potential problems (McEvoy 1984; Verser 1987). Further similarities in the employment relations in both systems include a high level of labor turnover and the individualized process of pay bargaining between employer and employee, in which unilateral determination by the employer is often the case (Curran et al. 1993; Gilman et al. 2002).

3.2.3 Financing Pattern and Innovation System

3.2.3.1 The Financing of Chinese Private Firms Depends on Internal Sources and Informal Channels

Self-financing and informal credit arrangements are the most common sources of finance for the Chinese private sector (Tam 2004). The start-up and growth capital for private firms are usually provided by the owner, with family or friends helping out. Accordingly, these firms start with personal or household savings, combined with loans from friends (Child and Pleister 2004). Most private firms continue to rely overwhelmingly on investments by their owners and on internal cash generation as they grow (IFC (International Finance Corporation) 2000, p. 32). Table 3.6 provides a glimpse of the financing patterns of the private sector.

As Table 3.6 shows, self-finance was the most important source, contributing over 93% of start-up capital, including owner's personal funds (69%) and funds from other individual investors (24.9%).

According to the survey by Garnaut et al. (2001), which includes private firms in Beijing, Shunde, Chendu, and Wenzhou, the surveyed firms started their business relying almost exclusively on self-financing (see Table 3.7). More than 90% of the initial capital was self-financed by the principal owners, the start-up teams, and their families. Other sources of financing, such as banks and other financial and nonfinancial institutions, played only a minor role.

Garnaut et al. (2001) further analyzed private firms' financing for post-start-up investments. A considerable number of private firms continued to rely overwhelmingly on internal sources, such as self-financing and retained profits for business operations and expansions (see Table 3.8).

The data from the Asian Development Bank 2003 (p. 23–4) reveal that the surveyed private firms in all cities uniformly face difficulty in getting bank or other loans. The most frequently cited financing sources are "individual or household investment," "internal capital," and "retained earnings."

Table 3.6 Source of private enterprise start-up capital, 1997

	Percentage of the total start-up capital
Owner's personal funds	69.0
Other individual investors	24.9
General public	1.1
Collectives	0.7
Government departments	1.0
Other enterprises	0.7
Foreign investment	1.3
Bank loans	1.3
Total	100.0

From Project Team on Studies on Private Enterprises in China (1999, p. 137)

Table 3.7 Sources of firms' initial capital (percentage of firms with valid data)

	Self-financed	Bank loans	Institution	Other
All	90.5	4.0	2.6	2.8
By city				
Beijing	96.1	0.3	2.0	1.1
Shunde	87.1	6.5	6.5	–
Chengdu	91.5	2.8	2.1	3.6
Wenzhou	97.3	1.1	0.1	1.6
Mianyang	73.2	17.9	–	8.3
Deyang	82.8	7.1	5.7	4.6
By years of operation				
≤3years	92.4	2.7	2.2	2.7
3–5 years	92.1	3.5	–	3.8
5–10 years	89.0	6.3	1.5	3.0
>10 years	83.1	5.7	9.9	1.3

From Gregory et al. (2000, p. 48)

3.2.3.2 Private Firms Receive Limited Bank Loans Conditioned on Hard Budget Constraints

While state enterprises obtained extensive loans from the state banks and faced soft budget constraints, private firms received only limited loans and operate under hard budget constraints (Chiu and Lewis 2006, p. 39).

As Table 3.9 indicates, loans remain the most important source of finance for all Chinese enterprises. Since the state-owned banks account for over 80% of the assets of the banking system, bank lending predominantly goes to the state enterprises, crowding out private enterprises. This exemplifies the problems that private firms face with respect to getting loans from banks (Tam 2004; IFC (International Finance Corporation) 2000, p. 31; Zhao 2005, p. 112).

As described above, private firms only have limited access to bank loans. This limited availability of credit can be gauged from the quite static and low proportion of lending to the private sector. As Table 3.10 shows, neither the banks nor the nonbank financial institutions have increased the proportions of credit to the private sector by any significant degree. Nonstate banks and nonbank financial institutions lent a higher proportion to the private sector than state banks did, but the share was still well below 1% (Tam 2004, p. 125).

Although the share of loans from banks and other financial institutions that were outstanding to the private sector has grown continually over the decade (see Fig. 3.2), it was still less than 1% of the total lending. Although the time series certainly underreports the share of bank lending to the private sector, it nevertheless suggests that the share of lending to the private sector is low (IFC (International Finance Corporation) 2000, p. 45).

The data on business financing by firm size (see Table 3.8 and Fig. 3.3) suggest two things. Firstly, that the larger the firm, the less it depends on self-financing and

Table 3.8 Sources of capital financing in surveyed firms (percentage of firms with valid data for 1998)

	Stock shares	Enterprise debt bonds	Loans from state-owned banks	Loans from foreign banks	Loans from credit unions	Informal channels	Profit retaining	Self-financing
Total	1.3	0.3	9.7	–	8.3	9.0	26.2	35.8
By city								
Beijing	0.6	–	3.0	–	5.3	11.1	23.1	45.6
Shunde	–	–	15.9	–	14.1	7.8	19.6	28.8
Chengdu	5.0	2.1	17.2	–	8.3	6.2	30.4	28.6
Wenzhou	2.3	–	19.2	–	1.7	6.5	44.5	29.4
Mianyang	–	–	26.2	–	23.0	9.6	14.1	11.7
Deyang	0.6	–	3.0	–	16.7	6.3	27.2	26.0
By size of firms								
<51	1.1	0.6	3.4	–	6.3	10.4	22.4	45.0
51–100	0.3	–	7.8	–	11.3	6.1	32.9	31.7
101–500	2.8	–	16.0	–	10.5	7.7	35.2	21.8
>500	2.3	0.4	25.0	–	9.7	4.2	30.2	23.6

From Gregory et al. (2000, p. 50)

Table 3.9   Structure of enterprise finance (percentage of annual flows)

	1995	1996	1997	1998
Loans from financial institutions	88.0	82.8	77.0	82.6
Direct finance	12.0	17.2	23.0	17.4
Shares	1.3	3.2	8.7	6.0
Commercial bills	8.8	12.0	12.6	10.3
Bonds	1.9	2.0	1.7	1.1

Source: Tam 2004, p. 125

Table 3.10   Loans to private enterprises and sole proprietorships (percentage of total outstanding loans)

	State-owned banks	Other banks and nonbank financial institutions
1997 Q1	0.30	0.56
1997 Q2	0.30	0.55
1997 Q3	0.29	0.54
1997 Q4	0.27	0.52
1998 Q1	0.27	0.52
1998 Q2	0.26	0.53
1998 Q3	0.30	0.54
1998 Q4	0.30	0.55
1999 Q1	0.32	0.55
1999 Q2	0.36	0.57
1999 Q3	0.38	0.59
1999 Q4	0.41	0.62

Source: Tam 2004, p. 125

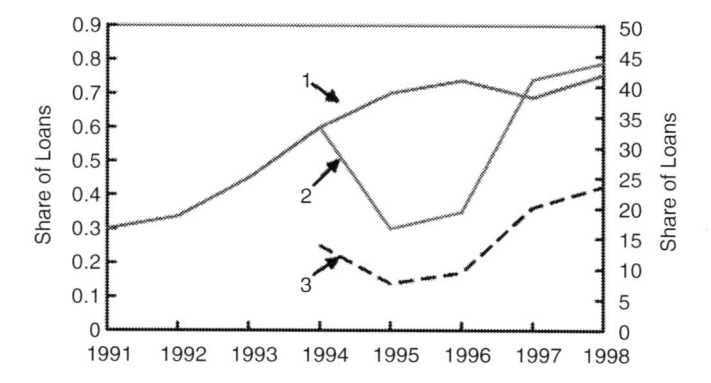

Fig. 3.2   Short-term loans to private enterprises. (1) Private enterprise loans as a share of all loans from all banks (*left axis*). (2) Private enterprise loans from state banks as a share of private enterprise loans from all banks (*right axis*). (3) Private enterprise loans as a share of all loans from state banks (*left axis*). Source: IFC (International Finance Corporation) (2000), p. 46

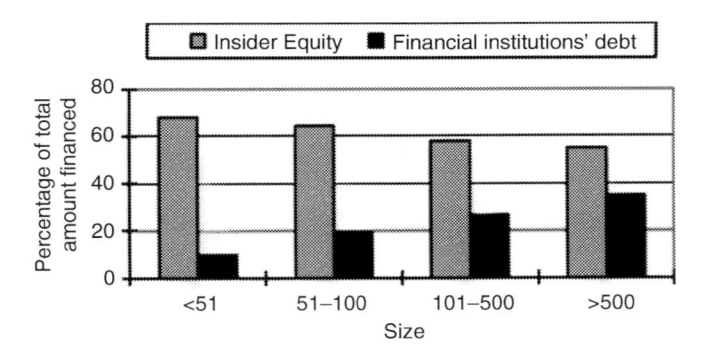

Fig. 3.3 Source of finance in surveyed firms, by firm size (From IFC (International Finance Corporation) 2000, p. 51)

informal financing. Secondly, that the larger the firm, the more it relies on commercial bank loan financing and issuance of shares on the market. The share of commercial bank loans increases with the firm size and becomes the second most important source of funds for the largest firms, after retained earnings (Garnaut et al. 2001, p. 54; IFC (International Finance Corporation) 2000, p. 51). Furthermore, a clear relationship between size and profitability of Chinese private firms can be identified. In 1998 about three-quarters of firms with fewer than 51 employees were profitable, but the figure rose to 93% for firms with more than 500 employees. Hence, the increase of the share of commercial bank loans with growing firm size indicates that banks provide more support for larger and relatively successful private firms and banks provide loans to private firms on the basis of their profitability (IFC (International Finance Corporation) 2000, p. 51–2).

Banks in China grant credit to private firms only according to the criteria determined by the market, such as profitability, which is similar to the way banks in liberal market economies act (Child and Pleister 2004). Based on the rule of the market, private firms receive commercial bank loans and operate under hard budget constraints (Chiu and Lewis 2006, p. 39).

3.2.3.3 The Chinese Stock Markets Play a Very Limited Role in the Private Firms' Financing Patterns

For China's enterprises the stock market is not a significant source of finance (Table 3.9). Access to stock markets has been closely controlled by the Securities Commission, which has given preference to state enterprises. To date, China's stock market has served primarily to finance state enterprises. Most listed companies in China are state enterprises. As a result, private firms have had limited access to the stock markets, either through initial public offerings or by buying into listed companies. Of the 976 companies listed on the two Chinese stock markets (Shanghai

Table 3.11 Nonstate firms listed via initial public offerings

Firm	Capital (thousands of shares)	Date of listing	Main business
Shenzhen exchange			
Wanxiang Qianchao	21,758	1994	Auto parts
Shishi Xinfa	6798	1996	Conglomerate
Hena Sida	8875	1996	Electronics, instruments
Lasha Pijiu	6600	1997	Alcohol
New Hope	14,002	1998	Agriculture
Shanghai exchange			
Dongfang group	35,479	1994	Conglomerate
Xinfu industry	31,280	1996	Clothing
XinChao industry	14,336	1996	Textile
Jiahe Gufeng	12,750	1997	Agriculture
Fuxin industry	15,070	1998	Biomedicine
Haixin Keji	19,800	1999	Computer

From Gao and Xu (2000) and IFC (International Finance Corporation) (2000, p. 47)

and Shenzhen stock exchanges), only 11 are nonstate firms (see Table 3.11) (IFC (International Finance Corporation) 2000, p. 31–47).

Private enterprises are normally prohibited from taking over listed state enterprises through acquisition. The only way for private enterprises to buy listed companies is to adopt a strategy called "to borrow the shell for the egg," that is, to buy shares of a shell company, which is a listed company with actually no net assets. Through the acquisition of shell companies, private enterprises can get listed. Thus, private firms that are unable to list on the stock markets try to gain access to the stock markets through the purchase of a shell company (see Table 3.12).

At the end of 2002, there were only 139 private companies listed on China's stock markets, accounting for 11.8% of all listed companies (Zhao 2005, p. 112).

3.2.3.4 Performance Criteria of Chinese Private Firms

In the Tentative Stipulations on Private Enterprises issued by the State Council, the Chinese private firm is defined as "a 'for-profit' organization that is owned by individuals," which indicates the primacy of profitability for Chinese private firms.

Because Chinese private firms mainly rely on self-finance, owing to their limited access to bank loans, which is conditioned on hard budget constraints, and their limited access to the Chinese stock markets, they have been operating under a tight liquidity constraint (Garnaut et al. 2001, p. 50). This tight liquidity constraint makes the profitability and turnover rate of its working capital the most important performance criteria for Chinese private firms. They are the main indicators of a private firm's financial position.

Table 3.12 Nonstate firms buying listed companies

Year	Seller	Original business	Buyer	Buyer's business	Share acquired	Holding (%)
1995	Huali Gaoke	Machinery	Stone Group	High-technology	2300	13.4
1997	Xiang Huoju	Industry	Xinjiang Delong	Real estate	3000	13.5
1998	Yinghe Dongli	Auto parts	Yinghe Gaoke	Computer	2058	29.0
1998	Tiange Group	Clothing	Fubei Zhengchang	High-technology, agribusiness	3000	20.9
1998	Jinlu Group	Chemical	Sichuan Santong	Building materials	3568	12.2
1998	Liao Wuzi	Trade	Shengyang Yingji	Tourism, real estate	4663	35.9
1999	Shen Jingxin	Real estate	Guangdong Yi'an	Information technology	1923	26.1

From Gao and Xu (2000) and IFC (International Finance Corporation) (2000, p. 47)

The turnover rate is calculated as the ratio of a firm's sales in a year to its stock of working capital in the same year. It therefore measures the frequency of the working capital circulation. A firm with a tight liquidity constraint tends to pursue a higher turnover rate in order to use its limited funds fully and efficiently.

The turnover rate of the working capital of Chinese private firms remained high, about 5.3 on average in the late 1990s. Such a high turnover rate may have been the result of a tight liquidity constraint and profit-driven efficiency (Garnaut et al. 2001, p. 57–8).

3.2.3.5 Price Competitiveness Is the Competitive Advantage of Chinese Private Firms

As mentioned in the previous part, in the Chinese private sector, long working hours, market-determined wages and benefits, the absence of employment welfare benefits, inadequate employment protection, and the hire and fire mode of employment relations are all prevalent because of cost concerns. Therefore, the labor costs in the Chinese private sector are found to be lower compared with those in the state sector. The public perceives the products of Chinese private firms as being generally cheaper. Lower costs and lower prices remain the key to a competitive advantage of Chinese private firms that operate in a highly cost sensitive business sector (Cooke 2005; Meng 2004; Child and Pleister 2004, p. 204).

In the CEO survey by Garnaut et al. (2001), the majority of the CEOs named price cuts and price competition as the main form of competition used among Chinese private firms. They also believed that an intensified price competition exists in the Chinese private sector (Garnaut et al. p. 47).

3.2.3.6   Innovation and New Technology Development in the Nonstate Sector

One of the main goals of the Chinese economic reforms was to raise China's indigenous technological capabilities. China adopted policies to create an indigenous technological capability: on the one hand, China develops capital-intensive and technology-intensive industries in the state sector; on the other hand, China develops information technology (IT) industries in the private sector (Segal 2003, p. 1).

State-controlled enterprises do not expand into the new technology sectors. The earliest nongovernmental enterprises entered market areas—information industry and bioengineering—that were completely new sectors where there was no competition from state-controlled enterprises (Segal 2003, p. 54). Most nongovernmental high-technology enterprises are involved in IT. The sector includes enterprises that are involved in personal computer, component, and peripherals production, software development, and Internet services. IT industries are not particularly capital intensive and do not initially require a large capital outlay (So 2004). There are few if any private entrepreneurs involved in the development of other technology areas like semiconductors, new energy sources, new materials, and photomechanical electronic integration because of the high entry costs, the high risk, and the continued dominance of state research laboratories and factories in those traditional technology areas (Segal 2003, p. 20–55).

The development of private enterprises has gradually shifted from a focus on traditional tertiary industries to one on primary industries, secondary industries, and high-technology industries (Wang and Shi 2007). Many private enterprises have entered the new high-technology sectors (Zhao 2005). In Beijing, Shenzhen, Zhejiang, Jiangsu, and many other provinces and cities, high-technology firms owned and founded by private individuals emerged, especially in the IT industries (Wang and Shi 2007; Tam 2004; So 2004).

China has been successfully building new technology nongovernmental enterprises to compete in ITs and its IT industries have grown rapidly. China's IT industries started to thrive in the early 1990s. Starting in the 1990s and until this day, the IT sector has been the fastest growing sector in the economy. The domestic IT market was worth $168 billion in 2000, 9 times larger than at the beginning of the 1990s. By 2005, at the end of the Tenth Five-Year Plan, China has invested $500 billion in the IT sector, raising the contribution of IT to GDP to 5%. Private IT firms have been vital to the sector's success, the development of ITs, and the "new economy" in China (Segal 2003, p. 2–3; So 2004).

Although IT industries took off at around the time when private enterprises were given legal status (in 1988), a few nongovernmental high-technology enterprises were registered as private because the policy implementation was biased against private firms. Those nongovernmental high-technology enterprises were categorized as *minying* ("people-managed"), or as nongovernmental, technology-based enterprises. As private ownership gained more legitimacy, and as property rights were reformed in the second half of the 1990s, most *minying* high-technology enterprises have become overtly privately owned. They transformed by re-registering themselves as private limited liability companies or by restructuring themselves into shareholding companies in accordance with the 1994 Company Law. Unlike most other private firms, IT firms are mainly formed by peer-group partners rather than by family members. This is probably because IT knowledge is usually shared between peers rather than between family members (So 2004).

3.2.3.7 Creating "China's Silicon Valley": The Beijing Model of High Technology Development in the Private Sector

Beijing has witnessed a rapid development of high-technology industries in its nonstate sector (IFC (International Finance Corporation) 2000, p. 2). In 2000, private high-technology firms accounted for one-quarter of all private enterprises in Beijing (Beijing Daily, 2 March 2000). Nongovernmental enterprises were at the center of Beijing's growth. By 1993, *minying* enterprises made up 10.2% of the total output value in Beijing. From 1988 to 1994, nongovernmental enterprises in Beijing received 32.5% of all awards given to national technology entrepreneurs, more than in any other part of the country (Segal 2003, p. 19).

As early as April 1984, the Haidian district government in Beijing held a meeting of more than 1200 science and technology personnel and declared that Haidian should become "China's Silicon Valley." It should rely on high-technology enterprises to promote industrialization. Individuals with a high level of educational achievement and technological know-how should become the main force in the technological development, and these entrepreneurs should be encouraged to set up their own nongovernmental enterprises. Also, the local government should act to maintain the autonomous enterprises.

The best example of the Beijing model comes from Zhongguancun, which is the center of Beijing's technological growth. In the 1980s, the growth of the *minying* enterprises was increasingly located on Zhongguancun, "Electrics Avenue," in Beijing's Haidian district. Central to the district's success were the technological and commercial abilities of the individual entrepreneurs. The governments allowed science and technology personnel to found their own private enterprises and these individual entrepreneurs were behind the success of the district (Segal 2003, p. 57).

Nongovernmental enterprises in Beijing were similar to the small, flexible, innovative, and privately owned technology firms found in the West, especially in Silicon Valley (Segal 2003, p. 51). These enterprises were self-managed and operated within the competitive private sector that was "market-led." Growing competition was felt among these nongovernmental high-technology enterprises. If *minying* enterprises fail, they may go bankrupt (Segal 2003, p. 58–62).

The governance structures of these nongovernmental enterprises had evolved along with the expansion of the enterprises. During the early 1980s, "management" meant not more than coordinating a group of close friends with similar goals. The founders and their small group of friends controlled decisions about business strategies, technology development, hiring, promotion, research cooperation, etc.

The enterprises reflected the talents of their founders, who often dominated the enterprises through the force of their personalities. Some nongovernmental high-technology enterprises grew rapidly and started to use the stock system as their governance structure. In 1988, the Beijing City Reform Commission approved Stone's use of the stock system, almost 5 years earlier than the promotion of a similar system at the national level. By 1994, 10% of all nongovernmental enterprises were using the stock system. After 1993, the operations of those enterprises were increasingly specialized and fanned out into marketing, research, sales, and personnel divisions, with a special focus on research and development. The division heads were responsible for day-to-day management decisions and reported to a general oversight office (*zongcai bangongshi*), which in turn reported to the board of directors (*dongshihui*) (Segal 2003, p. 73–6).

The Beijing "Silicon Valley" has promoted nongovernmental high-technology enterprises which are privately owned, responsive to market signals, and technologically competitive. Individual entrepreneurs have been successful in introducing and reproducing the market-based firm's governance structure supportive of technological innovation. Compared with the American Silicon Valley, where 8000 enterprises created an annual turnover of $200 billion, the Beijing Silicon Valley model has also been relatively successful considering its fewer years of development. In Beijing, 4000 nongovernmental high-technology enterprises registered $5.4 billion in terms of annual volume of business in 1999 (Segal 2003, p. 52–86).

3.2.4 Personal Networks Different from the Institutionalized Coordination in Coordinated Market Economies

3.2.4.1 Different from the Nonmarket Coordination in Coordinated Market Economies, Personal Networks in China's Private Sector Are Profit-Oriented and Market-Functioned

3.2.4.1.1 Instrumental Ties Model: Profit-Oriented Personal Networking

Personal networking, also referred to as personal relations or personal connection, expresses the notion of *guanxi* in Chinese and means that individuals connect with each other to facilitate the bilateral flow of transactions. It is assumed that personal networking implies mutual benefits for both parties and that it is decisive for business success (Jacobs et al. 2004). Individuals expect benefits of their engagement in networking because the membership of a network means having access to and being able to mobilize resources which are otherwise not available or only at a higher price (Bourdieu 1986; Coleman 1988; Erickson 1996; Lin 2001; Portes 1998; Jacobs et al. 2004). Subsequently, the personal networking mechanism describes processes by which individuals invest in personal relations in return for a personal benefit. The notion of social capital follows this line of argument when it is claimed that investment in personal relations leads to future returns (Lin 2001; Jacobs et al. 2004).

According to Schlevogt (2001), there is a greater emphasis on traditional Chinese culture (Confucianism) in the Chinese private sector than in the state sector. A Confucianism-influenced cultural environment scores high on the personal relations and performance orientation. Given performance orientation, personal networks can be explained by their instrumental value. Personal networks are exchange networks whose existence and maintenance depend on economic gains that are sufficiently high to make the continuation of the personal relationship worthwhile for all participants. Personal relations will be given up should the returns prove to be too small. "No *guanxi* connection can exist in the absence of utilitarian gains to the Chinese business partner" (Yeung and Tung 1996).

The study by Jacobs et al. (2004) offers evidence for the relevance of the instrumental ties model for the personal networking mechanism in the Chinese private sector. The instrumental ties model predicts that the recruitment of partners follows expected returns in an ongoing cooperation. Trustworthiness and mutual cooperation are seen as decisive factors without which no cooperation rent can be appreciated. The model also predicts that the personal relations in business will be evaluated in terms of the expected overall returns for the participants. Unsatisfactory overall returns will lead to an end of the personal networking (Jacobs et al. 2004).

In forming personal business relations, private entrepreneurs are motivated by economic calculations rather than by sentimental considerations. The instrumental ties model explains the configuration of personal networking in the Chinese private sector better than the sentimental ties model. In the former, mutual trust and mutual cooperation in business relations are coupled with economic calculations. Chinese entrepreneurs indeed consider social factors such as "mutual trust" and "mutual cooperation" to be as important as commercial interests. In particular, utilitarian gains are an essential part of *guanxi* connections in the instrumental ties model of personal business networking, while pure sentimental connections are dismissed as less crucial (Jacobs et al. 2004).

Chinese private firms working in an environment of competition in free markets will dismiss sentimental ties as a way to coordinate their personal networks. In addition to contractual relations and competition in the free markets, private firms engage in personal networking based on the instrumental ties model. In the instrumental ties model, the functional value of networking as assessed by its performance, i.e., expected outcome, is at the core of network formation. Therefore, networking becomes a benefit-oriented business activity. "Rational" behavior, or using an economic calculus, is not a contradiction to Confucianist values, which generally honor performance, as argued above. Overall efficiency can be secured as long as network participants consider networking in terms of performance and see the need for networks to compete for members. It seems that personal networking structures can function as efficiently as market contractual relations (Jacobs 1958).

3.2.4.1.2 Personal Networking for the Pursuit of Market Interest in the Institutional Environment Dominated by Interpersonal Trust

Because the lack of institutionalized trust constrains access to resources for Chinese private firms, entrepreneurs tend to make full use of personal contacts to acquire the initial endowment of a firm and seek full employment of all resources. Personal networking raises the probability of success and the expected level of profits in the new private sector (Krug and Mehta 2004; Krug and Polos 2004; Hendrischke 2004). To gain access to resources, private entrepreneurs need to form personal networks with those economic agents who possess or control the financial and physical assets and the human capital needed for starting production, for securing supply, and for accessing distribution channels (Cheng and Rosett 1991; Nee 1989; Boisot 1995). Personal networks render value to the private entrepreneurs, by reducing the level of risk, identifying profitable opportunities, giving access to resources, and increasing the expected net returns to a venture (Krug and Mehta 2004).

The institutional environment which lacks institutionalized trust also generates a high institutional uncertainty. This can be overcome by forming a personal network with those able to promote and sustain a stable business environment. Thus, private entrepreneurs need to form personal networks with agents of the judiciary, politicians, suppliers, customers, and other important business partners. These kinds of networks can be understood as means of creating and mobilizing the economic, social, and political capital required to lubricate the wheels of a private firm in an environment that is characterized by weak institutionalized trust and a high level of institutional uncertainty.

Networks are furthermore valuable to private entrepreneurs because they offer a trust-generating mechanism and because they reduce search costs. Therefore, networking increases business opportunities by overcoming institutional uncertainty and is a crucial factor in the determination of the level of profits. Private entrepreneurs seek out and tend to form personal networks with those who offer the highest expected returns (Krug and Mehta 2004).

Thus, to compete in an uncertain and volatile business system characterized by weak institutionalized trust and pervasive interpersonal trust, the Chinese private firm uses personal networking to search for partners and to maintain bilateral relations. In all these instances of showing market-induced behaviors and pursuit of self-interests, the firm takes advantage of personal networking and social relations to manage its business environment, with the unwitting consequence of being further constrained by them and of perpetuating institutional continuities (Zhou et al. 2003).

3.2.4.1.3 Market-Functional Personal Networking

The Chinese *guanxi* networks can be seen as assets and may be as crucial for establishing and operating firms as other forms of capital (Krug and Polos 2004).

Managers in Chinese private firms are described as not only in control of resources, technology, and personnel, but are also expected to control external relations with potential market partners and politicians. They need to command social capital, which is based on personal relations with economically valuable partners, and political capital, which is based on personal relations with politicians (Krug and Polos 2004).

Personal networking shows market rationality. Mutual trust and mutual cooperation that are assumed to bind the participants of networking do not, however, bind the network as a whole. The network does not owe loyalty to the individuals beyond what is useful for the network. Social capital can be utilized only within the network that shares it.

The inherent market rationality of the personal network makes it function as a market with the purpose of achieving economic gains and opens it up to competition and efficiency considerations. Therefore, social capital can be invested in and withdrawn from business ventures and will strive for return on investment.

The personal network has to result in social capital becoming an economic benefit for its participants. It therefore functions as a market for social capital. Personal networks are particularistic markets with a limited, albeit flexible, number of participants, defined by the options for entry and exit. Participants gain entry on the basis of their willingness to contribute to social capital, i.e., their willingness to trade useful contacts within the network. Exit from the networks happens by mechanisms of social exclusion, meaning that a member will be excluded when its inability to mobilize network resources is evident. In addition, the network as a market for social capital also helps to explain the low "exit" threshold that characterizes the Chinese private sector (Hendrischke 2004).

Chinese private entrepreneurs build up market-functional personal networks which need to compete (Jacobs et al. 2004). The mutual gains to networking are highest in the presence of a multiplicity of networks, where there is competition between networks. Therefore, individuals as network members have no incentive to see a single network (such as the Mafia) rise to dominance or to limit their allegiance to one single network. According to empirical analysis, no single network has the monopoly on all business transactions, and competition exists between networks (Krug and Mehta 2004).

3.2.4.2 The Personal Network in the Chinese Private Sector Is Different from the Institutionalized Coordination in Coordinated Market Economies

In China's state sector there exist strong state-based economic institutions, while the private sector is characterized by the lack of institutions, and the institutions are not yet depersonalized (Hendrischke 2004). To acquire resources, state enterprises depend on state-based institutions, while private firms lacking institutional links resort to informal personal networks (Zhou et al. 2003).

Unlike the private sector in Japan and continental Europe, the Chinese private sector has a few collective organizations between the family firms, on the one hand, and the government, on the other hand. In this respect, the nature of China's private sector business system is quite different from that in Japan and Europe (Whitley 1999, p. 179).

Because of the lack of secondary institutions that coordinate the relations among private firms, institutionalized trust and cooperation among private firms are generated only at a low level. Private firms emphasize flexibility and the unwillingness to enter into long-term commitments, except on a highly personal basis. The development of business alliances is inhibited by the difficulty in developing trust and mutual commitment. Although *guanxi* networks have been an important informal means of coordination among private firms, they tend to be highly personal, limited in stability, scope, and depth and are much less stable and significant than the interfirm alliances in Japan (Hamilton 1997; Numazaki 1992; Fields 1995; Gerlach 1992). Personal networks are not necessarily long-term-oriented or based on mutual obligations. Rather, personal networks are often managed in a way that helps to reduce risks, which in turn restricts commitments to other networking participants. Exchange partners may be numerous and selected on the basis of their personal competence and reliability. They usually do not form networks of long-term trust and reciprocal loyalty (Redding 1990; Whitley 1999, p. 149). Market relations can change rapidly, and flexibility is usually emphasized over long-term risk-sharing (Hamilton 1997, 1990). As a result, personal networks in China's private sector business system are less permanent and stable than those in Japan because of their little or no long-term commitment. Private firms prefer to develop a personal network with a variety of different partners rather than to become highly dependent on a small number of cooperations (Whitley 1999, p. 172).

3.2.4.3   The Personal Network Acts as an Informal Market-Supporting Institution

In China, governments possess considerable control over the allocation of resources through their control of the state enterprises, which also include state-controlled banks. State enterprises enjoy a preferential status in obtaining bank loans and other key inputs (Che 2002; Brandt and Li 2003; Li et al. 2006). Private businesses can, however, not fully rely on the markets to secure resources (Li et al. 2006, p. 560–4). Chinese private entrepreneurs have therefore been relying on the informal personal network as a kind of market-supporting institution. They form personal networks with politicians and important business partners such as suppliers, customers, and banks.

Political connections help private firms to secure favorable regulatory or tax conditions and to obtain access to resources, e.g., bank loans, which ultimately increase the value of the firms (Li et al. 2006, p. 560–5).

To alleviate information problems, many private entrepreneurs establish a personal relationship with a bank. According to the survey in IFC (International Finance

Corporation) (2000, p. 55), about 70% of the sample firms said that not having a good relationship with a bank minimized their chances of getting a loan. They therefore had to make an effort to form a tie with a bank. Half of the sample firms resorted to the informal market to finance their venture. Personal ties which form a closely knit network are also important in the financing in the informal market.

Private entrepreneurs also form personal networks with business partners to have stable trading relationships. According to the survey in IFC (International Finance Corporation) (2000, p. 29) and the study by Garnaut et al. (2001, p. 49), 84% of the companies in the CEO survey had stable suppliers, and 85% had stable customers. For the stable customers, 21% of the companies said that their customers were introduced by friends or family members, 19% said their customers were friends, and 3% said their business partners were family members; therefore, about 43% of the companies had some prior direct or indirect connection to their customers. For the stable suppliers, 24% said their partners were introduced by friends and family members and 10% said their partners were their friends; therefore, 34% of the companies had some connection to their suppliers. Private entrepreneurs can also establish business connections through their own marketing efforts. Around half of the private entrepreneurs establish ties with their business partners gradually through their own market efforts.

However, private firms also rely heavily on the "faceless" market to find customers and suppliers and to find greater opportunity to trade at arm's length with customers and suppliers (Garnaut et al. 2001, p. 49; IFC (International Finance Corporation) 2000, p. 62). For example, there is a quite efficient market for the supply of machinery and raw material for private firms, with no discernible intervention by the governmental agencies. Private firms freely choose their suppliers and set prices. Suppliers are found through market opportunities, and transactions take place through an on-the-spot exchange (Child and Pleister 2004).

The figures given above provide considerable insight into the role of personal networks in a private firm's market operations. Personal networking becomes as important as informal market-supporting institutions for private entrepreneurs. Private firms like to have a combination of the opportunities of the market and market-supporting networks (Garnaut et al. 2001, p. 49).

3.2.4.4   The Business Associations in the Chinese Private Sector Act as Market-Supporting Institutions

The business associations in China include those that initially recruited broadly among enterprises and industrial associations (IAs). In the former category are the China Enterprise Management Association (CEMA), which only recruits among state enterprises, and the All-China Federation of Industry and Commerce (ACFIC), which predominantly recruits private firms. The business associations in the Chinese private sector act as government agents and market-supporting institutions and are different from the associations for institutional coordination found in coordinated market economies.

The business associations in China are normally under government control. Almost all business associations are required to register and be affiliated with a government agency, and most of them have been founded by some branch of the government. The primary goal of the government when it set up associations was to have them assist in its regulation of the economy (Kennedy 2003). Most business associations in China are relatively underdeveloped. Both state and private enterprises primarily try to influence government policy through direct contacts rather than through associations. Chinese associations lack "restraining power" (*yuesuli*) over their members and are regarded as "not of much use" by their members, in contrast to the coordinating strength of associations in Japan and Europe (Kennedy 2003). Thus, Chinese business associations in the private sector actually act as government agents and market-supporting institutions, offering business-related help to private firms.

The All-China Federation of Industry and Commerce (ACFIC), now known as the China General Chamber of Commerce (CGCC), was established in 1950s as a (quasi) nongovernmental organization to represent the interests of the industrial and commercial business in China. It is a member of the Chinese People's Political Consultative Conference (CPPCC). The CGCC became the "new face" of the ACFIC in 1993, with the objective of serving better the emerging nonstate enterprises. The ACFIC defined its original objective as the "unification of all political fronts"; the new objective is to shift the emphasis more toward economic activities and nonstate enterprises. Members of the CGCC are predominantly private enterprises and individually owned enterprises (*getihu*). It has an extensive network of local chambers of commerce (LCs) throughout the country (Asian Development Bank 2003, p. 44). The CGCC and LCs act as a bridge between the private sector and the government and provide a wide range of services to its members (IFC (International Finance Corporation) 2000, p. 33), such as to nominate members to the CPPCC and People's Congress and to propose bills to the People's Congress to promote the interests of its members; to effect liaison with government officials on policies affecting nonstate business development; to organize economic events such as trade fairs, exhibitions, technology exchanges, training, and some fostering networking events; to support linkages between Chinese and foreign companies in economic and technological cooperation and trade; and to disseminate information on government policies, markets, new technology, etc. (Asian Development Bank 2003, p. 44–9). As the survey by the Asian Development Bank (2003, p. 26) indicates, private firms report positively on their interaction with CGCC and its LCs. They regard the CGCC and LCs as important sources of information, especially about government policies (for 85% of the surveyed firms) and markets (70%), and to a lesser extent about technology and clients, suppliers, or other important business partners; fewer than one firm in six also received information about financial services. Private firms also receive services from the CGCC and LCs, such as coordination with governments (63% of the survey firms) and commercial consultancy (14%). Some firms view LCs as potential sources for training and as help in dealing with governments.

As mentioned above, there are also IAs in China. Private firms consult the IAs for information on markets (predominantly), competitors, technology, financial services, and government policies. Private firms also receive services from the IAs, like commercial consultancy, training, and coordination with the government (Asian Development Bank 2003, p. 26; Child and Pleister 2004). IAs have played a significant role in helping firms exchange technical information and obtain technology-related consultations as well as setting national technical standards. Like the CGCC and LCs, IAs also served as vehicle for private firms to establish business relations. Because most of the IAs are dominated by state enterprises, private firms which produce intermediate products used by state firms find it helpful to join IAs. Through association contacts, they hope to find opportunities for forming a network with the larger firms and for subcontracting from the larger firms (Garnaut et al. 2001, p. 125; IFC (International Finance Corporation) 2000, p. 29).

Another official association for private firms is the Association of Private Firms. It is organized by the local Bureau of Industry and Commerce Management (BICM). Private firms have to join this association, and the BICM collects the membership fee. Oftentimes, the president of the Association of Private Firms is a deputy director of BICM. Most private firms regard the association as "not of much use" to them (Garnaut et al. 2001, p. 127; IFC (International Finance Corporation) 2000, p. 33).

3.2.4.5   Business Groups in the Chinese Private Sector: No Coordination Links All Member Firms Together

In the Chinese private sector, there are small groups of private firms (Fields 1995; Keister 2000, p. 68). Unlike in Chinese state enterprise groups, in which the state plays an active role in forming and maintaining business groups, private groups are more distant from the state. Private business groups tend to be more predominant in industries with a high proportion of private firms, that is, the groups are most common in low-technology and light-industry sectors (Keister 2000, p. 68–72).

The small groups formed voluntarily among businesses that were typically individual-based, family-based, or run by individuals with personal relations. It follows that the ownership and control of private business groups are in the hands of individuals, families, or groups of individuals tied by personal relations. Relations among private firms in the business groups include ownership relations, financing relations, trade relations, and joint production relations. The interfirm relations in private business groups tend to be informal, that is, groups lack a formal group-wide management system (Keister 2000, p. 68–9). In these business groups, firms tend to be organizationally separate from other firms, with each having a distinct management structure. Business groups have no formal unified management organization that links all the firms together. Each firm has a person who formally occupies the position of the manager. These firm managers are seldom linked into a larger formal management structure beyond the firms. Therefore, the day-to-day management of the firms is separated from the actual control of the group. Management is defined as a low-level activity and remains distinct from the control right and long-term decision-making affecting individual firms or the group. Control and decision-making are in the hands of the owners and of those in the inner circle. That control is kept by individual owners or by inner-circle groups of individuals lessens the possibility of a challenge to their centrality. Therefore, management tends to be formal and localized in each firm but not to be integrated through a group-wide management, whereas control and decision-making tend to be informal and to span the firms (Hamilton 1990, p. 144–7).

Thus, the private business group structure in China is different from that in Japan. In Japan, the predominant form of ownership in business groups is mutual shareholding among firms. There are no clear patterns of dominance among the major firms in the groups, but rather a mutuality of interests. Formal coordination links all the member firms together (Hamilton 1990, p. 143).

3.2.4.6 Summarizing the Nature of Networking in the Chinese Private Sector

In China, a business relation between private firms results from a combination of market relations and personal networks. Personal networks in China are different from the institutionalized coordination in interfirm networks in coordinated market economies because personal networks are benefit-oriented and function like a market with competition within and among networks. Such market-oriented networking is based on rational behavior and economic calculation. CGCC and other business associations are more like government-based market-supporting institutions, in contrast to the intermediate institutions in coordinated market economies which play a coordination role.

Personal networks in the business system where owner-managed firms dominate, like in the Chinese private sector, are different from institutional-coordination-based interfirm networks in business systems where alliance-controlled firms dominate, like in Japan and Germany. In comparing these two types of interfirm relations, the crucial issue is the extent to which economic activities are consciously and repeatedly coordinated on the basis of long-term organizational commitments. The personal networks in an owner-managed-firm-dominated business system, like in the Chinese private sector, do not imply such a high level of coordination based on long-term organizational commitments because they tend to be quite narrowly focused and based on personal relations. They also do not dominate the economy as their Japanese counterparts do (Hamilton 1990; Numazaki 1992). Such organizational coordination of activities and resources in the case of Chinese private sector business system is much weaker than in interfirm networks in Japan and Germany (Whitley 1999, p. 37–8).

Business groups in an owner-managed-firm-dominated business system differ from Japanese business groups in the extent of coordination between member firms.

In the business groups of the fragmented business system in the Chinese private sector, firms tend to be organizationally separate from other firms, have no formal unified management organization, and no coordination which links all the member firms together as in Japan (Hamilton 1990).

3.2.5   The Chinese Private Sector Is Not Supportive for Coordinated Industrial Districts

3.2.5.1   Market Competition Dominates the Chinese Private Sector

The Chinese private sector exemplifies a *fragmented business system*: it is not locked in an institutionalized coordinated production system, but primarily relies on the market mechanism.

On the basis of the analysis in the preceding part of the governance structure of Chinese private firms, it can be stated that the Chinese private sector is not characterized by an institutionalized coordinated production system, as in continental European countries and Japan. Namely, it differs in terms of employer–employee relations, interfirm relations, and firm's performance criteria, core competitiveness, and innovation system. Chinese private firms take advantage of the market mechanism to support the rapid growth of the private sector (Child and Pleister 2004).

The Chinese private sector encourages entrepreneurship, market competition, market-oriented business, and market-oriented institutional changes (Song 2004). Market competition among private firms is high (IFC (International Finance Corporation) 2000, p. 30). Among the sample firms in a survey (Garnaut et al. 2001, p. 46), 97% said the market competition in the private sector is intense and fierce. The sample firms in another survey (Asian Development Bank 2003, p. 37) also described the Chinese private sector as highly competitive. For a private firm, intense competition in the product markets, the capital markets, and the labor markets threatens at any time the subsistence of the firm. Bankruptcy, merger, acquisition, and other market mechanisms put pressure on the entrepreneurs. All these factors provide incentives and constraints for entrepreneurs in the private sector with a market-based firm's governance structure (Chen and Huang 2001). Market competition and market incentives that promote allocative efficiency and technological innovation have been primary factors in stimulating the emergence of an efficient and dynamic private sector, and they will continue to be needed to ensure the health of the market-based firm's governance structure in the Chinese private sector (Wang 2004b; Asian Development Bank 2003, p. 24).

In the Chinese private sector, atomistic private firms, fierce competition, and low thresholds for entry and exit characterize an almost neoclassical perfect competitive market, resulting in a fragmented business system. Those traits also make for a sharp contrast with the highly coordinated Chinese state sector (Schlevogt 2001) as well as the institutional coordinated industrial arrangements in continental European countries and Japan, as well as *coordinated industrial districts* (Whitley 1999).

3.2.5.2   The Business Environment of the Chinese Private Sector Suits a Fragmented Business System Rather than a Coordinated Industrial District

As Whitley (1999) mentioned, owner-controlled firms dominate in both the fragmented business system and the coordinated industrial district. This raises the question: Why is the Chinese private sector a fragmented business system rather than a coordinated industrial district system? Here, the ownership structure is not the only determining factor. The business environment of the specific business system is another determinative factor. The business environment of the Chinese private sector suits a fragmented business system rather than a coordinated industrial district. This can help to explain why the Chinese private sector is a fragmented business system rather than a coordinated industrial district, given that both of the business systems are dominated by owner-controlled firms.

The fragmented business system is dominated by owner-controlled firms that engage in market competition and short-term market contracting. The employment relations are short-term and dominated by external labor markets. In these business systems, the organizational integration of business activities is low for both intrafirm and interfirm. Low risk-sharing by firms with business partners and with employees is associated with short-term commitments to particular sectors or markets. That firms shift rapidly from one business to another exemplifies a low-commitment business system (Whitley 1999, p. 43).

Coordinated industrial district business systems, which are dominated by small owner-controlled firms, combine low levels of ownership integration with a more extensive interfirm integration and cooperation (Whitley 1999, p. 41). Such business systems exhibit a more organized integration of inputs and outputs within the production chains as well as a more sectoral cooperation. Firms remain small and owner-controlled, but rely on worker commitment to improve task performance and innovation. These kinds of business systems are exemplified by some European regional business systems, such as the postwar Italian industrial districts and Danish machinery firms, and some regional business systems in Japan, such as the machine-tool industry in Sakaki Township (Whitley 1999, p. 43, 84). We can get a clearer picture of the coordinated industrial districts when we compare them with the fragmented business system (see Table 3.13).

The fragmented business system, where opportunistic firms dominate, develops in a *particularistic* business environment with atomistic private firms, fierce competition, and low level of institutionalized coordination. The markets are weakly regulated. Trade unions and other associations are weak and bargaining is highly decentralized. Institutionalized coordination tends to be low and risks are difficult to share. The authority in businesses is concentrated in the hands of the private business owners. The organizational integration and the collective competences in such a business system are limited (Whitley 1999, p. 59–87).

Coordinated industrial districts are more organizationally integrated business systems where artisanal firms dominate. They develop in more supportive business

Table 3.13 Comparison of the characteristics of the fragmented business system with coordinated industrial districts

Business-system characteristics	Business-system type	
	Fragment	Coordinated industrial district
Ownership coordination		
Owner control	Direct	Direct
Nonownership coordination		
Alliance coordination of production chains	Low	Limited
Collaboration between competitors	Low	Some
Alliance coordination of sectors	Low	Low
Employment relations		
Employer–employee interdependence	Low	Some
Delegation to employees	Low	Some

From Whitley (1999, p. 42)

environments, that is, *collaborative* business environments, where institutional arrangements for managing uncertainty and trust are more strongly established and encourage collaboration between the economic actors. In other words, coordinated industrial districts normally develop and continue to be reproduced in the localities where institutions limit opportunism and provide a business infrastructure for collaboration to occur (Whitley 1999, p. 84; Friedman 1988; Kristensen 1992, 1996). Local governments work with local public institutions and local labor representation to restrict an adversarial price-based competition, to develop innovation strategies which are in favor of high-quality. Market regulation at the local level limits both firm entry and large customer attempts to enforce cost reductions and price competition, so that large firms cannot drive artisanal firms out on the basis of price, and customers cannot drive down prices so far that artisanal firms would be unable to compete on the basis of high quality related innovation (Whitley 1999, p. 59–84). Strong unions were also an important institutional feature in such an institutional environment. They ensure that employers have to compete on the basis of innovation and improvements to products rather than by reducing their wage costs. Coordinated industrial districts, which are dominated by artisanal firms, require a more trusting institutional environment than is experienced by the fragmented business system, which is dominated by opportunistic firms. The institutional infrastructure that generates trust between employers and employees and between the business partners, and that limits short-term opportunism, is important for artisanal firms to be able to pursue their strategic advantages through long-term commitments, continuing improvements, and innovations (Whitley 1999, p. 84–5). The collaboration between business partners and between employers and employees is also enhanced by the predominance of institutionalized authority relations in businesses (Whitley 1999, p. 62). This is different from the personal authority in businesses which is prevalent in the fragmented business system.

Therefore, the business environment of the fragmented business system, where opportunistic firms dominate, is different from that of the coordinated industrial

Table 3.14 Comparison of business environments associated with the fragmented business system and coordinated industrial districts

		Types of business system	
		Fragmented	Coordinated industrial district
Market regulation	The state control	Low	Considerable locally
	Strength of market regulation	Low	Considerable locally
Unions and bargaining systems	Union strength	Low	High
	Centralization of bargaining	Low	Considerable locally
	Strength of public training system	Low	High
Coordination and authority in businesses	Institutionalized coordination	Low	Some
	Personal authority	High	Limited
	Institutionalized authority	Low	Some
General	Typical business environment	Particularistic	Locally collaborative

From Whitley (1999, p. 60)

district, where artisanal firms dominate, as Whitley (1999) described. We further compare the differences between the two in Table 3.14.

On the basis of the analysis of the Chinese private sector, the business environment of the Chinese private sector is a particularistic business environment; thus, it offers the institutional context for supporting the fragmented business system rather than a coordinated industrial district.

3.2.5.3   The Wenzhou Case: The Chinese Private Sector Cannot Support the Forms of Coordination Typical for Industrial Districts

Being a fragmented business system with low trust, the Chinese private sector cannot support coordinated industrial districts. The Wenzhou case study illustrates this. After it had been arranged as a kind of coordinated industrial district for a short time, the family-based firms in Wenzhou transformed into joint-stock cooperatives with direct ownership arrangements and further developed into limited liability companies and joint-stock companies, showing the replacement of the specific markets by the vertically integrated enterprises with their in-home marketing.

Wenzhou is a prefecture-level municipality located in the southeast of Zhejiang province. The economic achievement of Wenzhou is the most impressive among the prefectures in China. From 1978 to 1997, the municipal GDP increased from 1.3 billion yuan to 60.5 billion yuan, and the annual per capita income of rural residents increased from 113.5 yuan to 3,700 yuan. These growth rates are more than double the national average and have been dominantly created by the private sector (People's Daily 1999; Sun 2003). The family as an entrepreneurial core for the development of private enterprises was the core element of the propaganda for the Wenzhou model (Liu 1992; Hendrischke 2004). Wenzhou became a much-celebrated city on a national scale because of its success in the development and flourishing of private enterprises, and family-based enterprises in particular (Hendrischke 2004). Since 1978, the development of the private sector in Wenzhou has gone through three stages: first scattered household businesses (1978–1992); then privately owned economy + specific markets (1993–1997); and then the formation of joint-stock cooperatives and corporations (from 1998 up to now) (Sun 2000, 2003; Wang and Shi 2007).

3.2.5.3.1 The First Stage: Scattered Household Businesses

In the late 1970s, as a component of the reform initiative, national policy on household manufacture and commerce was relaxed. Household industries and trade started to grow very rapidly in Wenzhou (Sun 2003).

3.2.5.3.2 The Second Stage: Privately Owned Businesses + Specific Markets

In this stage, the development strategy of Wenzhou was designed to aim for a coordinated industrial district. As of April 1985, the number of family firms in the industrial sector in Wenzhou amounted to 133,000. The development strategy could be summarized as "family firms, small commodities, specific markets, industrial clubbing districts," that is to say, Wenzhou chose the way of industrial clustering and the construction of specific markets to develop its family firms and to produce "small commodities." The term "small commodities" refers to those commodities with a small scale of production, a limited technology content, and lower costs of transport. The Wenzhou privately owned economy has focused on labor-intensive industries like the construction and manufacturing industries, including stationery, textiles, clothing, food, metal signs, plastic, general machinery manufacturing; and traditional tertiary industries like commerce, transportation, restaurants, logistic, and social services. Centering on numerous specific markets, family-based industrial plants developed into industrial clusters. Such industrial clusters were formed with regionally centralized clubbing of the same industries. Specific markets deepened industrial collaboration and stimulated the development of industrial clusters into industrial clubbing districts. These specific markets and the industrial collaboration formed the basis of industrial clubbing districts in Wenzhou (Wang and Shi 2007).

Except for the specific markets in this development stage, horizontal integration was employed. The development of scattered household businesses was severely constrained by their disadvantages in product marketing, input material search, license application and approval, and in the establishment of commercial trust and reputation. Meanwhile, the government monitoring of numerous household businesses in terms of license qualification and qualification control was too onerous. To solve these difficulties, horizontal integration was initiated. Under this arrangement, household firms attached themselves to an established larger enterprise, paying a fee for the use of its brands, stationery, bank account numbers, and receipt books, while household firms still kept their own property rights independently. Taxes were collected from the established bigger enterprises rather than from these attached household firms. Local governments delegated monitoring rights to the established bigger firms and obtained more administrative control over these previously scattered household businesses. At that time more than 60% of household firms joined this kind of horizontal integration. At the same time, such horizontal integration was still dependent on the specific market mechanism (Sun 2003; Wang and Shi 2007).

Specific markets with horizontal integration characterized the Wenzhou industrial clubbing districts in the second stage of development, which was termed "privately owned economy + specific markets." The specific markets provided a platform for lower transaction costs for a more specialized industrial division of labor. Compared with the way in which every family-based industrial plant invests in establishing in-home marketing networks, the practice of family firms to circulate their products in specific markets was to reduce the transaction cost, thereby improving the depth of industrial collaboration and division of labor (Wang and Shi 2007).

3.2.5.3.3 The Third Stage: Positive Replacement of Specific Markets by Vertically Integrated Enterprises

In the institutional environment of the fragmented business system with low trust, the uncertainty of transactions and the transaction costs are relatively high. Thus, the third stage of the Wenzhou industrial development demonstrated that the fragmented business system could not sustain the further development of the Wenzhou industrial clubbing district, which was supposed to be similar to the coordinated industrial district.

With the expansion of the scope and the explosion of the production scale of private enterprises, the volume of product transactions and transaction frequencies increases rapidly, which in Wenzhou's low-trust institutional environment led inevitably to a dramatic increase in transaction costs. Even the specific markets could not lead to lower transaction costs. As long as the private enterprises continued to expand their scale of production and business operation, the transaction costs in the specific markets for product distribution and sale became higher than for in-home marketing networks. Therefore, the private enterprises tended to establish in-home sales and marketing networks to lower the transaction costs. Accordingly, many bigger private enterprises have withdrawn from specific markets and established their in-home marketing networks, to reduce the transaction costs and attain market competitive advantages and to gain higher shares of local and national markets. This positive replacement of specific markets by enterprises with in-home marketing networks weakened the functions of specific markets and led to deterioration of their status (Wang and Shi 2007).

In such a low-trust institutional environment, the horizontal integration as described above also easily resulted in friction among the different property owners. The transaction costs of corporation collaboration increased very rapidly (Sun 2003; Wang and Shi 2007). The established bigger enterprises became increasingly interested in predatory rent maximization and less in effective services, which led to a dispute between them and the small household firms. Attached household firms behaved opportunistically to maximize their own profit at the cost of the business reputation of the established bigger enterprises. Products with poor quality and fake brand names produced by these business affiliation firms gave a bad reputation to all Wenzhou's firms. As a consequence, local governments started to reorganize the small household firms (Sun 2000).

Local governments encouraged the establishment of joint-stock cooperatives based on spontaneous initiations of joint-stock cooperation of household and small private firms (Sun 2000, 2003). The ownership arrangement of joint-stock cooperatives emerged and developed very fast in Wenzhou. In 1997, the number of joint-stock cooperatives in Wenzhou reached about 43,000, of which about 31,000 were industrial firms that produced about 86 billion yuan of output, accounting for over 70% of the city's total industrial output (Li 1997; People's Daily 1999). The arrangement of joint-stock cooperatives had obvious cost–benefit advantages, compared with the arrangement of specific markets with horizontal integration, which is characteristic for the fragmented business system, with a low-trust institutional environment. The disputes over the issue of sharing residual benefits and residual control rights between the established bigger enterprises and the attached household firms disappeared for a joint-stock cooperative. The previous quasi-market arrangement for sharing residual benefits and residual control rights was replaced by a direct ownership arrangement, the distribution of residual benefits was well defined by shares, and the exercise of residual control rights became better matched with the residual benefit rights, resulting in a significant reduction of transaction costs. The joint-stock form also created a legal position of private firms and economies of scale in terms of capital, production, and marketing (Sun 2003).

About 90% of the joint-stock cooperatives in Wenzhou originated from the voluntary joint-stock cooperation of private and household firms. Joint-stock cooperatives in Wenzhou had been dominated by management joint-stock ownership and employee joint-stock ownership, in which there was no community share or collective share. The joint-stock cooperative ownership arrangement can easily transform into a limited liability company and joint-stock company along with the expansion of the firm. Especially, the management joint-stock ownership made it easy for joint-stock cooperatives to transform themselves into limited liability companies and joint-stock companies. In 1997, 6738 joint-stock cooperatives with management ownership restructured themselves into limited liability companies and joint-stock companies. At the same time, in many employee joint-stock cooperatives, the tendency of increasing the concentration of shares owned by the managers had continued. In 1997 there were in total 10,868 limited liability companies and

15 joint-stock companies in Wenzhou. More and more joint-stock companies in Wenzhou had grown out of joint-stock cooperatives and had become limited liability companies (Sun 2003).

As we described above, the joint-stock form increased the size, economic scope, and economic scale of private enterprises, which in turn started to shift their marketing from the specific markets to in-home marketing networks to lower transaction costs. Horizontal integration of product specialization had also been transformed into vertical integration within enterprises. These enlarged enterprises integrated the specialized division of production, design, services, transportation, marketing, etc. The joint-stock cooperative ownership arrangement and vertical integration not only brought about the size expansion of enterprises and the development of modern corporations, but also meant the replacement of specific markets by vertically integrated enterprises (Wang and Shi 2007).

3.2.5.3.4 An Empirical Proof of the Replacement of Specific Markets by Enterprises: The Failure of the Development of Liushi Electrical Equipment Clusters in Wenzhou

In the early 1990s, the Liushi electrical industry was composed of family plants and specific markets. A rapid expansion of specific markets for low-voltage electrical equipment favored the growth of production and marketing in the Liushi electrical industry. Within a few years, more than 1400 electrical equipment manufacturers had clubbed together in 12 km^2 in Liushi town around this specific market; its volume of transaction and value of production were more than one-third of the national electrical equipment markets (Wang and Shi 2007).

From the end of 1996, the Liushi electrical industry started to experience the replacement of specific markets by vertically integrated enterprises. Small private firms integrated into joint-stock cooperatives to enlarge their economic scale and scope. These reorganized enterprises were big enough to have their own nationwide internal marketing networks. They therefore established in-home sales and marketing networks to reduce transaction costs, instead of trusting specific markets in the low-trust institutional environment. They no longer depended on specific markets to provide a platform for their product marketing. The transactions in the specific markets declined dramatically. By 1998, the level of transactions declined to only 10% of all transactions of the private enterprises in the Liushi electrical industry (Wang and Shi 2007).

3.3   Privatized SOEs, Collectives, and TVEs Converge to Direct Owner-Controlled Firms

3.3.1   Privatized SOEs Converge to Direct Owner-Controlled Firms

3.3.1.1   The Privatization of Small and Medium-Sized SOEs

Since the early 1990s, the focus of the Chinese SOE reform has shifted from delegation of the decision-making authority to the reform of ownership and corporate governance (Xu et al. 2005). From 1994, the Chinese government started to adopt the policy of "Keeping the large and letting go of the small" (*zhuada fangxiao*) (Chiu and Lewis 2006, p. 66). On the basis of this policy, two strategies have been adopted: corporatization and privatization. The aim of corporatization is to turn large SOEs from sole state ownership into modern corporations with a Western-style corporate governance structure without serious erosion of the dominant state ownership (Xu et al. 2005). The aim of privatization is to effectively privatize the small and medium-sized SOEs through selling, auctioning, merging, and bankruptcy (Chiu and Lewis 2006, p. 66). About 80% of firms owned by the governments at the county or lower administrative level had been privatized and put into the private sector (IFC (International Finance Corporation) 2000, p. 14). However, criticism about the loss of state assets tempered the government's enthusiasm for privatization. Some localities either stopped privatizing enterprises or lowered the profile of their privatization program. Despite the amendment in 1999 that gave the private sector legitimacy, privatization continued at a modest pace. The Chinese government places more emphasis on encouraging the development of the private sector than on privatizing the SOEs (Garnaut and Song 2004a, p. 93).

The privatization of small and medium-sized SOEs had taken a variety of forms. Except for mergers and bankruptcy (Chiu and Lewis 2006, p. 68), the other main forms are the following:

- *Open sale*. This form of privatization has been popular (Garnaut et al. 2005b, p. 50). Some SOEs have been sold directly to outsiders—individuals or private firms. Some SOEs have been sold to insiders—a management group. Since the 15th National Congress, such direct sales have become politically more acceptable. Progress in social security reform has also made it less difficult to sell SOEs to private owners (Tenev et al. 2002, p. 29). This is the most radical form of privatization because it involves transferring the firm's ownership to a single private owner or a management group (Garnaut et al. 2005a, p. 50).
- *Liquidation*. Liquidation is used to transfer ownership rights over physical assets such as land, buildings, and equipment to private owners (Tenev et al. 2002, p. 30).
- *Leases*. The lease contract commonly used in privatization is different from that adopted in the early years of the SOE reform. The early leases acted as incentives within the SOEs, but leases used later is to break up and privatize

SOEs. The lessee is a legal entity independent of the government. Some lessees are outsiders, while others are former managers or employees who have set up new companies and lease the buildings, land, and equipment from former SOEs. Leasing is adopted in cases where the lessee does not have enough money to buy the firm. It is another radical form of privatization (Garnaut et al. 2005b, p. 50).

- *Joint-stock cooperatives*. Conversion of SOEs into joint-stock cooperatives has been the most prevalent modality in privatization (OECD 2000, p. 57). In this case, the SOE shares are mostly sold to the employees, and thus the former SOE is transformed into a joint-stock cooperative (Chiu and Lewis 2006, p. 68; Tenev et al. 2002, p. 30; OECD 2000, p. 57).

3.3.1.2 Two Waves of Privatization: From Employee Ownership to Management Buyout

Privatization has occurred in two waves. It started in the mid-1990s and followed the model of employee shareholding adopted by Zhucheng. When Zhucheng abandoned this model and moved toward concentrated ownership through management buy-outs, other cities followed suit. The trend reflected the belief that it is necessary for the management to own the majority of shares in order for it to truly privatize an enterprise. Management buyout has been the most common form in the second wave of privatization (Garnaut et al. 2005a, p. 4).

3.3.1.2.1 The First Wave

During 1995–1998, in the early stages of privatization, joint-stock cooperatives were formed with employees as the most important shareholders (Tenev et al. 2002, p. 34; Chiu and Lewis 2006, p. 68). Most of the privatized enterprises emerged as 100% employee owned. Shares were widely dispersed throughout the firm (Tenev et al. 2002, p. 34; Garnaut et al. 2005b, p. 49). The shareholding of the senior management was relatively high and on average amounted to 20–30% of all employee shares. In a number of enterprises, top managers were able to amass significant blocks of shares, in some cases exceeding 50% of all shares. Overall, in this early period of privatization, the ownership structure was characterized by a significant dispersion of ownership (Tenev et al. 2002, p. 35).

For a firm to be registered as a limited liability company, the maximum number of shareholders should be less than 50, as stipulated by the Company Law. Firms with a larger number of shareholders, but which cannot meet the requirements for a joint-stock company, can become employee shareholding cooperatives. Shareholding cooperatives have been an innovative mechanism for the privatization of small and medium-sized SOEs in China (Garnaut et al. 2005a, p. 49).

The preference given to employee ownership in the early period of privatization reflected a number of factors: financial problems, which made direct sales difficult; de facto control by insiders, acquired during the process of enterprise reform; and political feasibility, which emphasized that the social impact of privatization should be less severe. Employee shareholding therefore satisfied three constraints: the government official's fear of making political mistakes, the manager's fear of losing power, and the workers' fear of losing jobs (Tenev et al. 2002, p. 30–2).

Because of employee ownership in the privatized enterprises, the channels through which shareholders/employees could monitor the senior management increased and were institutionalized. Despite some positive changes in enterprise behavior following the first wave of privatization, serious issues emerged in relation to incentive and governance practice (Tenev et al. 2002, p. 36). According to Tenev et al. (2002), the surveyed firms reported the prevalence of a short-term outlook, manifested by excessive dividend distribution accompanied by a lack of direct links between profitability and income growth. As a result, firms were unable to accumulate sufficient resources for long-term development. A common phenomenon among privatized enterprises was an excessive distribution of dividends in the early period of privatization. Well-performing privatized firms distributed all their profits in the form of dividends. Even though the dividend distribution began to slow down after shareholders had recouped their initial investments because of government intervention and deteriorating performance, wages continued to increase and remained significantly higher than before the privatization. In the privatized enterprises in Zhucheng, for example, dividends amounted to around 25% of employees' average annual salaries, and total incomes were about 2.4 times as much as before the privatization, without a corresponding increase in enterprise profitability.

Once shareholding employees had recouped their initial investments, their incentives to monitor the company's performance were reduced. Given the diffused ownership structure, employees were not motivated to spend the time and effort to inform themselves about factors affecting enterprise performance. Ordinary shareholding employees felt that their influence on the enterprise's decision-making was limited. Employees seemed to view their shareholder rights primarily as a tool for enhancing their job security. The privatized enterprises did not lay off staff and reduce overall employment during the early period of privatization. The diffused ownership structure was inconsistent with the actual distribution of power and control over key resources. For example, in some enterprises human capital was concentrated in a few key managers and technical personnel. Without control rights these employees had the incentive to withdraw these key resources and quit the enterprise.

The process of ownership transformation in employee shareholding cooperatives failed to produce a radical change in the relationship between enterprises and the government, despite some positive changes. Local governments retained some key powers that should have been transferred to the new owners. Surveyed enterprises presented numerous examples of government behavior inconsistent with the autonomy of a privatized enterprise. For example, the local government retained the right to appoint the enterprises' top management, policies on taxable salaries and dividends were under the direct control of the local governments, and local governments continued to act as arbitrators in the case of internal conflicts.

Thus, the low ownership concentration affected the efficiency of the decision-making process and caused problems like low management efficiency, missed business opportunities, and government intervention. Giving controlling ownership rights to the management, who have the power to withhold key resources, is one way of ensuring the continued existence of such enterprises. And for such an enterprise to be truly privatized, it is necessary for the management to own the majority of shares (Zingales 2000; Tenev et al. 2002, p. 36–9).

3.3.1.2.2 The Second Wave

Because of the aforementioned governance problems, the employee ownership structure was not conducive to the long-term development prospects of transformed enterprises. The solution lies in the concentration of ownership and further ownership transformation should be initiated to move in that direction. In contrast with earlier reforms, the driving force behind the second wave of privatization was the management (Tenev et al. 2002, p. 39). From 1998, in the second wave of privatization, actions were taken to increase the concentration of shares in the top management, through the purchase of old shares by the management from workers or the issue of shares (Chiu and Lewis 2006, p. 68). Managers have been able to buy a larger number of shares in the privatized firms. Some privatized firms have gone through second and third rounds of ownership transformation, further increasing the number of shares owned by managers (Garnaut et al. 2005a, p. 49).

The second wave of privatization resulted in ownership concentration—a higher concentration of ownership by the management through management buyouts, and in some cases the introduction of outside investors (Tenev et al. 2002, p. 39). Thus, the model that evolved, and which is now commonly employed, is concentrated managerial ownership of the privatized firm (Chiu and Lewis 2006, p. 68). On the basis of this model, privatized small and medium-sized SOEs converge to truly owner-managed private firms.

3.3.1.2.3 The Case of Shunde's Two Waves of Privatization

Shunde city began its privatization program in 1992, and it tried to maintain collective ownership and adopted employee shareholding as the main form of ownership transformation. Several problems were encountered with this form of privatization. First, employees might not purchase shares either because of insufficient money or because of insufficient faith in the firm's future. Second, the manager in an employee-held firm still played the role of an agent, and the firm still faced the monitoring problem experienced by state and collective firms. Third, free-riding was also a problem because workers could receive dividends from shares irrespective of the firms' performance. Fourth, uniform shareholding could not help to establish authority within a firm and could not help to solve a privatized firm's internal incentive problems (Garnaut et al. 2001, p. 22–96).

As a result, Shunde shifted to other forms of privatization after this initial experience, including listing on the stock market, management leasing, and management buyout. Two Shunde firms, Midea and Kelong, have been listed in the stock market in Shenzhen. Some firms were sold to a listed firm in another city.

Management leasing was used for firms with a large amount of net assets where the management did not have enough funds to buy it. In the cases of management leasing, the management purchased the equipment and leased the land and buildings from the local government.

Management buyout was the most important form of this second wave of privatization. Many firms that initially had been reorganized as employee shareholdings were truly privatized via management buyout, leading to the concentration of shares in the hands of the top management (Garnaut et al. 2001, p. 22, 96). They converged to effective owner-managed private firms.

3.3.2 Privatized Collectives Converge to Direct Owner-Controlled Firms

Another important development in the Chinese private sector was the transformation of a large number of collectives (including TVEs) into private enterprises or joint-stock companies (Song 2004).

3.3.2.1 About Collectives

Collective enterprises in China were collectively owned by local communities and local governments (Tian 2000). Many collective firms had been performing poorly and had faced problems similar to those of the SOEs, such as local government intervention and inefficient management (Song 2004). In the following, the transitional forms of collective enterprises will be discussed, that is, rented collectives, "red hat" collectives, and TVE collectives.

3.3.2.1.1　Rented Collectives

Many collective firms were rented out for private operation, encouraged by local governments in the hope that this would strengthen entrepreneurship and enhance performance. A private entrepreneur paid the collective a fixed rent and ran the firm as if it was his own. In many cases such entrepreneurs accumulated considerable capital assets, thereby reducing the share of the collective assets. Hence, the firm was gradually transferred into a solely privately owned firm (Song 2004).

3.3.2.1.2 "Red Hat" Collectives

Some private firms attached themselves to an established collectively owned enterprise to obtain representation. They paid a fee for the use of its name (and thus its license), stationery, letters of introduction, bank account numbers, and receipt books; some private firms gave enterprise shares to local government cadres, paid them positions as advisers, and positions as board members (Sun 2003; IFC (International Finance Corporation) 2000, p. 21); many firms registered as collectives were actually privately owned. All these kinds of firms were actually privately owned, but were regarded as "red hat" collectives, with the "red hat" enabling them to evade government prohibitions on private firms and ideological harassment by the government (Song 2004). "Red hat" could be helpful in securing access to land, assets, finance, and markets. "Red hat" could also help firms to take advantage of a favorable regulatory treatment and local government support, such as lower tax and government subsidy (IFC (International Finance Corporation) 2000, p. 20; Song 2004). On the other hand, local governments and officials could benefit from collecting fees and profit-sharing arrangements (Guo and Chen 2000, p. 140). Most of these "red hat" collectives had been transformed into private enterprises with the encouragement of the local governments, partly because of the governments' concern about the budgetary cost of supporting them (IFC (International Finance Corporation) 2000, p. 20).

3.3.2.1.3 Township and Village Enterprises

TVEs were collectively owned by a rural community and belonged to all residents of the rural community where they were located. A rural community could be either a township or a village, with each community having a number of such firms (Sun 2000; Chiu and Lewis 2006, p. 32). The local township and village governments had a majority portion in the initial investment and exerted dominant de facto control over the operations of the TVEs (Ding et al. 2004). A village enterprise was run by the village government and a township enterprise was run by the township government. In short, a TVE could be described as a community enterprise in which the community government had control (Chiu and Lewis 2006, p. 32).

TVEs as collective enterprises were characterized by three features: first, all enterprises within a community were owned collectively by the residents of that community; second, the decisions of the managers of the TVEs were restricted to day-to-day operations; third, the local government exercised control rights over TVEs on behalf of the residents of the community. Considering these points, collective TVE assets legally belonged to the community residents. The community government represented the owners of TVEs and had direct control rights over TVEs (Chiu and Lewis 2006, p. 113). Therefore, TVEs had an ownership structure similar to those of former SOEs, such enterprises were owned collectively and constituted an integral part of the local bureaucracy.

However, since the 1990s, these TVEs have been privatized under economic circumstances in which market liberalization was accelerated with Deng Xiaoping's southern tour in 1992 (Ito 2006). TVEs are now overwhelmingly privately owned (Chiu and Lewis 2006, p. 112).

3.3.2.2 The Incentives and Reasons for Local Governments to Privatize Collectives and TVEs

There were two major sources of incentives for local governments to privatize collectives, in general, and TVEs, in particular. The first one was that fiscal and financial reforms between 1994 and 1996 in China had hardened the budget constraints of local governments. A hard budget constraint means that local governments must survive using their own financial resources (Cao et al. 1999).

In 1994, the fiscal reform in China (a) introduced a clear distinction between national and local taxes, (b) established a national tax bureau and local tax bureau, each responsible for its own tax collection, and (c) determined that value added tax would become the major indirect tax to be collected by the central government and shared by local governments at a fixed ratio of 75:25. Before this reform, China did not have a national tax bureau, and all taxes were collected by the local governments. Local governments often reduced or evaded taxes supposed to be paid to the central government. After the fiscal reform, it became very difficult for local governments to reduce national taxes as in the past (Dong 1997).

Since 1995, the new Budget Law took effect. It prohibited the central government from deficit financing its current account. The central government was allowed to have deficit financing only in the capital account, but it had to be financed by government bonds. Local governments were required to have their budgets balanced. The law controlled strictly bond issuance and restricted borrowing in the financing market by local governments.

The monetary and banking reform in 1994 substantially reduced the local governments' influence on monetary policy and credit allocation decisions (Xie 1996a). Before the reform, 70% of the central bank's loans to state banks were made by the central bank's local branches. After 1994, the central bank's local branches were no longer under dual supervision, which meant that they were no longer reporting to both the headquarters of the central government and the local government of the region in which they resided. They were now only supervised by the headquarters of the central bank, which set the national monetary policy. In 1994, four major state banks became commercialized and adopted the international standard for bank assets and risk management (i.e., the Basel Accord). The internal management of these banks became centralized, which reduced the political influence of the local governments on their local branches in loan decisions (Cao et al. 1999).

The second major source of incentive for local governments to privatize collectives and TVEs was increased competition. Competition from the nonstate sector raised the competitive pressures on local collectives and TVEs. By the mid-1990s, the nonstate sector in China had become a major force in the economy, and both domestic nonstate firms and foreign firms had become the major sources of market competition. The competitive environment in China was becoming increasingly intense, especially after China's accession to the WTO (Gabriel 2006, p. 92). The interjurisdictional competition across provinces, cities, counties, townships, and villages had played an important role in inducing the ownership transformation (Montinola et al. 1995; Qian and Roland 1998; Qian and Weingast 1997). The interjurisdictional competition was put in place by the revenue-sharing contract between central and provincial governments, and between provincial and city or county governments, which was likened to "eating in your own kitchens" (*fenzao chifan*) and delegated the responsibility of balancing local revenue and expenditure to local governments (Sun 2000). Li and Zhang (1998) also used a theoretical model to show that competition among local governments for scarce resources had been a major reason for their privatization initiatives.

3.3.2.2.1 The Reasons for Privatizing TVEs

The "mechanism degeneration" of TVEs had been widely reported since the early 1990s (Ren and Du Ying 1990; China Information Daily, August 2, 1993; Ministry of Agriculture 1997). The term "TVE mechanism degeneration" refers to an increasing bureaucratization in TVEs by township and village governments, the softening of the budget constraints for their TVEs, and other trends which were like formal SOE mechanisms. The mechanism degeneration of TVEs had been linked to the problems inherent in TVE ownership and governance structure and justified demands for an ownership reform (Sun 2003).

The budget constraint for the community as a whole had been hardened. At the same time, the community government had to bear the unlimited liability for its TVEs; thus, the increasing opportunistic activities by individual TVEs, softening budget constraint to individual TVEs, and the building up of nonperforming loans could finally induce the bankruptcy of the whole community (Sun 2003). Financial crisis led community governments to make institutional changes (North and Weingast 1989; Yao 2004). To get rid of the unlimited liability for the TVEs, to capitalize community TVEs, and to avoid the risk of community bankruptcy, community governments initiated the privatization of TVEs in their communities (Sun 2003). Therefore, under the pressures of hard budgets, the financing burdens of TVEs, and fierce market competition from the nonstate sector, local governments became the promoters of privatization in consideration of providing incentives to entrepreneurs to improve the efficiency of firms, eventually to realize more income and tax for local governments (Sun and Lu 2004). In comparison with upper-level governments, township and village governments faced fewer political constraints, for example, the avoidance of layoffs was not a constraint; thus, township and village governments initiated the privatization of TVEs more freely (Sun 2003).

The mobility of nonstate capital investment also raised the opportunity costs for community governments bailing out inefficient TVEs (Jefferson 1998; Qian and Roland 1998). This helps to understand why some community governments started privatization when the performance of their TVEs was not in a state of crisis, but in a good condition. An example is Shunde county of Guangdong province. Because this kind of location has better investment opportunities, the opportunity costs of keeping inefficient public firms is high; therefore, privatization was started even when the TVE performance was good (Cao et al. 1999). Local governments that persistently bailed out inefficient TVEs not only failed to attract investment and skilled labor to their jurisdictions, but also found that their own resources and skilled labor had moved away from them (Sun 2000).

3.3.2.2.2   The Reasons to Privatize "Red Hat" and Rented Collectives

Both "red hat" and rented collectives had enormous problems with property rights. Both types of firms—the ones that were registered as collectives but were actually privately owned and those that were rented collectives which became privately owned—had been operating under informal property rights, without legal backing. Such "informal rights are characteristically ambiguous and therefore difficult to partition in the case of multiple and competing claims" (Nee and Su 1996, p. 114). As a result, disputes over property claims were easily generated, impeding long-term development (Song 2004).

Both types of collectives had associations with local governments or collective units, to evade the ideological bias and government regulations. In many cases, local governments suffered fiscal losses rather than benefiting from the firms. At the same time, the firms suffered from political interference in their operations. These firms made an entrepreneur's incentive asymmetric. If a firm made a profit, it was its own. If the firm incurred a loss, the government had to bear the burden. As a result, the local government accumulated a considerable amount of debt. The government officials called this "bleeding," and this became the most important reason for the local government to privatize the collectives to get rid of the burden of those firms. Privatization was therefore called "the project for stopping the bleeding" (Garnaut et al. 2001, p. 21).

In summary, local governments' incentives for privatization depended on the costs and benefits of the alternatives. The local governments started privatization when they came under hard budget constraints and faced market competition (Cao et al. 1999).

3.3.2.3   Privatizing Rented Collectives and "Red Hat" Collectives

The mid-1990s marked the watershed for collectives as they were privatized (Gibb and Li 2003). The local governments encouraged the privatization of rented collectives. By gradually increasing private assets while the share of collective assets in the business diminished, more and more rented firms changed from the basic property right arrangement of collective firms to being solely private owned (Song 2004).

In March 1998, the Chinese government issued a directive for "red hat" firms, requiring all "red hat" firms that were registered as collectives but in reality privately run to take off their red hats and show their private ownership by the following November (Yao 2004).

3.3.2.4   Privatizing TVEs

3.3.2.4.1   The Gradual Process of Ownership Transformation of the TVE Sector

By 1996, and in some cases as early as 1993, a widespread movement had begun to privatize TVEs (Yusuf et al. 2006, p. 98). The privatization was regarded as an "institutional innovation," which was adopted by local governments to follow the reform campaign in privatizing inefficient local TVEs wherever feasible (Ding et al. 2004). The nationwide campaign of privatizing TVEs aimed to clarify the property right relations and to prevent government administrative intervention in TVEs so as to improve their efficiency. The TVE ownership reform was a gradual process in which property rights were transferred to private individuals (Ito 2006).

In the earlier stage, by 1997, the ownership transformation of TVEs had taken diverse forms, of which the dominant one was the joint-stock cooperative. Table 3.15 shows the distribution of the different forms of ownership transformation of the TVEs. By 1997, 63.4% of TVEs had adopted the form of the joint-stock cooperative, 12.2% were sold to private investors, 4.7% were transformed into limited liability companies with management ownership or outside-investor ownership, 3.8 were merged, 1.6% were restructured into joint-stock companies, 0.7% went into bankruptcy, and 13.9% were leased to managers or re-registered back to private ownership (Sun 2003).

In the later stage of the TVE ownership transformation, the process accelerated. The 15th Party Congress was followed by the rapid privatization of TVEs

Table 3.15 Distribution of ownership restructuring of township and village enterprises (*TVEs*), 1997 (percent)

	Joint-stock cooperative	Selling	Limited liability	Merge and grouping	Joint-stock company	Bankruptcy	Others
In restructured TVEs	63.37	12.15	4.66	3.82	1.58	0.66	13.91
In total TVEs	21.23	4.07	1.56	1.28	0.53	0.22	4.66

The data are from the Ministry of Agriculture. In total, 33.50% of the community-owned TVEs restructured their ownership form by 1997. The category "others" consists mainly of leasing and the reregistration of "fake" collective TVEs back to private ownership
From People's Daily (1998)

throughout the country, many of which were sold to their managers (Garnaut et al. 2005a, p. 36). By the end of 1998, the majority of TVEs had gone through an ownership transformation (Zhao 1999).

3.3.2.4.2   The Evolution of Joint-Stock Cooperatives

In the nationwide property reform of the TVE sector in the mid-1990s, the majority of TVEs were transformed into joint-stock cooperatives (Ding et al. 2004). Shareholding cooperatives had been an innovative mechanism for the ownership transformation of TVEs in China (Garnaut et al. 2005b, p. 49). With the extensive conversion of TVEs into joint-stock cooperatives, a large portion of them had become privatized, although in many cases they remained registered as collectives (IFC (International Finance Corporation) 2000).

Use of the joint-stock cooperative as an experimental form for the ownership transformation of TVEs was initiated in 1987 in the Zhoucun District of Zibo City, Shandong province (Sun 2000). Under the joint-stock cooperative system, township and village governments, employees, and private individuals shared firm stocks (Ito 2006). However, in this experimental stage, the TVE ownership transformation was seriously constrained by the requirement that the majority of stock should be held by township and village governments, while the local governments should not intervene in the daily operation of the company (Vermeer 1996; Ding et al. 2004).

Following the decisive push for renewed reforms by Deng Xiaoping in 1992, the official restriction on share distribution between the township and village government and individuals became increasingly unpopular and has been gradually abandoned de facto since then. The removal of this restriction combined with the renewed reform impulse led to the rapid transformation of joint-stock cooperatives with majority local government shareholding into joint-stock cooperatives with majority employee shareholding (Yearbook of China's Township and Village Enterprises (1996–2001), p. 271–80; Wade 1988). Their stylized features can be described in the following four points:

a. Managers and employees owned a majority of the shares of the firm. The ownership shares were not freely tradable, although subscribed shares could be transferred within the community.
b. The local government could hold some shares in the name of community citizens.
c. Some shares were held by outsider individuals.
d. A representative form of governance was employed that was based on the voting principles of "one person, one vote" or "one share, one vote" or a combination of both.

The fact that the ownership shares were not freely tradable meant the individually subscribed shares were much closer to a venture capital investment with a simple profit-sharing scheme than to the shares of Western public companies. Specific to the profit-sharing scheme is that a fixed proportion of total profits is earmarked as the shareholding fund for the distribution of dividends (Sun 2002).

In comparison with the collective ownership of TVEs before the ownership reform, the joint-stock cooperative form reduces the costs of both monitoring and collective decision-making. Also, employee shareholding increased employee commitment to the firm (Dong et al. 2002). Employees could elect representatives to a board of directors, who in turn monitored management accountability. The direct employee participation in governance was confined to annual meetings, major constitutional changes of the firm such as mergers or splits of the firm, and issuance of bonds and shares. This arrangement helped to secure a professional management and to avoid inefficient decision-making induced by a highly participatory governance form (Sun 2002).

Even though there were some positive effects of the majority employee shareholding in this early stage of ownership transformation, the dispersed shareholding form in which local governments did not part with collective shares was just the beginning of a privatization initiative. Privatization was still incomplete and ambiguous property rights were maintained (Ito 2006).

Many Chinese township and village governments preferred to sell shares to managers rather than employees. This was the case because a large ownership role for the employees would reduce the pressures on the enterprise to focus on its financial objectives and to fully resolve the problem of "egalitarianism" and the deficiencies that TVEs were facing (Ho et al. 2002).

In many employee-owned joint-stock cooperatives, a tendency toward increasing concentration of share ownership in the hands of the core shareholders (mainly managers) started and has continued. The joint-stock form makes it easy for a cooperative to transform into a limited liability company or a joint-stock company along with the expansion of the firm and along with the expansion of shares held by managers. From 1994 to 1997, 6738 joint-stock cooperatives restructured themselves into limited liability companies or joint-stock companies (Sun 2003).

In 1994 the Tax Sharing System (TSS) was introduced and was a driving force for completing the privatization of TVEs. Before the TSS reform, the local governments were responsible for collecting all taxes and remitting a portion of this revenue to the next-higher level. In addition to this formal budget institution, an extra budget system was allowed and enabled local governments to enrich their fiscal coffers by promoting local industry and to spend the fiscal revenues at their discretion. The TSS overhauled this two-tier tax system and required lower-level governments to share tax revenues with upper-level governments. With TSS, collective assets became liable to state-controlled taxation, and this posed a challenge to local cadres. Consequently, the local governments decided to sell their assets to private individuals (Ito 2006).

Thus, in the later stage of TVE privatization, the process accelerated. The joint-stock cooperative had evolved and new types of joint-stock cooperatives emerged and become popular. Those are the joint-stock cooperatives in which the majority shares are held by several important key managers, and the joint-stock cooperatives in which one person (normally the general manager) holds the majority of shares and has full control of the firm; some successful giants even succeeded in listing themselves on the national stock exchanges. In the majority of such cases, the township and village governments simply sold the whole firm to managers or individuals and withdrew their interest completely. In these new types of joint-stock cooperative, where the majority of shares are held by a single person or a manager group, the governance control system actually converges a private-owner-managed firm system (Ding et al. 2004).

TVEs transformed into joint-stock cooperatives with an individual or a group of individuals holding the majority of shares have become truly private enterprises. With the privatization reform being deepened and the pace of reform accelerating, TVEs have already become overwhelmingly privately owned (Chiu and Lewis 2006, p. 112).

3.4 Innovation Highlight and Chapter Conclusion

The governance model of the Chinese private firms is quite similar to that of the firms in the US leading liberal market economies, that is, market-based firm's governance structure. Therefore, the innovation system developed in the Chinese private sector works also similar to that in the US leading liberal market economies, that is, a market-oriented innovation system. Based on the market-oriented governance model and innovation arrangement of the firms and the supportive start-up and venture capital market in Shenzhen, Chinese private firms have been quite successful in IT industry and high technology development. Many giants emerge in the private sector and become competitive global players like Huawei, Alibaba, Tencent, Jingdong, Xiaomi, etc. And Shenzhen becomes world well-known China's silicon valley.

There are also following supportive factors for the development of Chinese private sector, which cannot be found in the US leading liberal market economies.

The first is the positive externality. State sector that is under the state-controlled shareholding coordination spreads large positive externalities through research and development, learning by doing, and development of a local infrastructure and so on. This positive externality effect has great impact on the quick development of Chinese private sector. It also injects confidence into the private sector and makes the development a sustainable one.

The second is a balance between profit-driven and risk taken. In contrast to the managers in the managerial management in the USA that tend to place more emphasis on expansion and balance sheet performance while taking less consideration of risk, the owner-managers in Chinese private firms and personal networks tend to place more emphasis on the balance between the risk taken and profit driven. It also makes the development of Chinese private sector more sustainable.

It is based on such typical innovation system in the Chinese private sector, China is well on its way to being a global leader in 5G, ICT, AI, quantum computing, blockchain, and other key emerging and digital technologies. Its innovation has achieved substantial achievement across multiple other sectors, such as logistics, e-commerce, Fintech, Internet of Things (IoT), autonomous driving, digital health, and smart city. China is proactively shaping international standards for emerging technologies including blockchain, Internet of Things (IoT), and 5G, by securing leadership positions in international standard setting bodies (Shi-Kupfer and Ohlberg 2019).

We can see some example industries and a typical company Huawei that show Chinese private sector as a global leader. The first example industry is e-commerce. China accounts for over 40% of global transactions, and the penetration of e-commerce (in percent of total retail sales) stands now at 15%, compared to 10% in the USA. Alibaba has set up a global platform connecting sellers and buyers from more than 200 countries, with its total revenue growing by more than 200%.

The second one is Fintech. Chinese companies account for more than 70% of the total global valuations. The value of China's consumption-related mobile payments by individuals totaled US $790 billion in 2016, 11 times that of the USA. China's Fintech giants have been rapidly expanding in overseas markets. Alipay and WeChat Pay, the two popular third-party payment applications in China, are available at physical retailers in 28 countries and regions outside of China.

The third one is cloud computing. Alibaba cloud computing has set up 14 data centers globally, with overseas cloud computing revenue growing at 400%.

The fourth one is ICT exports. China accounts for 32% of global ICT goods exports and 6% in ICT services exports (Zhang and Chen 2019).

Huawei, the Chinese private telecommunications company, also embodies the global rise of Digital China. Huawei has developed quickly and expand into overseas markets. From 2014 to 2018, Huawei more than doubled its revenues to reach 108 billion USD. This tremendous growth was mostly driven by gains in foreign markets. In 2017, the company overtook Ericsson and owns the largest global market share in mobile infrastructure equipment. In 2018, Huawei became number one in global sales of mobile phones, beating Apple (Shi-Kupfer and Ohlberg 2019).

References

Asian Development Bank. (2003). *The development of private enterprise in the People's Republic of China*, Manila.

Boisot, M. (1995). *Information space: A framework for learning in organizations, institutions and culture*. London: Routledge.

Bourdieu, P. (1986). The forms of capital. In J. G. Richardson (Ed.), *Handbook of theory and research for the sociology of education* (pp. 241–258). Westport, CT: Greenwood Press.

Brandt, L., & Li, H. (2003). Bank discrimination in transition economies: Ideology, information or incentives? *Journal of Comparative Economics, 31*(3), 387–413.

Cao, Y., Qian, Y., & Weingast, B. R. (1999). From federalism, Chinese style to privatization, Chinese style. *Economics of Transition, 7*(1), 103–131.

Che, J. (2002). Rent seeking and government ownership of firms: An application to China's township-village enterprises. *Journal of Comparative Economics, 30*, 781–811.

Chen, J., & Huang, Q. (2001). Comparison of governance structure of Chinese enterprises with different types of ownership, *China & World Economy*, 6. Retrieved May 11, 2007, from http://www.iwep.org.cn

Cheng, L., & Rosett, A. (1991). Contract with a Chinese face: Socially embedded factors in the transformation from hierarchy to markets, 1978–1989. *Journal of Chinese Law, 5*(2), 143–244.

Child, J. (1994). *Management in China during the age of reform*. Cambridge: Cambridge University Press.

Child, J., & Pleister, H. (2004). Governance and management. In R. Garnaut & L. Song (Eds.), *China's third economic transformation: The rise of the private economy* (pp. 192–208). London: RoutledgeCurzon.

Child, J., & Lu, Y. (1990). Industrial decision-making under China's reform 1985–1988. *Organization Studies, 11*(3), 321–351.

Chiu, B., & Lewis, M. K. (2006). *Reforming China's state-owned enterprises and banks*. Cheltenham: Edward Elgar Press.

Coleman, J. S. (1988). Social capital in the creation of human capital. *American Journal of Sociology, 94*, 95–121.

Cooke, F. L. (2000). Manpower restructuring in the state-owned railway industry of China: The role of the state in human resource strategy. *International Journal of Human Resource Management, 11*(5), 904–924.

Cooke, F. L. (2002). Ownership change and the reshaping of employment relations in China: A study of two manufacturing companies. *Journal of Industrial Relations, 44*(1), 19–39.

Cooke, F. L. (2005). Employment relations in small commercial businesses in China. *Industrial Relations Journal, 36*(1), 19–37.

Curran, J., Kitchen, J., Abbott, B., & Mills, V. (1993). *Employment and employment relations in the small service sector enterprise—A report, ESRC Center for Research on Small Service Sector Enterprises*. London: Kingston University.

Ding, D., & Warner, M. (1999). 'Re-investing' China's industrial relations at enterprise-level: An empirical field-study in four major cities. *Industrial Relations Journal, 30*(3), 243–260.

Ding, D. Z., Ge, G., & Warner, M. (2004). Evolution of organizational governance and human resource management in China's township and village enterprises. *The International Journal of Human Resource Management, 15*(5), 836–852.

Dong, F. (1997). The 'budget law' and hardening government' budget constraints. In T. Xu & J. Li (Eds.), *China's tax reform*. Beijing: China Economics Publishing House.

Dong, X.-Y., Bowles, P., & Ho, S. P. S. (2002). Share ownership and employee attitudes: Some evidence from China's post-privatization rural industry. *Journal of Comparative Economics, 30*, 812.

Erickson, B. H. (1996). Culture, class and connections. *American Journal of Sociology, 102*(1), 217–251.

Fields, K. J. (1995). *Enterprise and the state in Korea and Taiwan*. Ithaca, NY: Cornell University Press.

Friedman, D. (1988). *The misunderstood miracle: Industrial development and political change in Japan*. Ithaca, NY: Cornell University Press.

Gabriel, S. J. (2006). *Chinese capitalism and the modernist vision*. London: Routledge.

Gao, S.-j., & Xu, G. (2000). *Sources of private equity capital for non-state firms in China*. Washington, DC: World Bank, Mimeo.

Garnaut, R., & Song, L. (Eds.). (2004a). *China's third economic transformation: The rise of the private economy*. London: RoutledgeCurzon.

Garnaut, R., Song, L., Tenev, S., & Yang, Y. (2005a). *China restructures: Letting the small go in China's state enterprises sector*. Washington, DC: World Bank and International Finance Corporation.

Garnaut, R., Song, L., Tenev, S., & Yang, Y. (2005b). *China's ownership transformation: Process, outcome, prospects*. Washington, DC: The International Finance Corporation and the World Bank.

Garnaut, R., Song, L., Yang, Y., & Wang, X. (2001). *Private enterprise in China*. Canberra, ACT; Beijing: Asia Pacific Press, The Australian National University; Peking University.

Gerlach, M. L. (1992). *Alliance capitalism: The social organization of Japanese business*. Berkeley: University of California Press.

Gibb, A., & Li, J. (2003). Organizing for enterprise in China: What can we learn from the Chinese micro, small, and medium enterprise development experience. *Futures, 35*, 403–421.

Gilman, M., Edwards, P., Ram, M., & Arrowsmith, J. (2002). Pay determination in small firms in the UK: The case of the response to the National Minimum Wage. *Industrial Relations Journal, 33*(1), 52–67.

Gregory, N., Tenev, S., & Wagle, D. (2000). *China's emerging private enterprises: Prospects for the new century*. Washington, DC: International Finance Corporation.

Guo, C.-x. (2000). Development of private companies & related governance structure. In A. Naiwu (Ed.), *Development and forecast of medium-sized & small chinese enterprise (1999)*. Beijing: Democracy and Construction Publishing House.

Guo, C., & Chen, D. (2000). Analysis and countermeasures on the management and control model of private enterprises in China. In H. Zhang & L. Ming (Eds.), *Development report on private enterprise in China* (pp. 122–148). Beijing: Social Science Literature Publishing House.

Hamilton, G. (1997). Organization and market process in Taiwan's capitalist economy. In M. Orru et al. (Eds.), *The economic organization of East Asian capitalism*. Thousand Oaks, CA: Sage.

Hamilton, Gary G. and Kao Cheng-Shu (1990), "The institutional foundations of Chinese business: The family firm in Taiwan", in Calhoun, Craig (ed.) Comparative social research: Business institutions, volume 12, a research annual, Greenwich: JAI Press Inc.

Heller, R. (1991, November). How the Chinese manage to keep it all in the family. *Management Today* (pp. 31–34).

Hendrischke, H. (2004). The role of social capital, networks and property rights in China's privatization process. In B. Krug (Ed.), *China's rational entrepreneurs: The development of the new private business sector* (pp. 97–118). London: RoutledgeCurzon.

Ho, S. P. S., Dong, X.-Y., Bowles, P., & Macphail, F. (2002). Privatization and enterprise wage structures during transition: Evidence from rural industry in China. *Economics of Transition, 10* (3), 659–688.

Holz, C. A. (2002). Long live China's state-owned enterprise: Deflating the myth of poor financial performance. *Journal of Asian Economics, 13*, 493–529.

Holz, A. C., & Zhu, T. (2002). Chapter 8. Assessment of the current state of China's economic reforms. *The Chinese Economy, 35*(3), 71–109.

IFC (International Finance Corporation). (2000). *China's emerging private enterprises: Prospects for the new century*. Washington, DC: IFC.

Ito, J. (2006). Economic and institutional reform packages and their impact on productivity: A case study of Chinese township and village enterprises. *Journal of Comparative Economics, 34*, 167–190.

Jacobs, G., Belschak, F., & Krug, B. (2004). Social capital in China: The meaning of *Guanxi* in Chinese business. In B. Krug (Ed.), *China's rational entrepreneurs: The development of the new private business sector* (pp. 166–188). London: RoutledgeCurzon.

Jacobs, N. (1958). *The origin of modern capitalism and Eastern Asia*. Hong Kong: Hong Kong University Press.

Jefferson, G. H. (1998). China's state enterprises: Public goods, externalities, and coase. *American Economic Review, 88*(2), 428–432.

Kao, J. (1993). The worldwide web of chinese business. *Harvard Business Review, 71*, 24–34.

Keasey, K., & Watson, R. (1993). *Small firm management: Ownership, finance and performance*. Oxford: Blackwell.

Keister, L. A. (2000). *Chinese business groups: The structure and impact of interfirm relations during economic development*. New York: Oxford University Press.

Kennedy, S. (2003). The price of competition: Pricing policed and the struggle to define China's economic system. *The China Journal, 49*, 1–30.

Kristensen, P. H. (1992). Strategies against structure: Institutions and economic organization in Denmark. In R. Whitley (Ed.), *European business systems: Firms and markets in their national contexts*. London: Sage.

Kristensen, P. H. (1996). On the constitutions of economic actors in Denmark: Interacting skill containers and project coordinators. In R. Whitley & P. H. Kristensen (Eds.), *The changing European firm: Limits to convergence*. London: Routledge.

Krone, K., Garrett, M., & Chen, L. (1992). Management communication practices in Chinese factories: A preliminary investigation. *The Journal of Business Communication, 29*(3), 229–252.

Krug, B., & Polos, L. (2004). Emerging markets, entrepreneurship and uncertainty: The emergence of a private sector in China. In *China's rational entrepreneurs: The development of the new private business sector* (pp. 72–96). London: RoutledgeCurzon.

Krug, B., & Mehta, J. (2004). Entrepreneurship by alliance. In *China's rational entrepreneurs: The development of the new private business sector* (pp. 50–71). London: RoutledgeCurzon.

Leung, F. F.-L. (1995). Overseas Chinese management: Myths and realities. *East Asian Executive Reports, 17*(2), 6–13.

Levine, M. (1997). *Worker rights and labor standards in Asia's four new tigers: A comparative perspective*. New York: Plenum Press.

Li, H., Meng, L., & Zheng, J. (2006). Why do entrepreneurs enter politics? Evidence from China. *Economic Inquiry, 44*(3), 559–578.

Li, S., & Zhang, W. (1998). Regional competition and the privatization of Chinese SOEs. *Economic Research, 12*, 13–22.

Li, S., Vertinsky, I., & Zhou, D. (2004). The emergence of private ownership in China. *Journal of Business Research, 57*, 1145–1152.

Li, D. (1997). The visible hands in the economic development of Wenzhou. *China's Rural Economy, 1*, 41–46. (in Chinese).

Lin, N. (2001). *Social capital: A theory of social structure and action*. New York: Cambridge University Press.

Lin, J. Y. (1992). Rural reforms and agricultural growth in China. *American Economic Review, 82* (1), 34–51.

Liu, Y.-l. (1992). Reform from below: The private economy and local politics in the rural industrialization of Wenzhou. *The China Quarterly, 130*, 293–316.

McEvoy, G. (1984). Small business personnel practices. *Journal of Small Business Management, 22*(10), 1–8.

McMillan, J., & Naughton, B. (1996). Elements of economic transition. In J. McMillan & B. Naughton (Eds.), *Reforming Asian socialism: The growth of market institutions* (pp. 3–16). Ann Arbor: University of Michigan Press.

Meng, X. (2004). Private sector development and labor market reform. In R. Garnaut & L. Song (Eds.), *China's third economic transformation: The rise of the private economy*. London: RoutledgeCurzon.

Ministry of Agriculture. (1997, April 24). The status of China's TVEs and the suggestions for TVE reform and development in the Future. *People's Daily* (in Chinese).

Montinola, G., Qian, Y. Y., & Weingast, B. R. (1995). Federalism, Chinese style: The political basis for economic success in China. *World Politics, 48*, 50–81.

Nee, V. (1989). Peasant entrepreneurship and the politics of regulation in China. In V. Nee & D. Stark (Eds.), *Remaking the economic institutions of capitalism*. Stanford: Stanford University Press.

Nee, V., & Su, S. (1996). Institutions, social ties and commitment in China's corporatist transformation. In J. McMillan & B. Naughton (Eds.), *Reforming Asian socialism: The growth of market institutions* (pp. 111–134). Ann Arbor: University of Michigan Press.

North, D., & Weingast, B. (1989). Constitutions and commitment: The evolution of institutions governing public choice in seventeenth-century England. *Journal of Economic History, 49*(4), 803–832.

Numazaki, I. (1992). *Networks and partnerships: The social organization of the Chinese business elite in Taiwan.* Unpublished PhD thesis, Development of Anthropology, Michigan State University.

OECD. (2000). *Reform China's enterprises.* Paris: Author.

Peng, Y. (2004). Kinship networks and entrepreneurs in China's transitional economy. *American Journal of Sociology, 109*(5), 1045–1074.

People's Daily. (1998) (in Chinese), July 25.

People's Daily. (1999) (in Chinese), March 30.

Portes, A. (1998). Social capital: Its origins and applications in modern sociology. *Annual Review of Sociology, 22,* 1–24.

Project Team on Studies on Private Enterprises in China. (1999). 1997 national sample survey of private enterprises-data and analysis. In H. Zhang & L. Ming (Eds.), *Zhongguo siying qiye fazhan baogao 1978–1998 (Report on the development of private enterprises in China 1978–1998)* (pp. 131–166). Beijing: Social Science Literature Press.

Qian, Y., & Roland, G. (1998). Federalism and the soft budget constraint. *American Economic Review, 88*(5), 1143–1162.

Qian, Y., & Weingast, B. R. (1997). Federalism as a commitment to preserving market incentives. *Journal of Economic Perspectives, 11*(4), 83–92.

Rainnie, A. (1989). *Industrial relations in small firms.* London: Routledge.

Ralston, D. A., Terpstra-Tong, J., Terpstra, R. H., Wang, X., & Egri, C. (2006). Today's state-owned enterprises of China: Are they dying dinosaurs or dynamic dynamos? *Strategic Management Journal, 27,* 825–843.

Ram, M. (1994). *Managing to survive: Working lives in small firms.* Oxford: Blackwell.

Redding, S. G. (1990). *The spirit of Chinese capitalism.* Berlin: De Gruyter.

Redding, S. G., & Wong, Y. Y. (Eds.). (1986). *The psychology of Chinese organizational behavior.* Hong Kong: Oxford University Press.

Ren, Q., & Du Ying, Q. J. (1990, March). An initial analysis of TVE survey in ten provinces. *Fazhan yanjiu (Develoment research)* (pp. 265–288). Beijing: Beijing Normal College (in Chinese).

Schlevogt, K.-A. (1998). *Power and control in Chinese private enterprises: Organizational design in the Taiwanese media industry.* Parkland, FL: Dissertation Publisher.

Schlevogt, K.-A. (2001). The distinctive structure of Chinese private enterprises: State versus private sector. *Asia Pacific Business Review, 7*(3), 1–33.

Scott, M., Roberts, I., Holroyd, G., & Sawbridge, D. (1989). *Management and industrial relations in small firms* (Research Paper No. 70). London: Department of Employment.

Segal, A. (2003). *High-technology enterprises in China.* Ithaca, NY: Cornell University Press.

Shi-Kupfer, K., & Ohlberg, M. (2019, April). China's digital rise: Challenges for Europe, *Merics Papers on China,* no 7.

So, B. W.-Y. (2004). State-business interaction in the IT sector. In R. Garnaut & L. Song (Eds.), *China's third economic transformation: The rise of the private economy* (pp. 209–224). London: RoutledgeCurzon.

Song, L. (2004). Emerging private enterprise in China: Transitional paths and implications. In R. Garnaut & L. Song (Eds.), *China's third economic transformation: The rise of the private economy* (pp. 29–47). London: RoutledgeCurson.

Stokes, D. (1998). *Small business management: A case study approach* (3rd ed.). London: Letts Educational.

Sun, L. (2000). Anticipatory ownership reform driven by competition: China's township-village and private enterprises in the 1990s. *Comparative Economic Studies, 42*(3), 49–75.

Sun, L. (2002). Fading out of local government ownership: Recent ownership reform in China's township and village enterprises. *Economic Systems, 26,* 249–269.

Sun, L. X. (2003). Ownership reform in the absence of crisis: China's township, village and private enterprises. In R. J. Mcintyre & B. Dallago (Eds.), *Small and medium enterprises in transitional economies.* New York: Palgrave Macmillan.

Sun, Z., & Lu, Z. (2004). From the government to enterprises. A summarization of the documents on the studies of Chinese private enterprises. *The Chinese Economy, 37*(6), 53–67.

Tam, O. K. (2004). Financing the private sector. In R. Garnaut & L. Song (Eds.), *China's third economic transformation*. London: RoutledgeCurzon.

Tenev, S., Zhang, C., & Brefort, L. (2002). *Corporate governance and enterprise reform in China: Building the institutions of modern markets*. Washington, DC: World Bank and the Institutional Finance Corporation.

Tian, G. (2000). Property rights and the nature of Chinese collective enterprises. *Journal of Comparative Economics, 28*, 247–268.

Tsang, E. W. K. (2001). Internationalizing the family firm: A case study of a Chinese family business. *Journal of Small Business Management, 39*(1), 88–94.

Turpin, D. V. (1998, February 6, 8). Challenge of the overseas Chinese. *Financial Times, Mastering global business series, part 2*.

Vermeer, E. B. (1996). Experiments with rural industrial shareholding cooperatives: The case of Zhoucun District, Shandong Province. *China Information, 10*(3/4), 75–107.

Verser, T. (1987). 'Owners' perspectives of personnel problems in small business. *Mid-American Journal of Business, 2*, 13–17.

Wade, R. (1988). The role of government in overcoming market failure: Taiwan, Republic of Korea and Japan. In H. Hughes (Ed.), *Achieving industrialization in East Asia*. Cambridge: Cambridge University Press.

Wang, J. F. (2000a). *Safeguarding woman's working rights and interests*. Paper presented in the International Seminar on the Legal Protection of Women's Employment Rights, April, Shanghai, China.

Wang, P. S. (2004a, May). *Farewell to Marx?* (pp. 20–22). Asia Inc.

Wang, X. (2004b). The contribution of the non-state sector to China's economic growth. In R. Garnaut & L. Song (Eds.), *China's third economic transformation: The rise of the private economy* (pp. 15–28). London: RoutledgeCurzon.

Wang, Z., & Shi, J. (2007). *Private sector and China's institutional transition: With the case studies in Zhejiang and Jiangsu*. Retrieved May 11, 2007, from http://www.economyandsociety.org/events/WANG_ZHIKAI_SHI_JINCHUAN_China_Capsm.pdf

Warner, M., & Ng, S. H. (1998). The ongoing evolution of Chinese industrial relations: The negotiation of "Collective Contracts" in the Shenzhen special economic zone. *China Information, 12*(4), 1–20.

Weidenbaum, M. (1996). The Chinese family business enterprise. *California Management Review, 38*(4), 141–156.

Weihrich, H. (1990). Management practices in the United States, Japan, and the Peoples Republic of China. *Industrial Management, 32*(2), 3–7.

Whitley, R. (1999). *Divergent capitalisms: The social structuring and change of business systems*. New York: Oxford University Press.

Wong, S.-L. (1985). The Chinese family firm: A model. *British Journal of Sociology, 36*, 58–72.

Xie, C. (1996a). *The complete book of enterprise property rights (Qiye Chanquan Shiwu Quanshu)*. Beijing: Jingji Ribao Chubanshe.

Xu, L. C., Zhu, T., & Lin, Y.-m. (2005). Politician control, agency problems and ownership reform: Evidence from China. *Economics of Transition, 13*(1), 1–24.

Yao, Y. (2004). Privatizing the small SOEs. In R. Garnaut & L. Song (Eds.), *China's third economic transformation: The rise of the private economy* (pp. 91–101). London: RoutledgeCurzon.

Yeung, I. Y. M., & Tung, R. L. (1996). Achieving business success in confusian societies: The importance of Guanxi (connections). *Organizational Dynamics, 25*(2), 54–65.

Yusuf, S., Nabeshima, K., & Perkins, D. H. (2006). *Privatizing China's state-owned enterprises*. Washington, DC: Stanford University Press and the World Bank.

Zhang, L., & Chen, S. (2019). *China's digital economy: Opportunities and risks*. IMF Working Paper, 2019 International Monetary Fund, WP/19/16.

Zhao, S. (2005). Changing structure of Chinese enterprises and human resource managemnet practices in China. In R. Smyth, O. K. Tam, M. Warner, & C. J. Zhu (Eds.), *China's business reforms: Institutional challenges in a globalized economy* (pp. 106–123). London: RoutledgeCurzon.

Zhao, X. (1999). *Competition, public choice and institutional change*, CCER (Working Paper No. C1999025). Beijing University.

Zheng, H. Y., & Lu, J. Y. (2001). An institutional analysis of the emergence of China's township and village enterprises. *Discovery and Research, 9*, 22–24.

Zhou, X., Li, Q., Zhao, W., & Cai, H. (2003). Embeddedness and contractual relationships in China's transitional economy. *American Sociological Review, 68*(1), 75–102.

Zingales, L. (2000). *In search of new foundations* (Working Paper No. 7706). Cambridge, MA: National Bureau of Economic Research.

Chapter 4
Dual Structure and Dual Convergence Drove Chinese Economic Catching-Ups and Innovation Engine Is Sparked

Abstract China's super innovation system and Chinese model were built up roughly in the period from the mid-1990s to the middle of the first decade in twenty-first century. This is also the period of Chinese catching-up. Building up such dual-structured Chinese model and China's innovation system, which are compatible not only with the US leading liberal market economies but also with the Germany leading European coordinated market economies, supported the dual convergence of the Chinese economy toward the two types of advanced economy. FDI and technology transfer drove the dual convergence. Thereby the catching-up got fueled, with the dual innovative capacity and competitiveness being enhanced in the Chinese economy. The further long-term sustainable growth of the Chinese economy has then quickly been driven by its own engine. A remarkable success of China's innovation follows up.

Keywords Innovation · Chinese innovation · Economic model · Chinese model · Business system · Corporate governance · Competitiveness · Chinese economic growth · Chinese catching-up · FDI · Technology transfer

Economic convergence implies that foreign direct investment (FDI) and technology transfer are based on similar economic models of the two economies, accompanied by a trend of fast economic growth of the follower that indicates a catching-up of the follower with the leader.

C. LIAO, *The Governance Structures of Chinese Firms*, Innovation, Technology, and Knowledge Management, https://doi.org/10.1007/978-3-030-52218-6_4

4.1 FDI and Technology Transfer Drive the Convergence Between the Economies with Similar Business Models / Innovation Systems

FDI can bring about a certain diffusion of technology, management style, and work practice and therefore implicate some convergence of the productive efficiency. If all these are based on different economic models and innovation systems of the two countries, it will still be difficult to observe economic convergence between the two economies. In contrast, if all these are based on similar economic models and innovation systems of the two countries, then the diffusion of technology, management style, and work practice and the convergence of productivity can be so greatly enhanced that FDI can promote the process of convergence and lead to economic performance convergence between the two economies. In this sense, FDI and technology transfer based on a similar economic model and innovation system actually mean economic convergence of the two economies.

Furthermore, if FDI is transferred from the two different types of advanced economy to an economy that follows a dual-structured business model and innovation system that is compatible with the two different types of advanced economy, then that implies a dual convergence of the economy toward these two different types of advanced economy. In this case, because the dual structure of the business model and innovation system makes it compatible with two different types of advanced economy, FDI and technology transfer tend to go to this economy with a strong trend. The economic convergences of this dual-structured economy toward different types of advanced economy happen at the same time. For such an economy, it is possible to further develop two different types of innovative capacity and core competitiveness, based on its dual convergence toward the two different types of advanced economies. With such overall innovation capacities and competitiveness, the country can produce a broader variety of goods and high technologies and can compete successfully in more sectors in the international markets. Economic indicators can show such a strong trend of economic convergence: FDI accompanied by technology transfer surges into the economy, and a strong trend of GDP growth is fueled. All these drive the economy catching-up quickly with the economies of leaders. The Chinese economy provides the typical case here.

4.2 The Dual-Structured Chinese Business Models / Innovation System Support China's Dual Convergence Toward and Catching-Up with Both the US Leading Liberal Market Economies and Germany Leading Coordinated Market Economies

Because the Chinese economic model and innovation system are dual structured and compatible with both the US leading liberal market economies and Germany leading coordinated market economies, FDI and technology transfer from both types of advanced economies to China are encouraged. They promote a dual convergence of the Chinese economy toward both types of advanced economy. During the process of dual convergence, the Chinese economy gains dual innovative capacity and core competitiveness. The dual structure and the dual convergence contribute to the remarkable catching-up of the Chinese economy.

4.2.1 Massive Waves of FDI Flow to China in Those Catching-Up Years

4.2.1.1 An Overview of Foreign Direct Investment in China in Those Years

From the 1980s onward, FDI steadily flowed into China. Especially after 1992, massive and strong waves of FDI poured into China. Table 4.1 shows the general trend of FDI in China during the period of 1984–2006. FDI that has actually been used reached a total amount of about US$70 billion in 2005 and 2006. China has become the largest recipient of FDI among the developing countries since the late 1990s, accounting for about 30% of the total FDI flow to the developing world (Tian et al. 2004). China has been the second largest FDI recipient in the world after the USA for many years (Madariaga and Poncet 2006).

The origins of FDI inflow to China are various, and FDI flows from economies with different business models. For example, Taiwan China, Hong Kong China, the USA, the UK, and Canada are the main source economies with a market-based firm's governance structure, while Japan, South Korea, Germany, France, and the Netherlands are the main source economies with a coordinated firm's governance structure. Table 4.2 shows the top sources of FDI in China.

Over two-thirds of China's incoming FDI flows into the manufacturing sectors. Within these manufacturing sectors, a big proportion of FDI flows into higher-value-added sectors such as semiconductors. FDI flows increasingly to the electronics,

Table 4.1 Foreign direct investment (FDI) inflows 1984–2006 (billion US dollars)

	Contracted	Utilized
1984	2.7	1.3
1985	5.9	1.7
1986	2.8	1.9
1987	3.7	2.3
1988	5.3	3.2
1989	5.6	3.4
1990	6.6	3.5
1991	12.0	4.4
1992	58.1	11.0
1993	111.4	27.5
1994	82.7	33.8
1995	91.3	37.5
1996	73.3	41.7
1997	51.0	45.5
1998	52.1	45.5
1999	41.2	40.4
2000	64.2	42.1
2001	71.1	48.8
2002	84.8	55.0
2003	115.1	53.5
2004	153.5	60.6
2005	–	72.4
2006	–	69.5

From The amounts of FDI from 1984 to 2005, Ministry of Commerce of the People's Republic of China, http://www.chinability.com/FDI.htm [30.10.2007]. The amount of FDI from 2003 to 2006, *Source:* UNCTAD, *World Investment Report 2007*; http://www.unctad.org/Templates/Page.asp?intItemID=3198&lang=1, or http://www.unctad.org/wir, or http://www.unctad.org/fdistatistics [13.11.2007]

Table 4.2 Top sources of FDI in China (billion US dollars)

	2001	2002	2003	2004	2005
Hong Kong	16.7	17.8	17.7	18.9	17.1
Virgin Islands[a]	5.0	6.1	5.7	6.7	9.0
Japan	4.3	4.2	5.0	5.4	6.5
South Korea	2.1	2.7	4.5	6.2	5.2
USA	4.4	5.4	4.2	3.9	3.1
Singapore	2.1	2.3	2.0	2.0	2.2
Taiwan	2.9	3.9	3.4	3.1	2.1
Germany	1.2	0.9	0.8	1.0	1.5

From Top Sources for Foreign Direct Investment in China (2007)
[a]Many foreign firms, including US companies, are registered in the Virgin Islands for tax purposes

telecommunications equipment, and chemicals sectors.[1] More and more multinational enterprises are locating their regional headquarters in mainland China. At the end of 2002, there were 70 regional headquarters and 37 international purchasing centers of foreign companies in Shanghai.[2] About 90% of multinational companies in Europe, the USA, and Japan have set a "China first" strategy. Four hundred of the *Fortune* 500 companies have made an influential direct investment in China. McDonald's alone has built 52 factories, ABB Group has established 20 joint ventures, Volkswagen has invested US$2 billion, key components of Boeing planes have been made in China, and so on. High profitability obtained by the early investors further encourages more and more foreign investment by multinational companies.[3]

Usually, FDI inflow is accompanied by technology transfer. Domestic firms can catch up with the advanced foreign firms on the level of technology and management skills through the externalities of FDI. As for the channels of technology transfer and spillover through FDI, there has been an increasing consensus among scholars on the four most outstanding forms of externalities. The first channel is the demonstration effect: domestic firms can learn superior production technologies and management skills from foreign firms located nearby. The second channel is the employment effect: foreign firms transfer their know-how and train their domestic workers, who may move to domestic firms later on and bring with them updated technology know-how and management skills. The third channel is the linkage effect: domestic firms may learn updated technology and management skills through backward or forward linkage across firms. The fourth channel is the competition effect: domestic firms are forced to update technology and management skills under the increasing competition pressure from foreign firms (Eden et al. 1997; Blomstrom and Kokko 1998; Gorg and Strobl 2001; Tian et al. 2004).

Empirical evidence is still limited on FDI spillovers in China, but it generally confirms that FDI generates positive spillovers (Tong and Hu 2003; Hu and Jefferson 2001; Madariaga and Poncet 2006). The studies on this issue show positive intra- and interindustry productivity spillovers within regions in the Chinese manufacturing sector (Wei and Liu 2006, Madariage and Poncet 2006), as well as a positive effect of FDI on the numbers of domestic patent applications in China (Cheung and Lin 2004).

Multinational companies emphasize the localization of research and development centers in China. Over 110 of the *Fortune* 500 companies have established research and development centers. At the end of 2003, Microsoft invested US$80 million in the China Research Institute, and further US$50 million flowed into the

---

[1]Foreign Direct Investment and Manufacturing Productivity in China 2002, p. 11. Internet publication: URL: http://www.bm.ust.hk/~ced/Yu%20CHEN.pdf [20.05.2005].

[2]The US-China Business Council 2003. Foreign Investment in China 2002, p. 2. Internet publication: URL: http://www.uschina.org/statistics/2003foreigninvestment.html [20.05.2005].

[3]Multinational Companies Adjust Strategies to China 2004, p. 2. Internet publication: URL: http://www.china-window.com/china_market/china_industry_reports/multinational-companies-a.shtml [23.05.2005].

Microsoft Asian Technology Center in Shanghai. Motorola set up the Motorola China Research Institute in Beijing in 1999. It has more than 18 research and development centers and has received investment of over US$1.3 billion since then, investing in advanced semiconductor materials, microcontrollers, code division multiple access technology, and chips for cell phones, and software.[4]

According to the standard approach from *Varieties of Capitalism*, firms in liberal market economies will be inclined to invest in foreign countries to secure cheaper labor, and they do not require special institutional infrastructure. In contrast, firms in coordinated market economies will not invest abroad only because of low-cost labor. The main reason for this is that they can get institutional advantages and core competitiveness from the special institutional arrangements in their home countries, and they are not willing to give up this opportunity only for cheaper labor (Hall and Soskice 2001). But if the host country's economic model is similar to that of their home country, then the firms may intend to invest there.

The facts on FDI and technology transfer witness that the Chinese economic model is compatible with both kinds of advanced economies; thus, Chinese enterprises can better attract, absorb, and adopt foreign capital and technology from both kinds of advanced economies,[5] which leads to the dual convergence effect. German and US FDI in China typifies this.

4.2.1.2   US Direct Investment in China

The USA is in the top position as a FDI contributor to China. US direct investment in China accounts for about 10% of China's FDI inflow in most of the years since the mid-1980s (see Table 4.3). Most multinational companies in the USA, such as General Motors, Intel, Microsoft, AIG, Ford Motors, General Electric, IBM, Mobil, DuPont, Hewlett-Packard, Procter & Gamble, Bell Atlantic, Lucent Technologies, and Motorola, have made prominent investments in China, indicating that China has indeed become an important investment outlet abroad for US firms. Smaller US firms have also invested in China; for example, the Aluminum Company of American, Sida Corporation, and Armstrong World Industries Delaware.

FDI from liberal market economies does not require special institutional infrastructure and institutional affinity. To enlarge markets for the expansion of the economic scale and to secure cheaper labor, liberal market economies make investments abroad (Hall and Soskice 2001, p. 56–7). China, with large markets and relatively cheaper labor, has become the favorite investment destination for liberal market economies, especially the USA. US investment in China is not

---

[4]Multinational Companies Adjust Strategies to China 2004, p. 3. Internet publication: URL: http://www.china-window.com/china_market/china_industry_reports/multinational-companies-a.shtml [23.05.2005].

[5]US Commercial Technology Transfers to the People's Republic of China 1999, p. 4. Internet publication: URL: http://www.bxa.doc.gov/DefenseIndustrialBasePrograms/OSIES/DefMarketResearchRpts/techtransfer2prc.html

Table 4.3 US direct investment in China, 1986–2006 (billion US dollars)

	US direct investment	Total FDI in China	Share of US direct investment (%)
1986	0.33	2.24	14.54
1987	0.26	2.31	11.36
1988	0.24	3.19	7.39
1989	0.28	3.39	8.38
1990	0.46	3.49	13.08
1991	0.32	4.37	7.40
1992	0.51	11.01	4.64
1993	2.06	27.51	7.50
1994	2.49	33.77	7.38
1995	3.08	37.52	8.22
1996	3.44	41.73	8.25
1997	3.24	45.26	7.16
1998	3.90	45.46	8.58
1999	4.22	40.32	10.46
2000	4.38	40.71	10.77
2001	4.43	46.88	9.46
2002	5.42	52.74	10.28
2003	4.20	53.51	7.80
2004	3.94	60.6	6.50
2005	3.07	60.3	5.07
2006	2.88	63.0	4.44

From China Department of Commerce statistical data, at http://www.mofcom.gov.cn/waimaotongji.shtml

locked into certain locations or industrial sectors, which shows that it does not require special institutional infrastructure. But the Chinese private sector, especially the privately dominated IT industries, attracts more attention from US investors.

Table 4.4 examines the distribution of US direct investment in China by sector and shows that the bulk is in the manufacturing industries. Two-thirds of US direct investment in China has gone to the manufacturing sector, half of which has been in privately dominated industrial sectors, such as computer, electronic products, and food sectors. IT industries attract the biggest portion of US investment in China (Fung 2004; Fung et al. 2004a, p. 74–5).

The US direct investment in China is profitable over time, and US firms performed better in China than in other foreign countries. In 2002, the return rate of US direct investment in China was 14.08%, in contrast to the average return rate of 8.15% of US direct investment in all countries (Fung 2004; Fung et al. 2004b, p. 117–63).

One important implication of US direct investment in China is technology transfer. The extent of the technology transfer can be approximately measured by the receipts and payments of royalties and license fees. As we can see from Table 4.5, the royalty and license fee transactions between the USA and China

Table 4.4 US direct investment in China by sector (million US dollars)

	1999	2000	2001	2002
All industries	9401	11,140	11,387	10,294
Mining	773	1404	1287	1514
Utilities	589	583	487	545
Total manufacturing	5787	7076	7698	6161
Food	280	286	330	392
Chemicals	995	1122	1045	1196
Primary and fabricated metals	223	157	140	121
Machinery	212	218	201	212
Computer and electronic products	2402	3500	3999	1942
Electrical equipment appliances and components	396	458	640	610
Transportation equipment	627	652	615	746
Wholesale trade	386	378	410	536
Information	46	79	105	99
Depository institutions	62	64	161	329
Finance (except deposit institutions and insurance)	11	43	D	29
Professional, scientific, and technical services	306	245	120	65
Other industries	1440	1267	D	1016

From Bargas (2000) and U.S. Department of Commerce, Bureau of Economic Analysis (2003a)
D the data in the cell have been suppressed to avoid the disclosure of data of individual companies

have been increasing dramatically, from US$113 million in the 1995 to US$723 million in 2002.

The US direct investors are advanced in manufacturing technologies, management techniques, corporate governance, and market institutions. Therefore, the US direct investment in China has accelerated the convergence of some of the Chinese economic sectors toward the American economy and enhance their efficiency, productivity, and competitiveness. Even though FDI from the USA does not require institutional affinity, the convergence effect needs the support from institutional affinity. Table 4.5 shows that the effect of technology transfer from the USA is distinctively strong in the Chinese privately dominated IT industries (general-use computer and software). This fact supports the convergence of Chinese IT industries toward their American counterparts.

4.2.1.3   German Direct Investment in China

In those catching-up years, direct investment in China from the EU had increased rapidly. The EU is one of the biggest foreign direct investors in China and is the largest provider of high technology to China. Among the EU countries, Germany is the top investor in China. Since 1980s, many famous German firms have invested in China. Bayer, Allianz, DaimlerChrysler, Siemens, Volkswagen, Henkel, and Bosch all invested and performed well in China. By 2002, the accumulated German direct

Table 4.5 Net receipts of royalties and license fees from China by the USA, 1995–2002 (million US dollars)

	1995	1996	1997	1998	1999	2000	2001	2002
Total net receipts	113	153	250	318	409	501	571	723
Total net receipts between affiliated parties	54	90	165	212	310	346	401	497
By US parents from affiliates in China	52	87	164	211	308	346	400	497
By Chinese affiliates located in the USA from Chinese parents in China	2	3	1	1	1	a	1	a
Total net receipts between unaffiliated parties	59	63	85	106	100	155	170	226
Industrial processing	31	43	52	47	32	44	43	48
Books, records, and tapes	1	1	1	b	2	3	4	5
Broadcasting and recording of live events	1	1	1	1	2	4	3	1
Franchise fees	4	5	5	5	5	4	b	3
Trademarks	8	7	6	5	10	17	9	20
General-use computer software	–	–	–	46	49	83	102	144
Other	14	6	20	1	0	0	b	6

From U.S. Department of Commerce, Bureau of Economic Analysis (2003b). For earlier years, trademarks are not listed as a separate item
[a]Less than US$500,000
[b]Figures have been suppressed to avoid disclosure of data of individual companies

investment in China had reached €8.48 billion, enabling Germany to take over the UK's position as the top investor in China (see Table 4.6).

Similar to the US direct investment in China, about two-thirds of German investment flowed into manufacturing sectors, such as automotive, electrical engineering, chemical, and mechanical engineering sectors. If measured in number of firms, manufacturing firms account for 74.7% of investment by German companies, while firms in the service sector account for 25.3% (Chen and Reger 2006). This characteristic is also demonstrated in Fig. 4.1. Unlike the US investors, German investors have long-standing business ties with China—10 years on average—and tend to invest in large-scale projects.[6]

Concerning technology transfer, 76.9% of German firms reported having transferred technologies to China through their subsidiary. There are three modes of technology transfer of German multinational companies: hardware transfer, on-site software transfer, and idea transfer (see Table 4.7). The first mode of technology transfer can increase the capacity of production to the international standard; the second mode can promote local learning of practical techniques and

---

[6]Foreign direct investment in China. Good prospects for German companies? China Special, 2004, pp. 1--3. Internet publication: URL: http://www.dbresearch.com/PROD/DBR_INTERNET_EN-PROD/PROD0000000000178546.pdf [23.05.2005].

Table 4.6 German direct investment in China (million US dollars)

Year	Contracted FDI	Actually used FDI	Accumulated Utilized FDI
1978–1993	1519	546	546
1994	1233	259	805
1995	1659	386	1191
1996	1000	510	1701
1997	628	1008	2709
1998	2374	987	3696
1999	1025	1347	5043
2000	2978	1251	6294
2001	1171	1261	7555
2002	915	928	8483
2003	1390	860	9343
2004	–	1058	10,401
2005	–	1530	11,931
2006	–	2003	13,934

From Ministry of Commerce of China Statistical data

Fig. 4.1 Destinations of German investment in China (2002). Source: From Deutsche Bank; Foreign direct investment in China. Good prospects for German companies? China Special 2004, p. 4. Internet publication: URL: http:// www.dbresearch.com/ PROD/DBR_INTERNET_ EN-PROD/ PROD0000000000178546. pdf

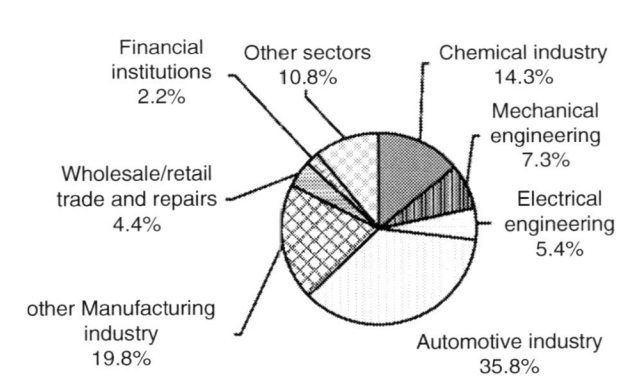

Destinations of German investment in China (2002)

Financial institutions 2.2%

Other sectors 10.8%

Chemical industry 14.3%

Mechanical engineering 7.3%

Wholesale/retail trade and repairs 4.4%

Electrical engineering 5.4%

other Manufacturing industry 19.8%

Automotive industry 35.8%

operation knowledge; and the third one may provide key opportunities for the recipient to catch up with the advanced technologies through gaining knowledge.

As Germany is a coordinated market economy, German investors consider institutional infrastructure more than those from liberal market economies, and German investors are likely to be more eager to maintain control of their own specific competitive advantages when they invest in foreign countries (Chen and Reger 2006). There are two main characteristics of German direct investment in China, which show that the Chinese institutional infrastructure is compatible with German direct investment and that the German production model can easily persist in China.

Table 4.7 Modes of technology transfer of German direct investment in China

Classification	Items	Nature
Hardware transfer	Complete set of technical equipment	Learning of production routine
	Key technical equipment transfer	
On-site software transfer	Technical document and on-site problem-solving	Learning of know-how
	Technical consultancy for production problems	
	Technical personnel and technical training	
	Management and quality control skills	
Idea transfer	Product prototype	Know-why-type learning
	Patent license	

Source: Chen and Reger (2006)

First, for German investors, investment incentives were regarded as rather unimportant when compared with location factors such as the local institutional infrastructure.

German investors consider social infrastructure and general location factors to be much more important than investment incentives. Thus, the preferred geographic locations of German companies in China are in those well-established industrial regions, where German investment may gain support from the institutional infrastructure (Chen and Reger 2006). German firms invest much more in the Shanghai-centered Yangtze Delta (48.93%), Beijing, and the surrounding industrial northeastern coast region (38.48%) than in the southeastern Pearl River Delta (8.17%) (see Table 4.8). Many more state-controlled enterprises are concentrated in the Yangtze Delta or in the industrial northeastern region, rather than in the southeastern coastal region, that is, Pearl River Delta. The northeast of China is famous for its state enterprises (Arvanitis 2006) and is China's heavy industrial center for iron and steel, oil, petrochemicals, shipbuilding, machine tools, aviation, and automobiles (Shenyang-U.S. Commercial Service China 2007). German investors get more support from the institutional infrastructure in the region where there are more state-controlled enterprises, and it seems easier for the German production model to persist in such regions than elsewhere. There are fewer state-controlled enterprises in the southeast Pearl River Delta (Arvanitis 2006; Wong et al. 2003), where there are even more investment incentives, but less institutional infrastructure, which German investors prefer.

As a result, almost all German firms that make investments in China have their representative offices in Shanghai. Also in the northeast, German investors invest in the traditional region of heavy industry, with numerous joint ventures having been launched with China's large state-controlled enterprises, which have traditionally operated there. The Volkswagen, BMW, and ThyssenKrupp joint ventures, the Degussa and Bayer subsidiary, as well as Adidas, Reebok, etc. have all invested there. Fewer German companies have located in the southern Pearl River Delta. German investors have so far greatly bypassed this area. Even though there are many more investment incentives there, especially in the Special Economic

Table 4.8 Geographical distribution of German direct investment in China

Typical district in China	Percentage of German Investment in China
Shanghai-centered Yangtze Delta	48.93
Shanghai city	39.00
Jiangsu province	7.70
Zhejiang province	2.23
Beijing and the surrounding northeastern region	38.48
Beijing city	26.47
Tianjin city	3.17
Hebei province	0.81
Shandong province	3.58
Liaoning province	3.17
Jilin province	1.28
Southeastern Pearl River Delta	8.17
Guangdong province	6.55
Fujian province	1.62
Other district	3.31
Sichuan province	1.35
Hubei province	1.28
Anhui province	0.68
Sum	98.92

Source: Chen and Reger (2006). German investments with shares of less than 0.50% are excluded, which means that the rest, 1.08%, of investment in terms of company numbers is scattered across 11 provinces and cities, and there are still six other provinces with no German investment at all

Zones in this area, only 25% of German investors have invested in Special Economic Zones. So it should be noted that free choice of location in a developing country does not always make it possible to attract German investment (Kreutzberger 2000a, b; Chen and Reger 2006). German investors rather choose to invest in regions with more suitable institutional infrastructure.

Similar to German direct investment, Japanese direct investment also preferred to be made in the north and northeast of China, where there are more state-controlled enterprises with a coordinated firm's governance structure as suitable institutional infrastructure for Japanese firms. Also similar to German investment, the majority of Japanese investment in China went into manufacturing sectors (Deng 1997).

Second, German companies that invest in China can get strong support from their steady supply chain cooperation. German companies therefore keep their institutional advantages by maintaining their specific firm's governance structure when they make investments in China.

German company operation in the supply chain in China is significantly positioned at mid and upper stream markets for China's domestic industrial buyers. German firms in China focus on industrial buyers in the Chinese market (75.1%), and they are upstream buyer oriented (66.7%). Most German companies (75.3%) also purchase semimanufactured products for their own production from the Chinese domestic market (Chen and Reger 2006, p. 411).

German direct investment in China is heavily localized in terms of both product output and material input, obtaining strong support from their steady supply chain cooperation. Because German direct investment relies on a larger share of purchasing of special-purpose parts, these special-purpose product supplies generally require longer-term interfirm relations. German subsidiaries are localized and well positioned in the Chinese market and have set up long-term interfirm relationships in the supply chain (Chen and Reger 2006).

According to the investigations in Chen and Reger (2006), Kreutzberger (2000a, b), and Liu (1997a), most important motives for German companies for investment in China were the prospect of entering into the local market and being well positioned for long-term cooperation in the supply chain, whereas low labor cost and lower production cost appeared to be the least important.

The major factors that are very important for the successful operation of German direct investment in China are a good relationship between the German and Chinese technical personnel and workers, the long-term relationship in the supply chain, and support from the local government. This runs contrary to the opinion that investment incentives and effective marketing were key factors for German investment success (Chen and Reger 2006; Chen 2005).

In terms of the major contributing factors to increasing the level of innovation at the subsidiaries in China, the most important choice is an active technology transfer between parent companies in Germany and subsidiaries in China, which is followed by intensive training of the local technical employees (Chen and Reger 2006).

An advanced production technology is regarded as the most important strength of the German subsidiaries and joint ventures for successfully competing in China. Therefore, technology transfer is very active, and localized firm's governance structure has been well organized. Most of the German companies have long-term strategies for their direct investment in China, and most of them consider their strategic investments in China to be successful (Chen and Reger 2006).

Likewise, for Japanese investors, the organizational capability perspective seems to have a more significant impact in determining the choice of destination of their investment. Japanese investors in China also maintain an organizational pattern similar to that of their domestic counterparts in Japan. Many Japanese direct investment firms in China adopt the form of the Japanese coordinated firm's governance structure, which generally involve collective decision-making, and retain their particular management method of dealing with internal and external relationships. Japanese investors keep their institutional advantages by maintaining the distinctiveness of their organization structure when they made investments in China (Deng 1997).

In short, German and Japanese investments in China link to the industrial destinations with institutional affinity, and this supports the convergence of certain Chinese industrial sectors toward their German and Japanese counterparts.

4.2.2   The Remarkable Achievement of China's Catching-Up

Those catching-up years are roughly from the mid-1990s to the middle of the first decade in the twenty-first century, when the dual-structured economic model and innovation system were built up. However, China's economic growth had been impressively fast since long. Since 1980, China's annual rate of real GDP growth had averaged around 10%. The economy still recorded 10% year-on-year growth in 2003, 10.1% in 2004, 10.4% in 2005, and surged to 10.7%, reaching a GDP of 20.94 trillion yuan (US$2.7 trillion) in 2006.[7] On the basis of the up-to-date exchange rate, China quickly became the world's third largest economy, just behind the USA and Japan in those catch-up years. On the basis of purchasing power parity exchange rates, China was also the world's second largest economy following the USA. Such a strong trend of growth and development shows that China had been quickly catching-up with the leaders in the world economy.

What is the role of FDI in China's economic development? What are the main channels through which FDI may contribute to the economic growth of China? Development economics initially focused on the impact of FDI on economic growth via capital formation. This argument, however, met strong criticisms. A number of empirical tests have been carried out on the impact of FDI on domestic capital formation and economic growth in developing economies. The studies found that FDI had no significant effect on domestic capital formation but had a significant positive effect on economic growth. FDI tended to substitute for domestic savings, rather than to supplement them. Instead of filling the "domestic savings gap," FDI might displace indigenous investment and have a negative effect on domestic investment (Griffin 1970; Weisskopf 1972; Areskoug 1976; Lee et al. 1986; Tian et al. 2004).

Many empirical studies are alike in their conclusion that FDI has almost no effect on domestic capital formation but has a significant positive effect on economic growth (Chen et al. 1995; Lardy 1995, p. 1073; Tseng and Zebregs 2002; Tian et al. 2004; Madariaga and Poncet 2006).

If FDI has no significant effect on domestic capital formation but has a positive effect on economic growth, it must contribute to economic growth via channels other than capital formation. Many new studies have found that the main channel is technology transfer and technology spillover, as inferred from the new theory of endogenous growth. New technology that is embodied in FDI manifests itself in the forms of new ideas, new products, advanced managerial skills, advanced production process, and advanced equipment and could spread out into the whole economy (Romer 1986; Tian et al. 2004). FDI has a positive effect on economic growth by bringing in new technologies and lowering the cost of innovation. By allowing FDI free access to the home market and to profit from the home market, the home country hopes to profit from the expected spillover effects (Ruffin 1993, p. 23; Tian et al. 2004). Technology transfer is not limited to the industries with FDI, because new

---

[7]NBS: China's GDP grows 10.7% in 2006, Nation Bureau of Statistics, January 25, 2007.

technology in FDI can spill over to the whole economy. These are called "externalities" in the new theory of endogenous growth (Tian et al. 2004).

As written in the preceding part, FDI and technology transfer between a developing economy and a developed economy can enhance the economic convergence effect, given that they have a similar economic model. Such an economic convergence effect helps the developing economy to catch up quickly with the developed economy. Because the Chinese economic model is dual structured, FDI and technology transfer from both US leading liberal market economies and Germany leading coordinated market economies can enhance the dual convergence effect. On the basis of such a dual economic convergence, the Chinese economy had been growing remarkably and catching-up quickly with the advanced economies in those years.

4.3 After the Dual-Structured Business Models / Innovation System Being Built Up and Chinese Economy Catching-Up, Chinese Economy Has Quickly Become Its Own Engine for the Economic Development and Innovation Enhancement

Dual structure, dual convergence, and catching-up showed a miracle of those years. The miracle is not going to stop there. Furthermore, as the engine of the Chinese economy is sparked, the Chinese economy gets on the track of further long-term development and innovation explosion.

4.3.1 China Furthers Its Long-Term Economic Development

As previously mentioned, because the Chinese business model and innovation system are dual structured and compatible with both US leading liberal market economies and Germany leading coordinated market economies, FDI from both types of advanced economies to China are encouraged. The dual convergence sparks the engine and sustains China's long-term economic development. Since 1980s, China has been one of the world's fastest growing economies for four decades, with real annual GDP growth averaging nearly 10% through 2010. Starting from the global financial crisis in 2008–2009, Chinese economy relatively slows down, it is driven by its own engine, and it is still much faster than the global average, also faster than the emerging markets and developing economies (see Fig. 4.2).

Due to the rapid and sustainable growth, China has emerged as a major global economic power in recent years. It is now the world's largest economy based on purchasing power parity (see Fig. 4.3), the world's second largest economy based on market exchange rate. Measured by purchasing power parity, China's

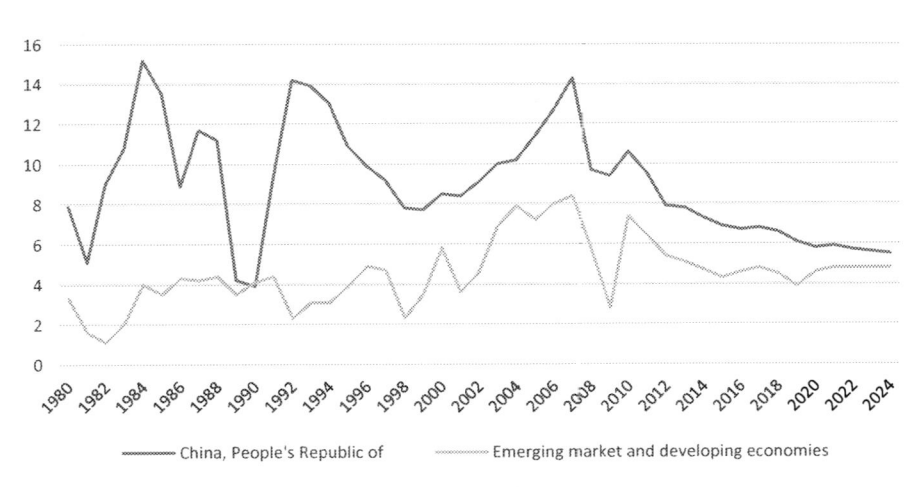

Fig. 4.2 China's real GDP growth rate. Source: IMF data mapper

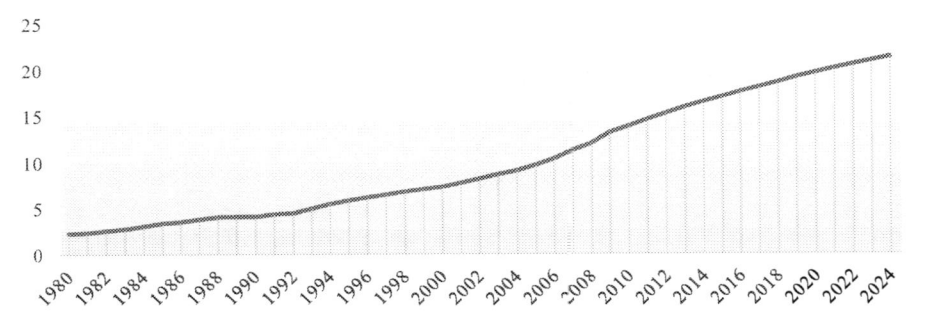

Fig. 4.3 China's share of world total GDP (based on PPP). Source: UNCTAD data center

share in world's total GDP has been steadily increasing from less than 3% in 1980 to above 20% in 2018. It will continue to rise up to about 25% by 2024 (see Fig. 4.3). China's GDP per capita also has increased from around US$400 in the early 1980s to above US$10,000 in 2019. Based on purchasing power parity, Chinese GDP per capita has been above US$20,000, making China into the high-middle-income group in World Bank's country category.

Since the early 2010s, China has also become the world's largest manufacturing center and the largest exporter for commodities (see Table 4.9, Fig. 4.4). China has built up one of the world's most complexed economy. According to Atlas of Economic Complexity published by the Growth Lab at Harvard University, China is ranked as world No. 19th using the Economic Complexity Index (see Fig. 4.5).

China is also the world's largest holder of foreign exchange reserve (see Table 4.10). By 2014, China alone had nearly $4 trillion foreign exchange reserve. In recent years, it reduced to US$3.1trillion but still way ahead of the second largest holder Japan.

Table 4.9 China's world
ranking of merchandise trade

Year	Export	Import
1980	30	22
1985	17	11
1990	14	17
1995	11	12
2000	7	8
2005	3	3
2006	3	3
2007	2	3
2008	2	3
2009	1	2
2016	1	2

Source: Database of Chinese Ministry of Commerce

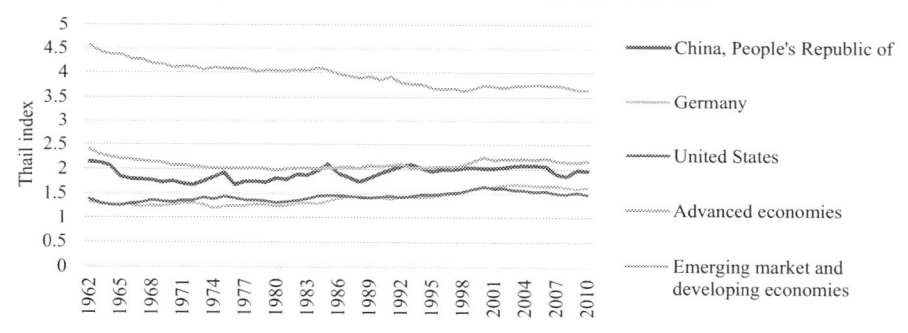

Export diversification of selected countries, economies

Fig. 4.4 China's Export diversification. Source: IMF data mapper

China is also making big progress in upgrading its economic structure, which
means steadily increasing the GDP share of service sectors and lowering the
GDP share of manufacturing sector. By 2018, value added of service sectors
already accounted for 52.2% of GDP in China. In the city like Shanghai, Beijing,
Guangzhou, and Shenzhen, GDP share of services already amounts to about 80%.

Besides upgrading the domestic industrial structure, China has been actively
integrating its economy into the global value chain (GVC) and improving its position
in GVC. China is now one of the hubs of the GVC alongside with the USA and the
European Union.

4.3.2 The Innovation Explosion Effect Follows Up: A Remarkable Success of China's Innovation

The dual convergence effect, based on the dual-structured Chinese model and
innovation system, not only helps the Chinese economy to catch up quickly with
the western advanced economies but also boosts its further development in science,
research, and innovation.

Economic Complexity Index (ECI) by country ranking

The ECI measures the relative knowledge intensity of an economy, The higher the index, the more economically complex a country is determined to be. In 2016, Japan was ranked top using the ECI.

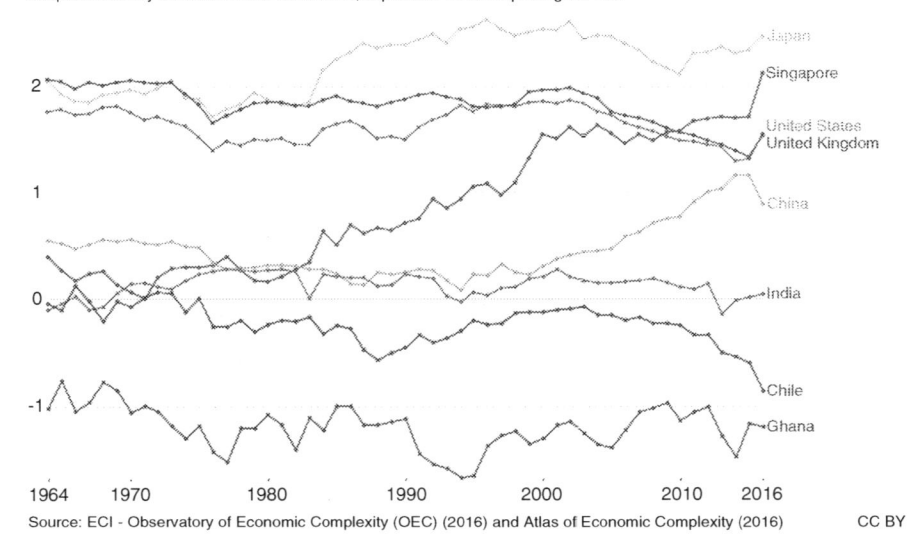

Source: ECI - Observatory of Economic Complexity (OEC) (2016) and Atlas of Economic Complexity (2016)   CC BY

Fig. 4.5 Economic Complexity Index of China, comparing with other countries. Source: MIT Observatory of Economic Complexity (OEC) (2016) and the Harvard Atlas of Economic Complexity (2016)

Table 4.10 World's top 10 foreign exchange reserve holder in 2018 (unit: USD, billion)

1	China	3143
2	Japan	1268
3	Saudi Arabia	489
4	Switzerland	826
5	Russia	464
6	Brazil	381
7	South Korea	397
8	Hong Kong	440
9	India	423
10	Singapore	376

Source: IMF data mapper

Due to the rapid economic growth, China has been able to steadily increase its spending on research and development. According to UNESCO's data on science and technology, China is already the largest spender on R&D in the world based on purchasing power parity. In 2018, Chinese expenditure on R&D reaches US$553.4 billion, higher than the USA (US$511.1 billion), the EU (US$379 billion), much higher than the developing counterpart India (US$66.5 billion) (see Table 4.11).

Even though R&D expenditure per capita in China is still relatively low, e.g., US $388 in 2018, but China's share of R&D expenditures in GDP is among the top

Table 4.11   World's top 20 countries in R&D spending

Country/ region	Expenditures on R&D (billions of US$ PPP)	Percentage of GDP PPP (%)	Expenditures on R&D per capita (US$ PPP)	Year
China	553.4	2.19	388	2018
USA	511.1	2.744	1586.35	2016
European Union	379	1.64	658.94	2016
Japan	165.7	3.147	1297.39	2016
Germany	118.8	2.94	1450.17	2016
South Korea	91.6	4.292	1518.47	2014
India	66.5	0.85	39.37	2015
France	60	2.256	905.8	2014
UK	44.8	1.701	692.9	2014
Russia	42.6	1.187	290.21	2014
Brazil	38.4	1.17	177.89	2012
Italy	27.4	1.287	452.14	2014
Canada	25.7	1.612	723.5	2014
Australia	23.3	2.12	986.86	2014
Spain	19.2	1.222	413.46	2014
The Netherlands	16.3	1.973	967.8	2014
Turkey	15.3	1.007	198.36	2014
Sweden	14.2	3.161	1468.1	2014
Switzerland	13.1	2.967	1647.9	2012
Israel	18.6	4.90	1973	2018

Source: UNESCO, data

10 countries in the world, ahead of many developed countries like Italy, Spain, Canada, and UK (see Fig. 4.6).

In past two decades, China has made a great progress in almost all indicators with regard to science, technology, and innovation, and in some areas it now leads the USA. In the span of about a decade, China has made much faster progress in innovation comparing to the USA (Atkinson and Foote 2019).

One indicator of innovation performance is the number of leading technology companies (software, hardware, Internet, telecommunications, and pharmaceuticals) and their market valuations. In 2009, China had only 2 technology companies among the top 100 companies in the world. And none of Chinese tech company could even made to top 50. By 2019, China had 15 companies among the world's top 100, including Tencent and Alibaba, which are already among top 10, not mentioning that some of the largest leading Chinese technology companies, such as Huawei, which are not publicly traded. China is therefore ranked second, following the USA with 54 leading tech companies (see Table 4.12 and Fig. 4.7).

Another indicator is patent applications. According to statistic data of World Intellectual Property Organization (WIPO), total world patent application by

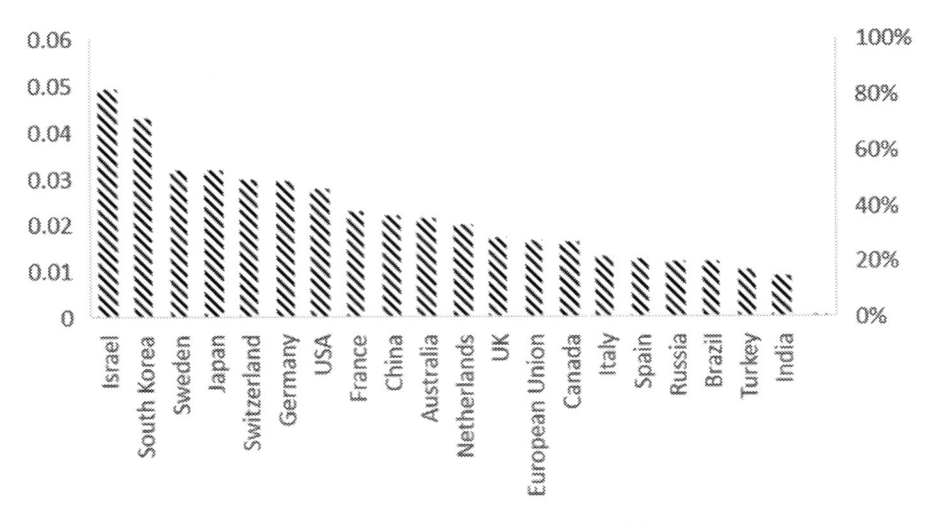

Fig. 4.6 Share of R&D expenditures in total GDP. Source: UNESCO

Table 4.12 Number of technology companies in world's top 100 largest by market capitalization in 2019

	Number of companies	Market capitalization ($bn)	Rank by market capitalization
USA	54	13,292	1
Greater China	15	3197	2
UK	6	870	3
France	5	696	5
Switzerland	3	774	4
Japan	2	298	6
Ireland	2	235	7
South Korea	1	234	8
India	2	233	9
Canada	2	208	10
Belgium	1	169	11
The Netherlands	1	166	12
Germany	1	142	13
Australia	1	131	14
Denmark	1	128	15
South Africa	1	102	16
Saudi Arabia	1	100	17
Brazil	1	100	18
Spain	0	0	N/A

Source: Bloomberg with PwC analysis (PwC 2019)

Fig. 4.7 Share of Chinese innovation Companies in the Global 100 (2009–2017). Source: Atkinson and Foote (2019)

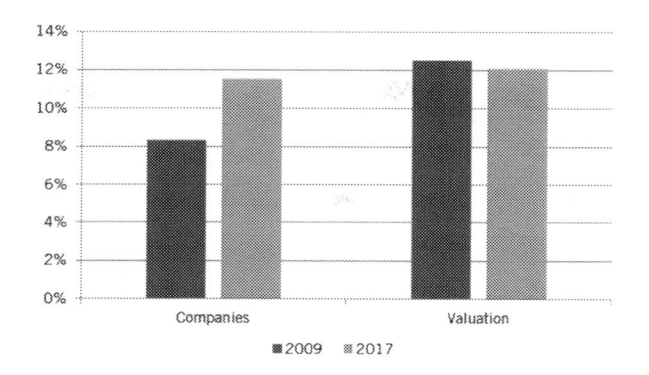

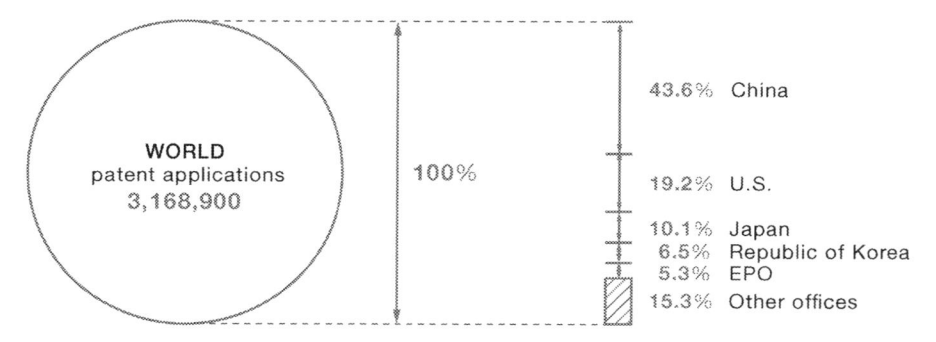

Fig. 4.8 Percentage share of total patent applications by top five countries. Note: EPO-European Patent Office. Source: WIPO statistic database, September 2018

September of 2018 reached 3,168,900 (see Fig. 4.8), of which China accounts for 43.6%, ahead of the USA (19.2%), Japan (10.1%), South Korea (6.5%), and the European Union (5.3%). Similarly, China is also leading in scientific publications. In 2016, there were 426,165 Chinese peer-reviewed science and engineering articles published, surpassing the USA for the first time (Atkinson and Foote 2019).

With the rapid strengthening on basic research, China has quickly improved its position in the World innovation. From many aspects, China is seen as one of the two world innovation leaders, just following the USA. This success is represented by both the Chinese private sector and the state sector.

From the private sector perspective, China is very successful in artificial intelligence (AI), 5G technology development, smart phone design and production, Fintech, E-commerce, Internet of things, etc. From the state sector perspective, China is leading in high speed railways, outer space exploration, drone, automotive driving, and catching-up very quickly in large commercial aircraft technology and biotechnology.

In 5G technology and services sector, two Chinese companies Huawei and ZTE are ahead of Intel, Samsung, LG, and Ericsson, as the top two 5G patent holders (see Fig. 4.9). Huawei, Xiaomi, Vivo, and Oppo are among the top smart phone designers and developers.

In the area of Fintech, China is seen as the world's leading mobile payment market with many world's most innovative mobile payment companies, including Tencent and Alibaba. By 2018, the market size of the digital payment in China reached US$1.9 trillion, much ahead of other countries, almost 10 times bigger than the market size of Japan and UK, and also bigger than USA, UK, Japan, and Germany all together (Table 4.13). More than half a billion people in China are paying with their mobile phones. That is equivalent to a penetration rate of more than 75 percent, the highest in the world. The two dominating payment apps Alipay and WeChat Pay are adopted widely by shopkeepers, cafes, restaurateurs, and consumers alike. In such a country like China, where a lot of small businesses cater to customers, the use of credit cards had never been widely adopted. With this

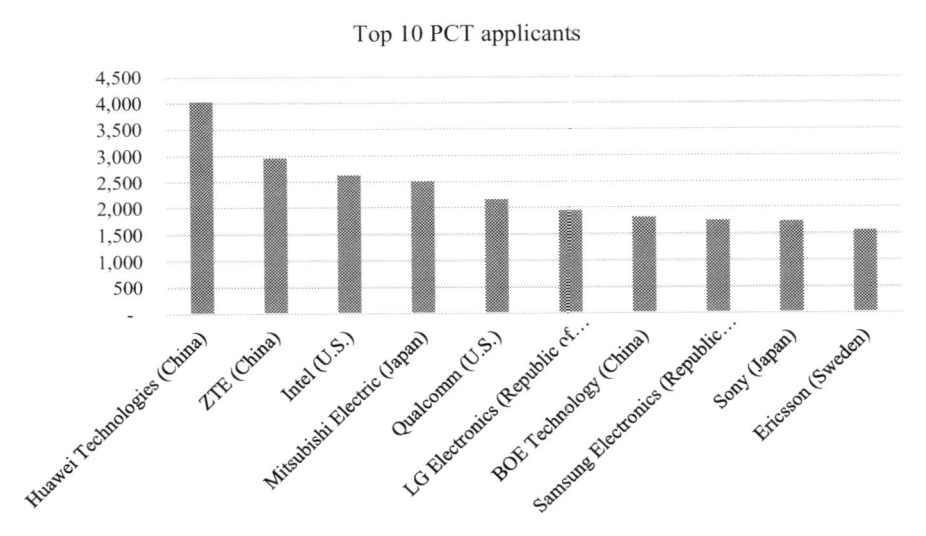

Fig. 4.9 World's leading 5G companies by patent applications. Source: WIPO Statistics Database, September 2018

Table 4.13 World's top five digital payment markets

1. China	US$1,928,753 m
2. USA	US$1,058,288 m
3. UK	US$176,077 m
4. Japan	US$173,136 m
5. Germany	US$127,443 m

Source: Technavio Blog. https://blog.technavio. com/blog/mobile-payment-companies-top-10

Table 4.14 Top AI software companies outside of the USA

Company name	Nation	Revenue (billions)[a]
ByteDance	China	150
Appier	Taipei	30
SenseTime	China	20
Kindred Systems	Canada	6
OrCam Technologies	Israel	6
Mobvoi	China	5.6
Preferred Networks	Japan	5
Prospera	Israel	5
Cambricon	China	2
Element AI	Canada	1.2

Source: Top artificial intelligence (AI) software companies in the USA and internationally https://www.thomasnet.com/articles/top-suppliers/ai-software-companies/

background, the businesses move directly from cash payment to payment by apps, creating a leapfrog effect (Buchholz 2019)

Artificial intelligence is another tech field, which will change our life dramatically in one decade or so. From everyday business to genomic editing, it will be in some ways touched by AI technologies. China has made tremendous strides especially in artificial intelligence. Businesses and government have collaborated on a sweeping plan to make China the world's primary AI innovation center by 2030, the serious progress already being made toward that goal (Amy Webb 2019) (Table 4.14).

China's success in innovation and technology is not only represented by the private sector but also by the state sector. Particularly in infrastructure, telecommunication, space exploration, nuclear power, and aviation industries.

China has developed the most advanced high speed rail technology. The Chinese high speed rail (HSR) consists of a network of passenger-dedicated railways, designed for speeds of 250–350 km/h (155–217 mph) that is faster than most of high speed rail in other countries. It is the world's longest high speed railway network and is also the most extensively used. China's high speed rail accounts for two-thirds of the world's total high speed railway networks. By 2019 December 29, HSR extended to 32 of the country's 34 provinces and municipalities, except for Macau and Tibet. The national network reaches 35,000 km (22,000 mi) in total length. The HSR building boom continues with the HSR network set to reach 38,000 km (24,000 mi) in 2025. In the meantime, China also started testing a magnetic levitation ("maglev") prototype train that runs at 600 km/h in 2019. Furthermore, China's Belt and Road Initiative shows the great innovation in connecting and building the global advanced infrastructure (Table 4.15).

Apart from the well-developed high speed railway system, China is also one of the few countries that has developed the capability to send human being to outer space. In commercial aircraft industry, the state-owned enterprise COMAC is one of the few producers of large commercial aircraft in the world, besides Boeing and Airbus. In nuclear and renewable energy sector, China is one of the leading powers in the world. According to the International Atomic Energy Agency (IAEA), in 2018

Table 4.15 World's longest high speed rail networks by 2019

Rank	Country/region	In operation (km)	Under construction (km)	Total (km)	Max. speed (km/h)
1	China	32,200	6007	38,207	350
2	Spain	3410	2110	5525	310
3	Germany	1571	1051.889	4692.889	300
		2070			250
4	France	2734	341.3	3802.1	320
		726.8			220
5	Japan	2764.6	657.1	3421.7	320
6	Sweden	1706	349.1	2055.1	205
7	UK	1527	230	1757	300
8	Italy	1467	890.96	2357.96	300
9	Turkey	1213	2287	3500	250
10	South Korea	1104.5	425	1529.5	305

Source: Data based on International Union of Railways with some corrections from news report

nuclear power generation in the world increased by 2.4%, of which 1.8% is due to a 19% increase in China. China is ranked third in the world both in total nuclear power capacity installed and electricity generated, accounting for around one-tenth of global nuclear power generated.

References

Webb, A. (2019). *China is leading in artificial intelligence—and American businesses should take note.* Retrieved from https://www.inc.com/magazine/201809/amy-webb/china-artificial-intelligence.html

Areskoug, K. (1976). Private foreign investment and capital formation in developing countries. *Economic Development and Cultural Change, 24*(2), 539–547.

Arvanitis, R. (2006). Technological learning in Pearl River Delta: The creation of an industrial space. In *Communication presented at the seminar - Globalisation and opening markets in developing countries and its impact on national firms: The case of China, Beijing, March 31 & April 1, 2006*, Institute of World Economics and Politics, Chinese Academy of Social Sciences.

Atkinson, R. D., & Foote, C. (2019, April). *Is China catching up to the United States in innovation?* ITIF report.

Bargas, S. E. (2000). Direct investment positions for 1999: Country and industrial betail. *Survey of Current Business, 80*(7), 57–68.

Blomstrom, M., & Kokko, A. (1998). *How foreign investment affects host countries?* (Policy Research Working Paper No. 1745). Washington, DC: International Trade Department, World Bank.

Chen, C., Chang, L., & Zhang, Y. M. (1995). The role of foreign direct investment in China's post-1978 economic development. *World Development, 23*(4), 691–703.

Chen, J. (2005). *Corporate governance in China.* London: Routledge Curzon.

Chen, X. D., & Reger, G. (2006). The role of technology in the investment of German firms in China. *Technovation, 26*(3), 407–415.

Cheung, K., & Lin, P. (2004). Spillover effects of FDI on innovation in China: Evidence from the provincial data. *China Economic Review, 15*, 25–44.

Deng, L. (1997). Understanding Japanese direct investment in China (1985–1993). *American Journal of Economics and Sociology, 56*(1), 115–127.

Eden, L., Levitas, E., & Martinez, R. (1997). The production, transfer and spillovers of technology: Comparing large and small multinationals as technology producers. *Small Business Economics, 9*, 53–66.

Foreign Direct Investment and Manufacturing Productivity in China. (2002), p. 11. Retrieved May 20, 2005, from http://www.bm.ust.hk/~ced/Yu%20CHEN.pdf

Fung, H.-G., Julius, H., Johnson, J. R., & Xu, Y. (2004a). Winners and losers: Foreign firms in China's emerging market. *The Chinese Economy, 37*(3), 5–16.

Fung, K. C. (2004). *United States Direct investment in China*, p. 2. Retrieved May 20, 2005, from http://www.aei.org/docLib/20040920_book273text.pdf or http://www.tdctrade.com/econforum/hkcer/hkcer041001.htm

Fung, K. C., Lau, L. J., & Lee, J. S. (2004b). *U.S. direct investment in China*. Washington, DC: The AEI Press (Publisher for the American Enterprise Institute).

Gorg, H., & Strobl, E. (2001). Multinational companies and productivity spillovers: A meta-analysis. *The Economic Journal, 111*, 723–739.

Griffin, K. B. (1970). Foreign capital, domestic savings and development. *Bulletin of the Oxford University Institute of Economics & Statistics, 32*(1), 15–27.

Hall, P. A., & Soskice, D. (2001). *Varieties of capitalism*. New York: Oxford University Press.

Hu, A., & Jefferson, G. (2001). *FDI, technological innovation and spillover: Evidence from large and medium size Chinese enterprises*. Waltham, MA: Mimeo, Brandeis University.

Katharina Buchholz, 2019. *China's mobile payment adoption beats all others*. Retrieved from https://www.statista.com/chart/17909/pos-mobile-payment-user-penetration-rates/

Kreutzberger, P. (2000a). *An OECD member country perspective: Experience of German investment promotion in China* (p. 2). Retrieved May 23, 2005, from http://www.oecd.org/dataoecd/11/25/1902830.pdf

Kreutzberger, P. (2000b, September 11–12). *An OECD member country perspective: Experience of German investment promotion in China*, Xiamen: OECD-China Conference on Foreign Direct Investment.

Lardy, N. R. (1995). The role of foreign trade and investment in China's economic transformation. *The China Quarterly, 123*(3), 1065–1082.

Lee, J., Rana, P. B., & Iwasaki, Y. (1986). *Effects of foreign capital inflows on developing countries of Asia*. Asian Development Bank Economic Staff Paper 30.

Liu, G. (1997a, March). Some issues concerning medium and small enterprise reform. *Zhongguo Gongye Jingji (China Industrial Economy)*.

Madariaga, N., & Poncet, S. (2006). *FDI in Chinese cities: Spillovers and impact on growth* (Working Paper No. 2006-22). CEPII.

Multinational Companies Adjust Strategies to China. (2004), p. 2. Retrieved May 23, 2005, from http://www.china-window.com/china_market/china_industry_reports/multinational-compa nies-a.shtml

PWC. (2019). *Global top 100 companies by market capitalization*. Retrieved from https://www.pwc.com/gx/en/audit-services/publications/assets/global-top-100-companies-2019.pdf

Romer, P. (1986). Increasing returns and long-run growth. *Journal of Political Economy, 94*(4), 1002–1037.

Ruffin, R. J. (1993). The role of foreign investment in the economic growth of the Asian and Pacific region. *Asian Development Review, 11*(1), 1–23.

Shenyang-U.S. Commercial Service China. (2007). Retrieved November 09, 2007, from http://www.buyusa.gov/china/en/shenyang.html

The US-China Business Council. (2003). *Foreign investment in China 2002* (p. 2). Retrieved May 20, 2005, from http://www.uschina.org/statistics/2003foreigninvestment.html

Tian, X., Lin, S., & Lo, V. I. (2004). Foreign direct investment and economic performance in transition economies: Evidence from China. *Post-Communist Economies, 16*(4), 497–510.

Tong, J. Y., & Hu, A. Y. (2003). Foreign investment and technology transfer: A simple model. *European Economic Review, 36*(1), 137–155.

Top Sources for Foreign Direct Investment in China. (2007). *World Trade, 20*(5), 16.

Tseng, W., & Zebregs, H. (2002). *Foreign direct investment in China: Some lessons for other countries*. IMF Policy Discussion Paper, 02/3.

US Commercial Technology Transfers to the People's Republic of China. (1999)., p. 4. Retrieved May 23, 2005, from http://www.bxa.doc.gov/DefenseIndustrialBasePrograms/OSIES/DefMarketResearchRpts/techtransfer2prc.html; http://www.fas.org/nuke/guide/china/doctrine/dmrr_chinatech.htm

U.S. Department of Commerce, Bureau of Economic Analysis. (2003a, September). *U.S. Direct Investment Abroad: U.S. Direct Investment Position Abroad on a Historical-Cost Basis*. Survey of Current Business.

U.S. Department of Commerce, Bureau of Economic Analysis. (2003b, October). *U.S. International Services: Royalties and license fees*. Survey of Current Business.

Wei, Y., & Liu, X. (2006). Productivity spillovers from R&D, exports and FDI in China's manufacturing sector. *Journal of International Business Studies, 37*(4), 544–557.

Weisskopf, T. E. (1972). The impact of foreign capital inflows on domestic savings in underdeveloped countries. *Journal of International Economics, 12*(1), 25–38.

Wong, K.-y., Shen, J., Feng, Z., & Chaolin, G. (2003). An analysis of dual-track urbanization in the Pearl River Delta since 1980. *Tijdschift voor Economische en Sociale Geografe, 94*(2), 205–218.

Conclusion

Different from the US leading liberal market economies (American model and innovation system) and the Germany leading coordinated market economies (European model and innovation system), a dual-structured economic model and its related dual innovation system are found in China.

China's state sector is dominated by the state-controlled shareholding-coordinated firm's governance structure with a state strategic innovation system, which operates with a logic similar to that in coordinated market economies: But the Chinese state strategic innovation system appears more powerful than the institutional coordination-based (incremental) innovation system in coordinated market economies; While the private sector is dominated by the market-based firm's governance structure with a market-oriented (radical) innovation system, which operates with a logic similar to that in liberal market economies: But the confidence and the positive externalities generated from the Chinese state sector help the private sector to avoid the market failure and crisis that occur inevitably in liberal market economies.

The connection between the institutional environment and the two types of strength, and the starting time of Chinese model of dual market economy and innovation system.

Chinese society is a Confucianism-influenced society with two basic institutional traits: highly centralized authority to the state and lack of institutionalized coordination. They support the two types of strength to grow: "coordination" by the state through its controlling shareholding, which matches the highly centralized authority to the state (the state coordination has affinity with the institutional coordination in coordinated market economies, only the types of coordination are different); and "the market mechanism," which matches the lack of institutionalized coordination similar to that in liberal market economies. Chinese reformers started to build up the dual market economy and innovation system from the mid-1990s. The topic of the book focuses on the critical 10-year period from the mid-1990s to the middle of the first decade of the twenty-first century, when the dual-structured Chinese model and the innovation system were built up.

C. LIAO, *The Governance Structures of Chinese Firms*, Innovation, Technology, and Knowledge Management, https://doi.org/10.1007/978-3-030-52218-6

Comparison between China's state-controlled shareholding-coordinated firm's governance structure and coordinated firm's governance structure in the Germany leading coordinated market economies, and the reason why the state strategic innovation in the former appears superior to the innovation in the latter.

In China's state-controlled shareholding-coordinated firm's governance structure, the coordination role is played by the state based on its controlling shareholding. The state-controlled shareholding-coordinated firm's governance structure is constrained within the state sector. In the coordinated firm's governance structure of coordinated market economies, the coordination role is fulfilled by the institutional coordination arrangements, whose coordinating mechanism covers the whole economy.

These two types of coordination have institutional affinity to each other. China's state-controlled shareholding-coordinated firm's governance structure has state strategic innovation system, which is similar to the coordination-based innovation system in the coordinated firm's governance structure of Germany leading coordinated market economies. But the former appears superior to the latter, considering the former has a state strategic view and state strategic financing based on the state controlling shareholding which the latter does not have.

Why can the dual-structured model and innovation system be established in the Chinese economy?

In the state-controlled shareholding-coordinated firm's governance structure in China, the coordinating mechanism is the coordination by the state through its controlling shareholding. It has clear coordination boundary and can be constrained within the state sector. Outside the state sector, private firms can develop a different kind of firm's governance structure—the market-based firm's governance structure, which matches the institutional environment in the private sector. Therefore, two different types of firm's governance structure and its related two different types of innovation system coexist in the Chinese economy.

Why cannot the US leading liberal market economies and Germany leading coordinated market economies support the dual structure?

Because the coordinating mechanisms in firms' governance structures of the two apply and cover the whole economy—they do not have clear boundary and cannot be constrained within a certain part of the economy—a different type of firm's governance structure has no ground to be rooted in each type of economy.

The state-controlled shareholding coordination is different from the state direction.

State-controlled shareholding coordination implies that the state plays a coordination role based on the state controlling shareholding. Only in the Chinese state sector, where the state continues to be the controlling shareholder, can the state play such a coordination role; while in the Chinese private sector, where there is no state-controlled shareholding, there is no state coordination.

State direction can be carried out without state ownership, like in some of the Asian countries, such as Japan, South Korea, and some other Southeast Asian countries. In such cases, the boundary of the "state direction" cannot be clearly defined. This type of state coordination normally applies and covers the whole economy and cannot be constrained within a certain part of the economy. Therefore, the state direction cannot support a dual-structured economic model as the state ownership coordination can.

Is the dual-structured Chinese model and innovation system consistent with the concept of institutional complementarities, i.e., will it generate friction between the two sectors?

The above explanation of the reason why a dual structure can be found in China also makes it clear that the dual-structured Chinese model and innovation system are consistent with the theory of institutional complementarities. Because of the clear coordination boundary between the two sectors, the institutional complementarities have been intact in each sector.

The consistency of the dual structure of Chinese model and innovation system with the concept of institutional complementarities minimizes friction between the two sectors. The friction is mostly generated when the institutional complementarities face challenge or are endangered. In the Chinese case, the institutional complementarities would be endangered if there were no clear boundary between the coordination mechanisms of these two sectors. As it has been found that the coordination boundary clearly divides these two sectors, the institutional complementarities in each sector are therefore intact, and it can minimize the friction.

Whitley's approach also supports this finding. His approach places high priority on the ownership dimension, which mostly determines all other dimensions in the firm's governance system. Therefore, the different ownership types determine the different institutional complementaries and its operating logics in different business systems. In China, different ownership between the state sector and the private sector results in different institutional complementarities and different operating logics between the two sectors which prevent the friction.

Interactions between the Chinese state sector and private sector are unlikely to generate a convergence effect between the two sectors.

Here the crucial point is that the convergence issue is only a political decision. Both sectors are embedded in the same cultural and historical institutional environment. What generates the basic difference in the running logic between the two sectors is state ownership. If the state keeps the controlling shareholding in the state sector, the state sector business system will keep state coordination arrangements and therewith retain a systemic logic different from that of the private sector. Even interactions cannot lead to the convergence of the different logics in each business system. Only if the state were to make a political decision and give up state ownership, would this change the configuration of the dual-structured Chinese model and innovation system and lead to the convergence of the state sector toward the private sector.

In reality, some more findings would contribute to this argument. First, both sectors are constrained within different industries and constitute different markets. Second, there is little competition-driven convergence between the two sectors. Competition is one of the most important factors for generating the convergence effect between competitors, especially when they are within the same markets (Hollingsworth and Boyer 1997, pp. 33–34). As the Chinese state sector and private sector constitute two different markets, the competition in-between is low (Garnaut et al. 2001, p. 49). Third, the sector boundary also minimizes the poaching effect between the two sectors. Fourth, neither can other interactions between the two sectors—such as some supply and demand linkages which exist between the state sector and the private sector (Garnaut et al. 2001, pp. 48–49)—generate the convergence. Both sectors value highly their own comparative advantages, because they support their firms to compete successfully in the respective industries. The convergence would make them lose their own particular comparative advantages which are valued by their particular industries. Fifth, Whitley's approach about different ownership types determining different logics of institutional complementarities also supports this point. The different ownership types between these two sectors result in different institutional complementarities which prevent the convergence. Last but not least, the intact institutional complementarities in each sector prevent the convergence. Because of the clear coordination boundary between the two sectors, the institutional complementarities in each sector are intact, and this prevents convergence.

The dual structure of the Chinese economic model generates a dual innovation system and dual core competitiveness, which is a strong support for Chinese economic development and growth.

Different economic models have different kinds of innovation capacity and core competitiveness; therefore, a particular economic model only enhances competitiveness in certain industrial sectors, but limits the capacity to compete in others (Hall and Soskice 2001). The US leading liberal market economies have a market-oriented (radical) innovation system and market competitiveness, but they are constrained to develop a coordination-based (incremental) innovation system and organizational competitiveness like that in coordinated market economies. The Germany leading coordinated market economies have a coordination-based (incremental) innovation system and organizational competitiveness, but they are constrained to develop a market-oriented (radical) innovation system and market competitiveness like that in liberal market economies.

In contrast, the dual structure of the Chinese economy generates a dual innovation system and dual core competitiveness, which is the strong support for Chinese economic development and growth. The state-controlled shareholding-coordinated firm's governance structure in the state sector generates a coordination-based state strategic innovation system, which is similar to but also superior to the incremental innovation system and organizational core competitiveness in Germany leading coordinated market economies. While the market-based firm's governance structure in the private sector generates the market-oriented innovation system and market competitiveness similar to that in the US leading liberal market economies. The dual innovation system and the dual core competitiveness have enabled the Chinese economy to compete more successfully than liberal market economies and coordinated market economies, which have only one type of innovation system and core competitiveness, respectively. With such an overall innovation system and competitiveness, Chinese economy can develop successfully in much broader industrial sectors, technological sectors, and scientific research fields than the US leading liberal market economies and Germany leading coordinated market economies. Table (in conclusion) summarizes the results of the comparison of different types of innovation system and core competitiveness based on different firms' governance structures between Chinese state firms, Chinese private firms, German firms, Japanese firms, US firms, and UK firms.

Chinese economic growth has been overwhelmingly supported by endogenous factors and driven by domestic sources. China's economic growth can therefore sustain high single-digit growth rates for decades, unfettered by world market limitations (Keidel 2008). Even though the contribution to Chinese economic growth from exports and trade surplus has become a common assumption, it has just occupied a secondary position.

China's state coordination through the state controlling shareholding is based on the corporatization of state banks and state enterprises and the Company Law. In the meantime, the state shareholder function is scientifically separated from the state regulation function. Therefore, the state-controlled shareholding coordination does not stifle economic initiative and productivity gains as in the former central planning economic system. In contrast, it helps the state sector to implement long-term development strategies and also helps to sustain confidence in the economy. Based on the state coordination and the advance in macroeconomic management, China's policy-makers have increasingly shown an ability to manage cyclical ups and downs, to make a sustainable economic growth.

China's state-controlled financial system pursues a combination of developmental and commercial goals. After the reform during the mid-1990s, it becomes economically efficient. In the meantime, because of the state-controlled shareholding coordination, it also directs credits to state strategic industries and public investments, especially in infrastructure. China's financial system is not only a strong support for, but also a source of confidence in, optimistic economic development and growth.

China's "scientific development" strategy, which is based on state coordination and academic studies, promotes the goal of a combination of economic growth with goals involving environment protection, social welfare systemization, even-handed courts and judicial proceedings, professionalization, and nongovernmental civil society empowerment. Especially, civil society empowerment is an important element for improving the institutionalized trust in the private sector, and thus for the development of the Chinese private sector from personal management toward managerial management. With such a successful development, Chinese dual-structured economic model has been updated to a more advanced stage: market-based firm's governance structure with advanced managerial management (instead of previous personal management) in the private sector and state-controlled shareholding-coordinated firm's governance structure in the state sector.

Extraordinary poverty reduction and rapid income improvement everywhere in China markedly weaken the significance of the modest increase in interregional gaps and the gaps between social groups. This is also a sign of policy success (Keidel 2008).

Table (in conclusion): Comparison of the dual-structured Chinese model and its super innovation system with coordinated market economies (Germany and Japan) and liberal market economies (the US and the UK) (Including the following five sub-tables)

Sub-table 1 Comparison according to the dimensions of economic model, business system, coordinating type, and ownership and control

Economic model	*Coordinated* market economies with *coordinated* firm's governance structure		Chinese *dual-structured* market economy with *dual* firms' governance structures		*Liberal* market economies with *market-based* firm's governance structure	
Business system	Alliance-controlled firms-dominated business system		Coordination-based firms-dominated state sector	Direct owner-controlled firms-dominated private sector	Direct owner-controlled firms-dominated business system	Market arm's length controlled firms-dominated business system
	German firms	*Japanese firms*	*Chinese state firms*	*Chinese private firms*	*UK firms*	*US firms*
Coordinating type	Institutionalized coordination	Institutionalized coordination	Coordination of the state through its controlling shareholding	Market coordination	Market coordination	Market coordination
Ownership and control	Cross-shareholding; interlocking directorship; concentrated shareholding with a few block shareholders; rarely trading their shares; rare hostile takeover; insider-dominated corporate governance; "voice" instead of "exit" as corporate control; consensus decision-making; long-term managerial contract	Cross-shareholding; interlocking directorship; concentrated shareholding with a few block shareholders; rarely trading their shares; insider-dominated corporate governance; "voice" instead of "exit" as corporate control; consensus decision-making; lifelong managerial contract	SASAC and its local organizations as shareholders of state assets; the state as direct or indirect (through state-controlled enterprises) controlling shareholders; cross-shareholding; interlocking directorship; concentrated shareholding with majority of state shares being not allowed to be traded; the power to appoint and to remove the top management by state shareholders; insider dominated; "voice" instead of "exit" as corporate control	Firms owned and controlled by individual, family, or groups of individuals; owner-managed firms	Firms owned and controlled by individual or family; personal management or family-managed	Arm's length control type of ownership; clear ownership boundaries; widely held shares; market for corporate control; hostile takeovers; top management unilateral control; freedom to hire and fire; freedom to impose a new market-oriented strategy; typical managerial management

Sub-table 2 Comparison according to the dimension of employer–employee interdependence

	German firms	Japanese firms	Chinese state firms	Chinese private firms	UK firms	US firms
Employer–employee interdependence	Long-term labor contract; high employment protection; employee representatives in works council and supervisory board; co-determination structure; highly skilled labor; substantial work autonomy; collective wage bargaining; highly centralized trade unions and associations; industry-specific skill training	Long-term employment relations and job security; participatory work management; consensus decision-making; employee loyalty; job rotation and flexible labor assignments; intensive on-the-job and firm-specific training; seniority-based wage and promotion system; small gap in the distributions of the profits and wages; company welfare capitalism; common company unions	Employee representatives in the supervisory board; codetermination structure; long-term labor contract; employment protection; seniority-based wage system; state- and company-based welfare benefits; legal role of labor union and worker's congress; collective contracting and collective wage bargaining	Market-oriented employment relations; procedural informality; short-term employment contract; high level of labor turnover; inadequate employment protection; unattractive worker training; unilaterally determined employment terms and conditions by owner-managers; market-oriented wage and benefits; inadequate employment welfare benefits; lack of labor unions and collective bargaining; individualized process of pay bargaining between employer and employee	Fluid external labor market for employment; short-term employment contract; high level of labor turnover; substantial amount of job movement among firms; lack of investment in skill training; unilateral determination by employers; procedural informality; individualized process of pay bargaining between employer and employee; lack of trade unions, works councils and collective bargaining	Fluid external labor market for employment; short-term employment contract; unilateral freedom for management to hire and fire employees; considerable job mobility from firm to firm; substitutable workers with narrow job assignments and skills; lack of incentive by both employers and employees to invest in specific training and skill development; high degree of distrust between labor and capital; weakly developed business associations, trade unions, and collective actions

Sub-table 3 Comparison according to the dimension of inter-firm relations

	German firms	Japanese firms	Chinese state firms	Chinese private firms	UK firms	US firms
Inter-firm relations	Representatives of other firms on the supervisory boards of firms; cross-shareholding-induced consensus decision-making; inside information sharing and network monitoring among firms; close relationships with suppliers and clients; business associations and collective coordination	Cross-shareholding encouraged long-term relation; main bank-centered business group; interdependence among member firms in the business group; long-term stable relationships between producers and suppliers; clustering and cooperation among complementary firms; trade associations' coordination roles	State-owned enterprise groups resemblance to the Japanese business groups; cross-shareholding and interlocking directorship among member firms; finance company for the group; primarily dealing with suppliers and clients within the group; state coordination role in the group through the state's controlling shareholding	Lack of institutionalized coordination; short-term opportunistic market relation; a combination of market relations and personal networks; personal networks as informal market-supporting institution; benefit-oriented personal network functioning like a market; market-based logic of personal network different from the institutionalized coordination in coordinated market economies	Lack of institutionalized coordination; short-term and opportunistic market relations; loose contractual cooperation	Standard market relationships; enforceable formal contracts; lack of collective coordination, business networks and associations; high degree of distrust and instability between the firms and their suppliers; opportunistic relationships among producers and suppliers; a low degree of cooperation among competitors; hard-nosed bargaining over prices

Sub-table 4 Comparison according to the dimension of firms' financing pattern and performance criteria

	German firms	Japanese firms	Chinese state firms	Chinese private firms	UK firms	US firms
Firms' financing pattern and performance criteria	Access to finance that is not dependent on balance sheet financial data; bank-based financing; substantial proportion of shares by banks; banks exercise the stock voting rights and serve on the supervisory boards of firms; long-term relationship between banks and firms; less well-developed security markets; "inside" information sharing and networking reputation monitoring; exempt from fluctuation of the equity markets; long-run returns and long-term growth instead of the maximization of current returns as the main performance criteria	Bank-based financing; long-term bank–firm relationship; bank-centered business group; important role of banks in corporate governance; poorly developed equity and bond markets; nonexposure to fluctuations of the stock market; long-term growth instead of short-term profit maximization as the main performance goal	Access to financial capital which is independent of short-term profitability; bank-based financing; combination of development and commercial goals of banks; important role of banks in corporate governance; state controlling shareholding-based coordination between banks and firms; preferential access to stock market; majority state shares not allowed to be freely traded; nonexposure to fluctuation of the stock market; insider-dominated corporate governance; state strategic innovation; Long-term strategies oriented development and innovation instead of short-term profit maximization; the pursuit of stakeholder value instead of shareholder value	Self-financing; limited bank loans with hard budget constraints; limited access to the stock market; short-term maximization of profitability, high turnover rate of working capital, as well as family wealth as the most important performance criteria	Little need to seek investment from financial institutions; insignificant role of banks in firms' investments; the initial investments from the founding families; financing expansion of firms from retained earnings or by issuing debentures or other non-voting securities; profits and a large income instead of long-term growth as primary performance objectives	Less dependent on the bank system; arm's length banking system; heavily dependent on liquid financial markets; strongly dependent on the valuation of firms in equity markets; publicly available balance sheet information for dispersed investors to value the company; well-developed venture capital markets; current profitability, share price, as well as short-term profit maximization as the main performance criteria

Sub-table 5 Comparison according to the dimension of firms' innovation system and core competitiveness

	German firms	Japanese firms	Chinese state firms	Chinese private firms	UK firms	US firms
Firms' innovation system and core competitiveness	Coordination-based incremental innovation system; organizational competitiveness; rapid diffusion of the latest technology to the production of traditional products; better competing on the basis of high performance and high quality rather than cost; productive efficiency based on the long-term commitment of major stakeholders for collective learning and intensive horizontal cooperation; lack of allocative efficiency; lack of market-oriented innovation and competitiveness; highly	Coordination-based incremental innovation system; organizational competitiveness; lack of market-oriented radical innovation and competitiveness; productive efficiency instead of allocative efficiency; enormously successful in improving upon existing products; less successful in developing new products; well competing in machinery, electronic products, cars and trucks, and machine tools; less competitive in IT industries	Coordination-based state strategic innovation system similar to incremental innovation system; organizational competitiveness; productive efficiency based on the long-term commitment of major stakeholders for collective learning and intensive horizontal cooperation; rapid diffusion of the latest technology to the traditional products; better competing on the basis of high performance and quality rather than cost; lack of market-oriented innovation and competitiveness; lack of allocative efficiency;	Market-oriented competitiveness; lack of organizational competitiveness; market-oriented innovation system; lack of coordination-based incremental innovation; allocative efficiency; lack of productive efficiency; highly competitive in cost-sensitive businesses, such as consumer electronics and other consumer goods; highly competitive in the new technological sectors, such as IT industries and bioengineering; less competitive in developing heavy industries and	Market-oriented competitiveness and innovation system; allocative efficiency; lack of coordination-based innovation and organizational competitiveness; lack of productive efficiency; the large industrial firms cluster in much the same broad categories as those in the US do, but concentrate in different sub-divisions; produce consumer goods instead of industrial ones; compete well in the production of branded or packaged products—food, drink, and tobacco; devise new	Market-oriented competitiveness; market-oriented radical innovation system; allocative efficiency; excellence in developing new products and industries; highly developed commercial applications of creative innovations; highly competitive in the production of low-cost standardized products; lack of coordination based incremental innovation and organizational competitiveness; lack of productive efficiency; less successful in improving upon the

(continued)

	German firms	Japanese firms	Chinese state firms	Chinese private firms	UK firms	US firms
	competitive in machine tools and automobiles industries; less competitive in IT industries		highly competitive in heavy industries and capital intensive technological sectors, such as power, steel, chemicals, machinery, automobiles, and infrastructures; less competitive in IT industries and consumer electronics	capital intensive traditional technology areas, such as new energy source, new material, automobile	technology in packaging and branding products	products; lack of the ability to achieve a high level of quality competitiveness; compete well in IT, nuclear power, pharmaceuticals, soft drinks, breakfast cereals, soaps, paper, advertising, and entertainment industries

The dual-structured Chinese model and innovation system support the dual convergence of the Chinese economy toward both kinds of advanced economies (US leading liberal market economies and Germany leading coordinated market economies). Foreign direct investment and technology transfer sparked this dual convergence.

Even though the concept of institutional divergence and continuity of business systems does not support arguments for the convergence among different business systems, it can support the argument for the dual convergence of the Chinese economy toward both advanced liberal market economies and coordinated market economies. Such a dual convergence is sparked by foreign direct investment and technology transfer and the dual institutional affinity.

Therefore, the dual-structured Chinese model not only generates a dual institutional advantage, a dual innovation system, and dual core competitiveness but also generates a dual convergence effect. All these joint strengths contribute to the remarkable Chinese catching-up and the development of China's super innovation.

The future of the Chinese economy.

The future of the Chinese economy is mainly based on the political decision. If the state makes a political decision to give up state ownership, it will change the configuration of the dual market economy into a liberal market economy. Because currently the dual-structured Chinese economy has already reached a strategic equilibrium, such a shift will not likely happen. Dual-structured Chinese model and innovation system will then get further stabilized. As a strong base, they will sustain the development of the future Chinese economy and the remarkable achievement of its super innovation.

Can dual-structured Chinese model and innovation system be intentionally replicated in other countries?

The determinative factors for the setup of the dual-structured Chinese economic model are the state-controlled shareholding coordination, which inherently has a clear coordination boundary and a market economy framework. The replicability of the dual-structured Chinese model in other economies lies in the probability of their setting up state-controlled shareholding coordination, because the market mechanism is an easy mode of a coordinating mechanism and can be easily set up in any contemporary economies. The US leading liberal market economies could have the potential to intentionally build up the dual-structured economy, especially when facing an economic crisis. The government stock injection plan and the nationalization of financial institutions in liberal market economies (the USA, the UK) during the financial crisis in 2008—the effort towards this direction—could build up dual system. The effort has been indeed proved quite successful in lifting the economy out of the recession. And as a positive experience, this effort will be repeated in the next similar crisis situation. If these liberal market economies further nationalize some of their strategic industries, they will successfully build up the dual structure. The US style of dual structure would probably show advancement in the sense that its private sector has much mature venture capital market and its private sector develops in much broader high-technology fields than the Chinese private sector (however, the Chinese economy has reached the goal of developing into a more advanced dual structure with managerial management integrated into its private sector that secures its position as one of the leading powers in the world economy). For coordinated market economies, it would be more complicated to develop a dual structure because of its extensively internal institutionalized coordination, which is not supportive of the liberal market concept. In the meantime, the nationalization of the banking system in the financial crisis in 2008 could only lead to a double coordination (its original institutionalized coordination and the established state ownership coordination in the financial sector), but not the dual structure. The state direction in some other coordinated market economies (like those in South Korea and other Southeast Asian countries) also belongs to the state coordination strategy. Such kind of state coordination can be played by the state government without being based on state ownership. It does not have a clear coordination boundary and its role covers the whole economy; therefore, it also cannot support the dual structure as can the state-controlled shareholding coordination in the Chinese state sector. The socialist developing countries, which plan to duplicate the Chinese economic development strategy, have the potential to do so. The strong precondition is to start a reform and open policy and to build up a market economy framework.

Comparison of the Chinese economy with the US leading liberal market economies and the Germany leading coordinated market economies, regarding the stability to avoid an economic crisis and the capability to control crisis.

Chinese dual structure has stronger stability than coordinated market economies and liberal market economies. Chinese state ownership coordination in statist financial system and in capital control mechanism keeps the risks in the financial markets and the housing markets under control. The state controlling shareholding can instill the confidence into the economy, and can generate positive externalities, eg. state-controlled shareholding coordination initiates building infrastructures for the whole economy. Confidence and positive externalities contribute to the correction of market failure, stabilizing the economy and avoiding the crisis. At the same time, the owner-manager managing style involving managerial management in Chinese private firms tend to place more emphasis on the balance between the risk taken and profit driven than managers in the managerial management in the USA. The managers in the managerial management in the USA tend to place more emphasis on expansion and balance sheet performance, while taking less consideration of risk. Liberal market economies inevitably face with market failure and economic downturns. Coordinated market economies have stronger internal stability than liberal market economies, but cannot avoid an economic crisis induced by external influential factors or world markets. Their institutionalized coordination has less ability to keep the critical situation under control than Chinese state ownership-based coordination. The housing market crisis in Japan in the 1990s and the financial crisis in 2008 in many liberal market economies and coordinated market economies are examples. The Chinese economy is an example of how China successfully avoided the East Asia financial crisis in the late 1990s and the worldwide financial crisis in

2008. China also has shown its stronger capability to control crisis compared with other countries, for example, the coronavirus crisis and its induced worldwide economic downturn in 2020.

Chinese dual-structured model is a business model rather than a political economic model.

Because Chinese dual-structured model is based on the analysis of firms' governance structures and business systems, it is actually a business model/economic model. The institutional environment and the institutional advantage is here culture-related rather than politics-related.

The institutional advantage of dual-structured Chinese model and innovation system.

This book proves that Chinese economy is a dual-structured market economy. It also indicates the institutional advantages of the dual-structured Chinese model and innovation system. First, it shows the institutional advantage of the private sector in building up its market-oriented innovation system (similar to the US innovation system), in supporting private high-technology firms, and in developing new high technology. Second, it shows the institutional advantage of state coordination through its controlling shareholding in the state sector in building up the state strategic innovation system (similar to but superior to coordination-based innovation system in Germany leading European countries) and developing state high-technology programs, in keeping the market risks in control and injecting confidence in the economy, in avoiding the economic crisis and successfully controlling the crisis. Third, such a dual innovation system in China can amplify the innovation effect. For example, private firm Huawei can develop the most advanced 5G technology based on the market-oriented innovation system, and Chinese state-controlled telecommunication companies can build quickly the infrastructure and 5G stations based on state strategic innovation system, covering 5G net in the whole country and quickly applying 5G technology. Therefore, such a new high technology can be developed and applied much more quickly than in other countries. In the USA, Ciscos and other private telecommunication companies develop 5G technology based on the market-oriented innovation system, but AT&T, Verizon, and other private firms cannot build up so quickly the infrastructure covering 5G net in the whole country for applying the technology, as Chinese state-controlled telecommunication companies do. In coordinated market economies like Germany, a typical coordination-based incremental innovation system cannot quickly bring up 5G such kind of new high technology, and private firms cannot quickly build up infrastructure covering 5G net in the whole country for applying the technology, either. In reality, we see that Chinese Huawei, Xiaomi, and many other private smartphone producers can produce and sell 5G smartphones earlier than Apple.

References

Garnaut, R., Song, L., Yang, Y., & Wang, X. (2001). *Private enterprise in China.* In *Canberra, ACT; Beijing: Asia Pacific Press, The Australian National University.* Peking: University.

Hall, P. A., & Soskice, D. (2001). *Varieties of capitalism.* New York: Oxford University Press.

Hollingsworth, J. R., & Boyer, R. (1997). Coordination of economic actors and social systems of production. In J. R. Hollingsworth & R. Boyer (Eds.), *Contemporary capitalism: The embeddedness of institutions.* Cambridge: Cambridge University Press.

Keidel, A. (2008, November 3). *The global financial crisis: Lessions for the United States and China. Carnegie Endowment for International Peace.*

Index